RED LIGHT TO STARBOARD

RECALLING THE *EXXON VALDEZ* DISASTER

RED LIGHT TO STARBOARD

RECALLING THE *EXXON VALDEZ* DISASTER

ANGELA DAY

WSU
PRESS

Washington State University Press
Pullman, Washington

WASHINGTON STATE UNIVERSITY

Washington State University Press
PO Box 645910
Pullman, Washington 99164-5910
Phone: 800-354-7360
Fax: 509-335-8568
E-mail: wsupress@wsu.edu
Web site: wsupress.wsu.edu

Library of Congress Cataloging-in-Publication Data

Day, Angela, 1971-
  Red light to starboard : recalling the Exxon Valdez disaster / Angela Day.
    pages cm
  Includes bibliographical references and index.
  ISBN 978-0-87422-318-7 (alk. paper)
1. Oil spills–Alaska–Prince William Sound Region. 2. Exxon Valdez (Ship) 3. Tankers–Accidents–Alaska–Prince William Sound Region. I. Title. II. Title: Redlight to
starboard.
  TD427.P4D3935 2013
  363.738'2097983–dc23

                                                                    2013043116

WSU PRESS

Fine Quality Books from the Pacific Northwest

Contents

To Walt and Gloria Day

Preface

H E HEARD A CRY THAT SOUNDED LIKE A BABY, and then he saw it. Next to his boat, an oil-soaked sea otter struggled to stay afloat. Bobby Day gripped the edge of his fifty-foot seine boat in anger and disgust. It was the spring of 1989 near Naked Island in Prince William Sound, Alaska. In the few short weeks since the *Exxon Valdez* ran aground on a charted reef, his life had decidedly gone off course. He was not alone. His story gives voice to the ten thousand fishermen whose lives and livelihoods were affected by the grounding of the *Exxon Valdez*.

My interest in writing this book began with a desire to provide an account of the fishermen's shared experience. I was initially inspired by the man I love and his family, who never considered themselves remarkable even though I thought they were. The Days were settlers and pioneers in a rugged Alaska and they supported development of the oil industry. Their values and actions helped to shape the terminus of the Trans-Alaska pipeline and its place within the community of Valdez. Bobby Day's support of the oil industry in the early 1970s put him at odds with his fellow fishermen. When the *Exxon Valdez* ran aground nearly two decades later, they were bound together by shared emotional and financial challenges and a common struggle for survival.

As I sought to tell this story of the causes and consequences of a disaster, I encountered questions I could not answer, riddles I could not solve. With so many laws in place to prevent such a disaster, how did it happen? What emerged from my research is an account entwined with the regulatory and governance failures that gave rise to the spill, politics surrounding oil development, coziness between the government and oil industry, and the unheeded warnings sounded by local citizens and industry insiders. Many of the failings that gave rise to this disaster are common to other tragic accidents in retrospect. Yet the impacts of such disasters are uniquely personal, shaping the lives and futures of people and their communities. I found rich lessons to be gleaned from the failures that gave rise to this accident, as well as the responses to it.

The writing of this book took many years, and in the end, it shaped me as much as I shaped it. My search for knowledge and understanding of this and similar events led me to graduate school, first for a master's in public administration, and then a doctorate in political science. Researching the factors that give rise to catastrophic accidents and their impacts has become my life's work. But this is not a scholarly book in the sense that it sets forth a theory and seeks to prove it. Rather, my goal was to tell a story and to see what can be learned from it. I began by writing down recollections shared by my family over late summer evening dinners. I checked and verified memories by digging through boxes of records, court documents, and newspaper accounts. Recordings of town hall meetings, transcripts released by the National Transportation Safety Board, investigations and reports prepared by government agencies, copies of speeches collected in a family notebook, and records housed in the government publications section of the University of Washington library allowed me to incorporate original dialogue into the narrative of the book.

I also interviewed friends and members of the community of Valdez who lived through and shaped the events detailed in the book. Of course, one cannot remember with precision exact conversations among friends and family members, but I have in places attempted to reconstruct those conversations. Close family members and friends reviewed an early version of the manuscript and assured me that I have captured the tone and intent of those conversations, based on their recollections. With one exception, all other dialogue or remarks in quotations are drawn from original or secondary materials and sources are cited in endnotes.

I am indebted to many who helped me gain knowledge about the facts and locate evidence. John Devens and Stan Stephens shared their memories of the spill, and their efforts to envision and carve out of democratic principles a mechanism for preventing future accidents. Ross Mullins shared historical documents from the Cordova District Fishermen United, and videos of town hall meetings in Cordova. Although this book centers on the story of one fisherman, Mullins' insights contributed to an understanding of the shared perspectives and experiences of fishermen throughout Prince William Sound.

Riki Ott's writings and presentations at the University of Washington also provided insights into the causes and aftermath of the spill from the perspective of the fishermen. Her training as a scientist added expertise and heft to the fishermen's concerns and frustrations in the wake of the spill. Dan Lawn spent patient hours with me on the sunny patio of a coffee shop, and on the phone. His first-hand knowledge of the politics and pressures that quashed the voices of those raising concerns prior to and following the spill proved an invaluable resource.

Valdez public radio station KCHU shared countless hours of recordings of town hall meetings in the days and weeks following the spill. They provided me with an index of the recordings, a workspace in their studio office, and recording equipment so that I could take copies with me. The Alaska Forum for Environmental Responsibility provided access to historical documents related to oil development, spill prevention and response, and Congressional investigations. Gloria Day supplied me with a notebook full of historical records, articles and speeches made by public officials.

Tom Carpenter shared his knowledge about the struggles of citizens, a government regulator, and industry insiders to warn of an impending disaster, and the reactions of those in positions of power who sought to stymie their efforts and silence their voices. Jon Brock and John Boehrer taught me about the power of a story as a means for learning lessons and crafting solutions to challenging public policy problems. They gave me the tools I needed to tackle this project, and helped me find the words and confidence I needed to complete it. I will always be grateful for their mentorship. I am also indebted to my editor, Beth DeWeese, for her good instincts, suggestions and support, and to the entire team at the Washington State University Press. I am grateful to Editor-in-Chief Robert Clark, Director Edward Sala, and Marketing Manager Caryn Lawton for their enthusiasm and support for this project, and designers Nancy Grunewald and Pat Brommer for giving these words and images a distinct look and feel.

My life and this book have been inspired by Walt and Gloria Day. Their pioneering spirit and commitment to the public interest provided the foundation upon which modern-day Valdez was built. Walt passed away in 2001 but his example and spirit live on in his community and family. Gloria remains a source of strength and support to all who know her, and her keen memory is a treasure. Most of all, it has been an honor to tell the story of Bobby Day.

Map courtesy of Prince William Sound Regional Citizens' Advisory Council (PWSRCAC).

1

Red, Right, Returning

PRINCE WILLIAM SOUND, ALASKA: MARCH 24, 1989

A T THE END OF A DEEP, PROTECTED FJORD, across from the town of
Valdez, the fateful voyage of the *Exxon Valdez* began on a chilly,
misty Alaskan night. Workers at the Alyeska Marine Terminal loaded
fifty-three million gallons of North Slope crude oil onto the tanker,
tied at its berth. Over tundra and three mountain ranges, a forty-eight-
inch pipe had delivered the oil to the terminal's temporary storage
tanks, almost an acre apiece in size. From the depths of Prudhoe Bay
to Valdez Bay, the North Slope crude had traversed an eight-hundred-
mile path, at times raised high above the permafrost or buried in rock.
It was still warm as it settled into the cargo hold of the *Exxon Valdez*.

Across the bay to the north of the terminal, warm yellow light
spilled onto the snowy lawn of the town's civic center. Inside, Alyeska
employees celebrated and congratulated each other at their annual
safety awards banquet. In the city council chambers three blocks to
the northwest, Mayor John Devens convened a group of thirty citizens who had become concerned about the possibility of a major oil
spill in Prince William Sound. Representing Alyeska, local tourism
operators, environmentalists, and fishermen, the citizens learned that
ships calling on the Alyeska terminal comprised 13 percent of the
nation's tanker traffic, but accounted for 52 percent of the accidents.

Mayor Devens asked Dr. Riki Ott, a local activist and fisher-
woman who also held degrees in fisheries and marine toxicology, if
she would speak to the group. Fog and low clouds prevented her from
flying to Valdez, so she spoke to the group via speakerphone from her
log cabin in Cordova, seventy miles to the southeast. As the group
gathered around the phone on the center of the conference table, Ott
led a discussion about the possible effects an oil spill might have on
the environment, local economy, and on the lives and livelihoods of
local residents.

The group agreed that they couldn't rely solely on state regulators, elected officials, or the oil companies to prevent and respond to an oil spill. As local citizens who would be most affected by a spill, they resolved to secure their own oil-spill response equipment and seek ways of incorporating their input into the regulatory process. They also resolved to lobby the state for an additional environmental regulator in the Valdez office. Ott concluded the meeting with a chilling admonition, "Gentleman, it is not a matter of if you will have an oil spill, it is a matter of when."[1]

As Dr. Ott concluded her remarks to the group gathered in the council chambers, workers untied the lines securing the *Exxon Valdez*. The massive tanker, almost a thousand feet long, slowly maneuvered away from the terminal and was underway about two hours before midnight. Her dark hull sat low in the water, her long bow broad and flat. In the dark of the night, only the white house on the stern was perceptible as the ship crept down the bay.[2]

On the bridge, harbor pilot Ed Murphy manned the controls. Common to many ports worldwide, a harbor pilot's sole job is to guide ships through inland waters, in and out of port. The Valdez pilots are well paid, their salaries derived from fees charged to the owners of the ships. Twelve miles down the section of the fjord known as Port Valdez the tanker approached the Narrows where Potato Point juts into the passage, allowing only three quarters of a mile through which to pass. As an added challenge, a tall pinnacle-shaped rock known as Middle Rock juts upward in the center of the narrow passage. At a careful pace of six knots, the tanker passed unscathed through the narrow neck of land. In years past, the harbor pilot would have stayed aboard until a point further out into the Sound, but as was customary in 1989 he bade farewell at Rocky Point, not far outside the Narrows.

The ship was to proceed on a course south through Prince William Sound toward the Gulf of Alaska in shipping lanes outlined on navigational charts as plain to a tanker's captain as a marked lane on a freeway. The ship's loran (long-range navigation system) received signals from stations located throughout the state, which provided coordinates of the ship's location that could then be identified on navigational charts. Radar provided an additional tool for the crew to identify approaching boats, islands, or coastline.

The current that night was reportedly thick with icebergs calved from nearby Columbia Glacier. Otherwise known as "growlers" for the sound they make as they scrape along the side of a boat's hull, they can be large enough to merit slowing a ship's pace, or worse, forcing a diversion from the marked shipping lanes. In a routine maneuver, Captain Joseph Hazelwood radioed the Coast Guard station in Valdez for clearance to divert to the inbound shipping lane to avoid the heaviest ice. The officer on duty granted permission and the turn commenced. Then the captain left the bridge in charge of third mate Gregory Cousins and went to his cabin. As the ship's master, it seemed he always had paperwork to complete. He may have intended to finish some of it before they disembarked but perhaps time ran short. While not yet in open waters, his departure from the bridge was a clear violation of company policy.

With the light at Busby Island already in sight, Cousins was to complete the turn back into the outbound lane when they were abeam of the light. Although the third mate had already completed a full shift, he volunteered to work one more hour, a decision he would surely regret. Not wanting to make a mistake, Cousins went to the chart room adjacent to the bridge to carefully plot his location and coordinates for the turn he was to make. He studied the sketchy outline of floating icebergs on the ship's radar.

Minutes passed and the opportunity to turn the massive length and weight of the tanker was ticking away. The lookout person that night was Maureen Jones, who came somewhat breathlessly through the door to the outside deck.

"Sir," she said. "There's a buoy light on the starboard side. It should be to port sir."

"Right," he said. "Thank you." Quickly, he finished the notes he'd been making. He turned to the helmsman, and ordered a turn ten degrees to the right. It was the equivalent of directing a car back into its own lane after passing. Cousins called to the Captain's quarters to report he was commencing the turn back to the outbound lane.

"Fine," Hazelwood responded. "You know what to do then?" The captain was looking at forecasts of a storm brewing in the Aleutian Island chain. With some calculations, he might be able to figure a way around it. A bottle of Moussey non-alcoholic beer rested atop some of the papers stacked on his desk and he took a sip. Alcohol was prohibited on board but supervisors probably figured the small amount of alcohol contained in Moussey was better than being tempted by the real thing. He was likely focused on his paperwork, and perhaps satisfied when Cousins said everything was under control.

Again, Maureen Jones burst through the door. "That light, sir, it's still on the starboard side. It should be to port sir." Though she tried to maintain a tone of respect for her superior officer, her voice was thick with sarcasm and fear. The rule "red, right, returning" is ingrained in anyone who has spent time at sea. The red buoy light marks the channel, and ships coming into port should be able to see the red buoy to their right-hand or starboard side. Jones noted the red buoy light remained on the right as the ship *departed* the port. Her 'red light to starboard' declaration would prove to be the last of a litany of signals of impending disaster. It served as a metaphor for the unheeded warnings that fishermen and citizens, and whistleblowers at the Alyeska Terminal and the Department of Environmental Conservation (DEC) had sounded over the past decade.

Cousins decided to increase the turn to twenty degrees. The digital red numbers of the fathometer began to race ever faster, showing a water depth too shallow to escape. His turn was too late. A hasty call to the captain's cabin was cut short as the words, "Sir, I think we have a serious navigational problem…" rushed from his mouth. A horrifying slam of steel onto solid rock, a scraping and jarring, a continual crashing and rocking that must have seemed to go on forever, interrupted that feverish call. Listing slightly the tanker came to rest perched there on Bligh Reef. A rock impaled in her midsection on the starboard side, the *Exxon Valdez* was spurting oil three feet above the water line at a rate of 14,000 gallons a minute.

As Prince William Sound emerged from a cloak of darkness on March 24, 1989, shades of pale spring light revealed the scene of the tragedy. The giant vessel, grounded on the underwater rocks of Bligh Reef, looked out of place in the vast expanse of water, mountains and sky, like some rude intruder who had lost its way. The twenty-eighth voyage of the newest supertanker in Exxon's fleet had gone dreadfully wrong.

In the early dawn, lights from the *Exxon Valdez* shimmered across the water in wavy uncertain beams. Around the ship, oily waves thickly licked her side. Seals perched on a nearby buoy marker as if observing the scene. Icebergs, once a mystic shade of light turquoise, were stained dark as if to foreshadow the fate of the Sound.

The oil boiling furiously from the bowels of the ship would ultimately create a wake of death and destruction. To what extent, and how long it would impact the rugged Alaska coastline, no one could guess. Already the oil slick extended southwest from the tanker over an area three miles long and two miles wide. The water was unusually still on that early spring day. It was breathtakingly quiet, too quiet.

2

Hard Aground

SITKA, ALASKA: MARCH 24, 1989

IT WASN'T LIKE HE SLOWLY CAME TO A GROGGY, half-awake consciousness. He didn't have to will himself to get up and grope for the coffee pot in the dark hours before dawn. A stiff easterly wind hadn't rocked his fishing boat, pulling him from an exhausted sleep. This was different. Bobby Day's eyes opened wide and he saw his suitcase on the floor. He didn't have to wonder where he was. His mind was instantly clear. A hotel room in Sitka. Waiting for a herring season opener. It was March 24, 1989. He lay still, wondering if someone had knocked on his door. It wasn't like him to be so wide awake at this early hour if he didn't have to be. Every one of his senses seemed sharp, ready. For what?

His hand fumbled for the switch on the unfamiliar lamp. The dim yellow rays fell across a small table still cluttered with cards, pistachio nut shells, and empty beer bottles, remnants of a pinochle game ended only a few short hours earlier. With the remote control outstretched toward the TV, he pushed the 'on' button. The polished professional voice of the CNN reporter said she had breaking news. Her young face was attractive even as she willed a somber expression. A supertanker was hard aground on Bligh Reef, in Prince William Sound Alaska. Exact amounts had not been confirmed, but oil was escaping into the water. Though he couldn't possibly realize the significance of it, one wrong turn by an oil tanker had changed the entire course of Bobby's life.

It was hard to believe, he thought. Bligh Reef? The charted shipping lanes lay atop a deep channel at least a mile from the submerged reef. Something must have gone desperately wrong with the weather or perhaps there had been a mechanical failure. Many friends had warned this would happen someday. Someday is right now, he thought, still trying to equate the notion with reality. Images from the past echoed in his head: an energy crisis two decades ago, Americans waiting in gas lines. At the time, he wondered if these images could somehow have been staged by politicians and oil companies in an effort to push construction of the Trans-Alaska pipeline through. He wondered this, even though he had publicly supported oil development. Those voices in favor of development had promised less dependence on foreign oil if North Slope oil was extracted and shipped to markets Outside—a term Alaskans used for the lower forty-eight states. Those opposed feared that extraction of a non-renewable resource could ultimately come at the cost of marine resources that had for so long been the state's primary economic driver.

Environmentalists, politicians, fishermen, and oil company executives had waged a war over their differing perspectives about economic opportunities, environmental risks, and how oil development would ultimately affect the lives of Alaskans. In the end, with promises to extract oil leaving only a tiny environmental footprint, and a commitment to use Alaskan oil exclusively for domestic use, the eight-hundred-mile pipeline was constructed in three short years.

Bobby fought down the concern rising quickly inside him. He knew the counter-clockwise currents would take the oil right down the western shoreline of Prince William Sound. Herring season was due to open in the Sound in a couple of weeks and salmon season would follow. It couldn't have been a worse place or time in the delicate cycle of birth and renewal.

He reached for the phone and dialed his brother's number in Valdez. Pat Day finally answered, his voice thick and groggy in the early morning darkness. When Bobby told him the news he simply responded, "You're kidding." No one could have imagined a fully loaded tanker running onto a charted reef and Pat was no exception. Fearing Pat might roll over and go back to sleep, Bobby urged him to get on the phone and see what he could find out.

A hot shower calmed Bobby's nerves only slightly. He dressed in Levis and his favorite blue Pendleton wool shirt. He paced the room, his hand absently guiding the electric razor over his face. After a pat with Old Spice aftershave, he grabbed his white baseball cap and left the old Sheffield House Hotel. He turned his collar up against the stiff wind, grey eyes observing every detail around him. The early spring sky was turbulent in the breaking dawn. High puffy clouds tumbled and parted above him like airy drifting mountains.

The town of Sitka lay sprawled along the coastline as if expanding up into the mountains behind would have been too great an effort. The main street parted and went around the ancient Russian Orthodox Church in the center of town. The buildings were both old and new, reflecting the hundred-year history of the oldest Russian trading post in Alaska. His back to the town, Bobby strode the few short blocks to the boat harbor. His stride was as steady and flat-footed as his temperament, giving him away as a man accustomed to being at sea. His neck and shoulders were thick and muscular, hips thin. His short stature was not readily apparent until meeting him face to face.

He walked out onto the dock and stepped onto his boat, the *Lady Lynne*. The new fifty-foot LeClerque Marine fishing vessel was in spotless order as usual. The Department of Fish and Game would likely open the Sitka herring season tomorrow. He had a lot left to do today, but the first item on his agenda was a fresh pot of coffee. As he waited for the pot to brew, he flipped through the channels on the marine radio. He wondered if anyone had seen the tanker or had any more details.

The coffee maker gurgled and spluttered. Impatiently, he pulled the pot out as the last drips of coffee hissed on the hot plate. The smell and taste, and the hot cup in his hands were like a pacifier. He glanced out the window to see who else might be on the dock. He saw someone heading toward one of the float planes tied nearby. He recognized his pilot, and he remembered the day he hired her only a few years ago.

Lori Egge's thick blonde braid fell over her shoulder and landed hard against her face as she leaned over to pick up her gas can. Fine wavy wisps of hair had escaped the straw-colored braid, brushing against her cheek and falling over her eyes in the chilly, stiff wind. She hoisted the five-gallon can and climbed up over the wing of her Cessna. The can weighed half her hundred and ten pounds but she showed little sign of strain. Deftly she guided the fuel into the small opening on top of the wing. She made it look easy.

Her cheeks were flushed in the chilly spring air, the collar of her Levi jacket turned up to defend the wind. Her hands were puffy and red. She could have been feminine, perhaps, in another setting, but her attractive face had a set of tough, determined blue eyes. What her petite frame lacked in size was all but made up by her drive. Bobby had learned long ago that an offer to help would be met with rebuke. She could handle it, thank you.

Lori competed in a man's world. The life of a spotter pilot is tough and physical. In a way, she had to be better than a man to earn respect. She was a good pilot and Bobby knew it. It wasn't just her skill, but a determination and toughness that told him she had what it takes. In those early days her tiny plane seemed to lack the power to rebuff a strong breeze. When the wind blew hard it looked as though she was standing still in the sky. She knew how to handle a plane, but spotting fish from the air was something she had to spend time teaching herself. A spotter has to be able to detect fish beneath the water, but more importantly, know if they are can be caught in that spot, if rocks will rip the net, or if a nearby boat is about to scoop them all up. That art and instinct, once developed, can yield a spotter pilot a sizeable amount of money.

Bobby had watched her those first few years as she camped on empty beaches in her tent and tried to make a name for herself as a spotter. When the wind howled out of the north, she opened a cold can of beans and a packet of pop tarts and rolled her gas barrels around her tent for protection. But she never did get a job with a top boat. Not only was she a rookie but the only woman fish spotter at the time. He figured she deserved a fair break when he hired her. Now he wondered what would become of her if an oil spill truly threatened the herring fishery.

He filled his coffee cup and walked out the dock toward her plane. Lori was bent over, tightening the line securing her plane to the dock. When she saw him, she stood up, hands rubbing the small of her back.

"Good morning," she said brightly.

"Morning," he said.

Her eyes focused on his face, as angular and strong as if it were chiseled from granite. She sensed coolness, a preoccupation. Warmly she asked, "You want to go up and see if there is any fish showing up today?"

"Lori," he said, "There's been a terrible accident. It's finally happened." He proceeded to tell her what he had learned on the news that morning. It didn't take him long to fill her in on the few details he knew.

"Well," she responded, "I guess all we can do is wait and see what happens." Ever the pragmatist, she suggested they might as well focus on figuring out where the fish might be when the Sitka herring season opened sometime in the next few hours.

After some thought, he responded, "Sure, let's go check it out."

She busied herself readying the plane for takeoff. Bobby walked back to the boat to top off his coffee. Better put a lid on the cup, he thought. It was bound to be a bumpy ride today. As he refilled his cup he listened as familiar voices crackled over the marine radio. Fishermen confirmed the tanker was hard aground in the waters of Prince William Sound over four hundred miles away—a place as familiar to Bobby as his own face in the mirror. For twelve years now tankers had become a part of that landscape. But he couldn't quite get his mind around a picture of a stricken tanker on the reef. The deep emerald waters of the Sound were not only a part of his soul, they were the lifeblood of his career and his father's before him. He craved information.

As Lori accelerated across the rough dark waters of Sitka Channel, she gently rocked the plane so the first float would break suction with the surface of the water. Then they were free, buoyed only by the turbulent air under the wings. They climbed sharply, the water falling quickly behind. It was a sensation that always made Bobby feel exhilarated and free. From the air, any setting can take on a completely different perspective, as if everything is summarized, blending each small detail that seems tiny and insignificant by itself into a meaningful picture—a perspective he needed for his own life right now, he thought.

They banked to the right and he studied the dark gray waters dimpled with whitecaps. On any other day, he would be patiently scanning for schools of elusive herring. His eyes were sharp and practiced. He had spent so much time searching for them over the years he could almost feel their presence before he saw them. Fishing was more than his livelihood, it was his passion.

He chided himself for his inattentiveness. Bobby's mind was everywhere but the water below. Numbers ran through his head again. The past few years had been prosperous and he had invested heavily back into his business. The payments and insurance on his two boats were over a hundred thousand a year, but the equity in them was high. The horse ranch Bobby had built north of Seattle was sucking up more money than he had anticipated. Still he could manage. Even if the oil closed some seasons that year, he could refinance.

The puffy clouds surrounding the plane were tall and substantial looking. He couldn't remember a sky that had ever looked so dimensional——it seemed like a world apart from the one below. Scenarios rushed through his mind. Maybe the oil would be quickly contained, leaving nothing but a scare and promises of precautions in the future. How much oil could one of those tankers carry, and how much could really escape? He tried to reason but his mind was anything but rational. Something in his gut told him it was going to be bad. A sense of dread and helplessness like he had never known was taking hold of him. Going back to the place of his childhood in Prince William Sound would break his heart, but returning to Seattle would offer little comfort. Clouds, water, the sky in front of him all ran together as tears blurred his eyes. He wished they would never land, just continue on to a place he couldn't define.

3

"We're Going to Be Here for a While"

BLIGH REEF: MARCH 24, 1989

IT HAD BEEN TWELVE HOURS SINCE the grounding of the *Exxon Valdez*. Frank Iarossi, president of Exxon Shipping Corporation, absorbed the scene through the window of his corporate jet. It must have seemed a sharp contrast between the stricken tanker and an otherwise tranquil setting. According to the oil spill contingency plan, the scene at Bligh Reef should have been alive with activity. Oil boom and skimmers were to have arrived within five-and-a-half hours after grounding. He learned en route, via the sky-to-land phone, that the tanker had already lost over 200,000 barrels—eight million gallons— of crude. Yet no oil boom surrounded her, no skimmers hummed over the black slick like waterbugs devouring an evening meal. The situation looked anything but under control.[1]

Frank Iarossi graduated from the Coast Guard Academy in 1959. He served on active duty for ten years, earning master's degrees in mechanical engineering and naval architecture while on active duty, and later, an MBA. In his twenty years with Exxon, it wasn't the first time he had awoken to the sharp ring of the telephone in the middle of the night. He had just returned home to Houston from a spill in Hawaii. The eight hundred barrels the *Exxon Houston* spilled was quickly attended to and had been declared a "model response" by the Coast Guard. No doubt he was confident that Exxon's twenty-eight-volume response plan would ensure successful containment and cleanup of this spill.

As president of Exxon Shipping Corporation, Frank Iarossi was responsible for eighteen tugs and nineteen ocean-going tankers. Throughout his entire career with Exxon, no major spills had occurred. The *Valdez*, built in 1986, was the newest supertanker in the fleet. But the sight of the tanker helplessly, even precariously, perched on the reef, must have taken his breath away. How different it must have looked from the six-foot replica inside the glass case in his office.

The Exxon jet flew between the mountain peaks at the narrow entrance to Valdez Bay and began its descent to the airport. Nestled at the bottom of steep mountains on glacial silt, the tiny airport was unaccustomed to the sight of sleek corporate jets. With a tight-knit population of 3,000 people, the town was about to experience an influx of Outsiders not seen since the construction of the pipeline itself. The modest two-story Westmark Hotel situated on the edge of the bay opposite the pipeline terminal was to become corporate headquarters for Exxon's response in Valdez. In the makeshift office at the Westmark, Iarossi was briefed about the events of the grounding. Behind thick glasses, his dark eyes were calm and absorbing. One of his assistants told him Captain Hazelwood wasn't on the bridge when the grounding occurred.

The Exxon manual clearly stated a captain should remain on the bridge "whenever conditions present a potential threat to the vessel such as a passing in the vicinity of shoals, rocks or other hazards presenting any threat to safe navigation." It didn't take long for investigators to uncover and reconstruct the details of the grounding from the Coast Guard recordings. When Hazelwood radioed the Coast Guard station for permission to change lanes, the officer on duty granted the request. Hazelwood radioed in return, "Once we're clear of the ice at Columbia Bay, we'll give you another shout, over." The Coast Guard officer responded, "Roger that, sir, be awaiting your call,"[2] but then the officer left his desk. He poured a cup of coffee and proceeded to chat with the new officer coming on duty at midnight. The next thought given to the *Exxon Valdez* was the ring of his telephone and a stressed voice, or was it slurred? Captain Hazelwood relayed an unbelievable message.

"Yeah, this is the *Valdez* back," Hazelwood said in a low mutter. "We should be on your radar there. We've fetched up hard aground north of Goose Island off Bligh Reef, and evidently we're leaking some oil, and we're going to be here for a while."

The officer turned his attention to the images of Prince William Sound on his computer screen. It was still hard to believe, even as he saw the tiny ship's green image inches outside the shipping lanes marked on his screen. It did indeed look as if the tanker was atop Bligh Reef. He blinked and breathed heavily into the phone as he responded. *"Exxon Valdez*, uh, Roger."

Joseph Hazelwood must have known without a doubt that his career as a captain was over, as certain as the jarring of steel on rocks. Bolting from his desk chair at the time of the impact, he had climbed up stairs that seemed to be a moving target. In the bathroom just off the chart room, he vomited in the toilet. He then approached the bridge with the air of a man accustomed to being in control.

"Hard Right!" he yelled to the helmsman, Robert Kagan. "Hard Left!" Captain Hazelwood then tried ramming ahead and backward. He continued, perhaps hoping the ship could be commanded off the reef, and continue unscathed to its destination in Long Beach, California. By 1:00 a.m. Steve McCall, the Coast Guard Commander, had arrived in the office and requested a report on the situation from Hazelwood.

The captain responded, "We're working our way off the reef. We've, ah, the vessel has been holed and we're ascertaining, right now we're trying just to get her off the reef and we'll get back to you as soon as we can."

"Take it slow and easy," McCall advised. "You know, I'm telling you the obvious, but take it slow and easy, and we're getting help out as fast as we can."

Concerned, McCall then asked about the stability of the ship— whether it had sustained enough damage, lost enough oil, or taken on enough water to be in danger of sinking or breaking up.

"We're [in] pretty good shape right now, stability-wise, and, ah, trying to extract her off the shoal here," Hazelwood said. "You can probably see me on your radar, and, ah, once we get under way, I'll let you know, do another damage control assessment."

"Before you make any drastic attempt to get away, make sure you don't, you know, start doing any ripping," McCall said. "You got a rising tide, about an hour-and-a-half worth of tide in your favor. Ah, once you hit that max, I wouldn't recommend doing much wiggling."

"Major damage has kind of been done and we kind of rock and rolled over it," Hazelwood said. "We're just kind of hung up on the stern here. We're just, ah, we'll drift over it. Ah, I'll get back to you."

"Captain of the port out," McCall said.

At the Valdez Coast Guard Station, a series of hectic, tense meetings took place in the hours after the grounding. Finally, Coast Guard Lieutenant Commander Falkenstein and Chief Warrant Officer Delozier boarded the patrol boat *Silver Bullet,* bound for Bligh Reef in the darkness before dawn. They were accompanied by Dan Lawn from the Department of Environmental Conservation. It was three o'clock in the morning and Lawn was angry. Angry at the way the oil companies had pushed back against his agency's regulatory oversight, angry that this had happened on his watch, and even angry at himself for not having done more to prevent what he knew would one day happen.[3]

When the brightly lit tanker punctuated the darkness that still enveloped the Sound, her dark hull and white house personified for Lawn the unheeded memos he had written to his supervisors. It laid bare the breakdown in the political and regulatory system that had failed to prevent a fully-loaded tanker from grounding on a charted reef.

Lawn had feared such an incident for years but he still wasn't prepared for the strong, toxic fumes fouling the air. He braced his stout frame against the side of the boat, rubbing his salt-and-pepper beard. The tanker was still a quarter of a mile away. It was a smell that didn't belong in this wild place. The stench overcame him and his head ached. His mind pounded as he thought about how many times he'd warned of this scenario. How many times a memo to his supervisor had gone unread or received no response. The years of frustration gripped him, clinging as fervently to him as the smell of tragedy.

Dan Lawn came to Alaska in 1974 as an engineer to help design and build the pipeline terminal. As an employee for the Alaska Department of Environmental Conservation (DEC), he was now a policeman for the oil industry, particularly the Alyeska Pipeline Company. The company was a consortium of seven companies, at the time including BP, ARCO, Exxon, Mobil, Amerada Hess, Phillips, and Unocal. The state of Alaska did not want seven different oil companies responsible for maintaining equipment, and responding to potential oil spills. The Alyeska consortium was officially responsible for submitting detailed, site-specific spill prevention and response plans to DEC.

As time passed, Lawn found his job becoming more difficult. More than 8,700 tanker trips had been made to Port Valdez since the pipeline began pumping oil in 1977. Spill prevention and precautions were becoming more relaxed. In 1986, the DEC demanded that Alyeska provide a response scenario for a hypothetical 8.4 million-gallon spill. Alyeska protested that the odds of a spill of that magnitude were only one in 241 years. Their statistics were a little off, Lawn thought grimly as the *Silver Bullet* sidled up to the massive *Valdez*.

The two Coast Guard officers and Lawn climbed the Jacob's ladder up the steep hull and onto the deck, their nostrils, lungs, and eyes burning from the fumes. They found Hazelwood leaning up against the wheelhouse window, smoking a cigarette. Delozier suggested he may want to put his cigarette out. With all the fumes present, he feared it could cause an explosion. Hazelwood quickly complied. As Lawn would later recall from his field notes, Hazelwood was "fairly quiet, pensive. His hand was up to his face."

As if it wasn't apparent, Officer Falkenstein asked, "What exactly is the problem here?" Hazelwood answered somewhat sarcastically, "I think you're looking at it."[4]

The Coast Guard officers traded glances and stepped a few paces away to the starboard bridge. One of them suggested that they ought to run a sobriety test on the crew. After some discussion and calls back to the station to determine whether they had the authority to do that, the officers had a qualified person on the way to perform the tests. A thought perhaps resting in the back of their minds—as for all of the players in the unfolding drama—was that of culpability. Who was liable for what, who was negligent, overstepped boundaries, neglected to follow procedure, or was in some way reckless. Although they were likely worried, the Coast Guard officers might not have suspected the potential for one of the biggest legal battles in American history.

The executives at Exxon headquarters in Houston, however, could no doubt see it coming like a freight train. Data from the ship's monitoring system was feeding directly to their offices and it was clear they were facing the biggest oil spill in U.S. history. The massive amount of oil surging into the cold, clear waters of Prince William Sound was creating yet another worry about the tanker's stability. The weight of the full cargo and ballast tanks versus empty ones created a precarious imbalance. Now it seemed that the ship was in serious danger of rolling over or breaking up as its eleven oil-storage compartments became unbalanced. More than forty million gallons of oil remained on board.

According to the contingency plan on file with the DEC, Lawn knew that equipment and workers were to be mobilized within five and a half hours of a spill. As he stood on the deck of the ship, he watched in horror as oil boiled out from below the surface of the Sound. He looked anxiously to the horizon for any sign of approaching lights from Alyeska's response boat. At 4:00 a.m. he used the ship's satellite phone to call the Alyeska terminal. Their time was nearly up.

When Larry Shier, Alyeska marine supervisor answered the phone, Lawn said, "What is going on? This ship is still leaking. You need to send out every piece of equipment you've got right away."[5] Shier assured him that the equipment was on its way and would be there by first light. Alyeska's plan acknowledged that "speed in deploying booms is essential in order to contain the maximum amount of spilled oil," and assured, "the necessary equipment is available and operable to meet oil spill response needs... Rapid and effective operations are necessary to limit the spread of oil."

At the terminal, the response barge rested in the dry dock, scheduled for repairs for a cracked hull it had sustained in a storm in early February. The deep-sea boom and skimmers that would normally have been ready to load on the barge were stored in a warehouse under several tons of lightweight harbor boom. The barge was declared to be seaworthy despite the crack and the equipment was no sooner loaded onto it, than a change in priorities set in motion a new set of tasks.

Based on reports from Officer Falkenstein aboard the *Valdez*, Coast Guard Commander Steve McCall called Alyeska at approximately 3:30 a.m. to advise them that "lightering" the ship's cargo—transferring it to another tanker—should commence immediately. The inflatable lightering fenders and related gear would have to be found. After about an hour's search, a worker noticed a corner of one of the fenders peeking out from under a snowdrift. Workers then unloaded the deep-sea boom and skimmers and loaded the lightering equipment onto the barge.

As dawn crept over Prince William Sound, Alyeska officials flew over the spill to assess the damage from 700 feet above. Lawn again called Shier. "You need to get that equipment to Bligh Reef. The oil is moving away from the ship and has to be contained immediately."[6] Shier assured Lawn that boom and skimmers were on the way, even though they had actually been removed from the barge and replaced with lightering equipment. The boom and skimmers would remain on the dock for another four hours.

According to Lawn, "I told them where to go with their goddamn boom and with their cleanup equipment, and to get their butts out here! They told me they were coming, that they had all the stuff coming, and they'd be right out there. And we waited, and we waited, and we waited, and we waited."[7]

On the afternoon of Good Friday, Alaska Governor Steve Cowper's plane approached the airport in Valdez. Just over fourteen hours had passed since the grounding of the tanker on Bligh Reef. At the airport's single gate, Valdez Mayor John Devens awaited the Governor. As he waited for the plane to arrive, Alyeska president George Nelson noticed him and motioned him over to a quiet corner. The mayor expected him to apologize for the slow response to the spill, but Nelson instead leveled criticism for the outcome of the citizen's oil-safety meeting the night before. The citizens had resolved to request an additional DEC regulator in Valdez. Nelson asked the mayor, "What did you do last night, asking for more DEC involvement? You trying to cause trouble? That's not playing fair. We expected more of you Devens."[8]

Still reeling from Nelson's unsettling remarks, Devens greeted the Governor and DEC Commissioner Dennis Kelso, who flew in from Juneau. Cowper and Kelso then flew from Valdez to Bligh Reef on a float plane where a Coast Guard boat ferried them over to the grounded tanker. The two men were greeted by the tense faces of Coast Guard officers who wasted no time in helping them into bright orange survival suits. They said if she started to go, it would take only thirty seconds for the supertanker to roll over.

Cowper's Alaska was supported almost eighty-five percent by royalties from oil. The population that elected him paid no state sales or income tax. In fact, they received a yearly "permanent fund" distribution just for being a resident of the state. No doubt, this was the last thing he ever wanted to see on his watch. As he surveyed the scene, Governor Cowper consulted with Dan Lawn, asking him for his perspective on what had gone wrong. Lawn railed that oil companies hadn't lived up to their promises and that the state had been too afraid to exercise the powers granted to them, to shut down the pipeline if the oil companies wouldn't comply with regulations.

The barge carrying skimmers and deep-sea boom finally left Valdez at 11:00 a.m. and arrived at Bligh Reef at 2:30 p.m., more than fourteen hours after the spill. As they stood on the deck of the *Valdez*, Kelso and Cowper observed two skimmers that had been filled to capacity within minutes. Having no place to empty their catch in order to resume skimming, they had little to do but stand by. Although the skimmers had short boom that appeared to direct some of the oil within their grasp, there was no deep-sea boom on the leading edge of the slick as described in the contingency plan. Kelso explained to the Governor, "Alyeska's contingency plan is very specific about what kind of equipment they would have here within five and a half hours. It's quite clear that what was promised has not been delivered."[9]

Since first light, the slick had grown from six to eighteen square miles. As he weighed the magnitude of the scene, the Governor finally exclaimed, "I've never seen such a goddamned mess in my life."[10]

4

According To Plan

VALDEZ: EASTER WEEKEND 1989

A SOMBER, MOSTLY WELL-BEHAVED GROUP of citizens began to gather at the Valdez Civic Center on the evening of Good Friday. In Subarus, pickups, and other four-wheel-drive vehicles, they parked outside the angular, modern-looking building. Although the calendar said it was nearly April, the taste of winter was yet in the air. Plowed, dirty mountains of snow dotted the parking lot, melting and running across the pavement, shiny in the evening lights.

They were conservative folks, hardworking, with the independent attitude of those who lived in a rugged land—a land whose sheer size and emptiness dwarfed those who inhabited it. Their clothes reflected a familiarity and cooperation with their surroundings. Lace-up leather boots or slip-ons, turtlenecks or wool shirts, faded jeans, polar fleece and down jackets. Since the bigger town of Anchorage was a six-hour drive away, most residents shopped at the local independent stores such as Days, Sugar and Spice, or Southcentral Hardware.

When Frank Iarossi arrived with other representatives from Exxon, all dressed in dark suits, the feeling of division was almost palpable. It was as if two opposing teams were meeting, set apart by their uniforms. When Governor Cowper arrived, he was dressed in the same manner as the Alaska locals and his alliance to their team would become more evident as the evening wore on.

Perhaps the frustrations of some Department of Environmental Conservation employees over the past few years were weighing on the Governor's mind. Maybe he feared the media would dwell on the coziness between state officials and the oil industry, the safety and preparedness cutbacks of the previous decade, and the apparently broken promises for protecting the environment. Or maybe it was the realization that even though Exxon and the other oil companies had made the state he governed wealthy, it was people like the ones in this room who had elected him. Tonight that distinction would become clear.

Frank Iarossi began by expressing regrets, on behalf of Exxon, for any inconvenience and anxiety the oil spill, now less than twenty-four-hours old, would cause them. He seemed genuine in his concern, dark eyes engaging, even compassionate. He seemed to believe he could reassure his audience that everything was under control. Exxon, he said, accepted full responsibility for what had happened, including full financial and operational responsibility for the cleanup. They wouldn't stop until the Sound was clean, he told them, even if it meant wiping off every single rock.

Since the completion of the pipeline in the mid-1970s, many of the people in Valdez made a living derived from the oil industry. Whether they worked across the bay at the oil terminal, or owned a local business that prospered in the now thriving economy, most felt that oil development truly benefited them. At the same time, their hearts were still most loyal to the beauty that surrounded them. Hunting and fishing still provided the lifestyle they were accustomed to. The spirit of the old "sourdoughs" who settled at the end of the tiny fjord and developed the town was still very much alive. The affinity the hardy locals felt for their land ran stronger than economic motives. That evening, they were concerned, uncertain about what the days and months would bring. Their fear and anger could hardly be concealed.

Why was the ship still leaking oil? Where was Alyeska with retaining boom, and clean up equipment? What was being done in these critical early hours to keep the situation from worsening? The sullying and polluting of their surroundings felt akin to a personal violation.[1]

Frank Iarossi assured them that Exxon was mobilizing skimming equipment, dispersants, and planes from around the globe, but that the first priority was to secure the more than 40 million gallons of crude oil that remained aboard the ship. The meeting remained mostly calm and cordial until questions about the upcoming fishing season were raised. Then the crowd of 125 people came to the ragged edge of control.

A stocky, dark haired man stood up. Ray Cesarini, owner of Sea Hawk Seafoods, a local processing plant, feared for his livelihood and that of local fishermen. He said, "I flew [out over the spill], with Chuck

LePage at two-thirty this afternoon, and there wasn't even a Kleenex in the water to clean up that oil." He said he had heard that morning on the radio that a decision had already been made to use chemical dispersants on the oil and speculated that was the reason there was no containment boom around the ship. Cesarini suspected Exxon and Alyeska had no intention whatsoever to skim the oil.

What about the fishing season that was supposed to start in a few weeks' time, Cesarini asked? Not only are the herring due to return to the Sound to spawn, but millions of salmon fry would soon emerge from streams and hatcheries. A chorus of gruff voices joined his. The oil companies had promised that oil and fishing could exist in harmony together. Now what about those whose livelihoods depended on fishing?

Riki Ott, who had flown over from Cordova earlier that morning stood and said, "You mentioned that Exxon is assuming all financial responsibility for the spill, which I think is a very positive step. But I would also like to point out that after the majority of the spill is cleaned up off the water and it looks like there is no more oil around, the oil can still be down in the water column and the fisheries resources can still be affected weeks after the spill looks like it is cleaned up. Now, I am interested to know whether the company is going to cover our fisheries resources. If, when the herring fishery opens, and our fishermen deliver to the local processors, and assuming they have a DEC person there, the DEC person discovers that hydrocarbons have been stored in the lipid levels of the herring or herring roe...."

Iarossi interrupted to assure her, "I said we would assume full financial responsibility. I didn't put any qualifications on it. If it is a claim that is associated with the spill, we've assumed full financial responsibility."

Pressing, she reminded him that the nature of the damage might not be known for years or even decades to come. Still, Iarossi remained steadfast, "We'll be just as concerned as you would be, so we'll be talking a lot with you and making all the checks that are necessary. We aren't going to be leaving for a long time."

Another member of the audience stood to question Iarossi. What about the talk of using dispersants, weren't those toxic to marine life? Iarossi quickly came to the defense of chemical dispersants, because they were his most powerful tool for making the oil disappear. "No, it is not toxic. It is totally non-toxic. I think the EPA agrees with that. Clearly."

Riki Ott interrupted him. In fact, dispersants only made the oil sink into the water column, she claimed. It suffocates the fragile marine organisms that support the food chain. Not only that, she said, the fish pick it up in their gills and retain the toxins in their systems. What consumer would want to purchase a fish from Alaska? The oil was bad enough, Ott said, and the use of dispersants would ruin the image of any fish sold in the entire state for years to come! It is not out of sight, out of mind. Using dispersants doesn't mean that the oil disappears, she exclaimed.

At that point, Iarossi said he preferred to defer questions about dispersants to Exxon's chief environmental scientist. Dr. Alan Maki, he said, was qualified to understand these complexities. Ott pointed out that she too had academic credentials relative to oil and sediment pollution as well as fisheries biology. At this, the crowd broke into a hearty applause.

Dr. Maki joined Iarossi at the podium, and explained that in fact, dispersants only speed the natural deterioration of the oil. It breaks the oil molecules apart so they can mix in with the water column. This speeds the natural evaporation, breakdown from light, and biodegradation. Dr. Maki pointed out, if the slick were left to its own devices, it would remain a cohesive mass floating on top of the water and would travel farther. This would affect sensitive coastline and beaches to a greater degree.

Iarossi glanced toward the Governor, who had just arrived back in town from Bligh Reef. He was standing alongside the Coast Guard Commander. No doubt Iarossi hoped he would still have full clearance for spraying dispersants in certain zones tomorrow. The skeptical crowd began to talk amongst themselves. Governor Cowper stepped forward. He addressed the crowd, "Everybody realizes the risk that dispersants pose to marine life. We are already seeing some effect on marine life just because of the oil. I want to assure everybody that dispersant is not going to be used in anything other than a carefully targeted way. We want to make sure that we check back with the fishing community, that we check with the Department of Fish and Game, and do as little damage as possible. You can't use dispersants without doing damage to marine life, that is clear. But we want, if possible, to keep oil off the beaches."

Frank Iarossi paused as if trying to divine the governor's intent. Was this for the benefit of the gathering tonight? Or was the state really having second thoughts about the use of dispersants? Only a few hours earlier, the Coast Guard said he had clearance for dispersant use in certain zones, only to then say that a test was needed? He didn't know it yet, but such indecision and uncertainty of authority would plague the cleanup process. One thing he was certain of, the longer the oil was in the water, the less effective dispersants would be.

Standing before the crowd gathered in the Civic Center, the Governor concluded by assuring them the question of dispersants was, "One of a whole lot of questions going to be asked and answered as a result of this disaster. This is not going to happen again. Once is too many times. We were assured, of course, that it would never happen."

As Frank Iarossi and Governor Cowper faced the citizens of Valdez that night, the faces of reporters brought the evening news to the people across America. As they watched their televisions at dinnertime, they learned of the growing magnitude of the spill in Prince William Sound. There was a possibility the captain was drunk, reporters said. Many stations had footage of the stricken tanker pitifully out of place in her breathtakingly beautiful surroundings.

After the press conference that Good Friday evening, Iarossi drove around the end of the bay to the Alyeska terminal, where he again announced that Exxon accepted responsibility for the cleanup of the spill, including removing the remaining oil from the *Valdez* and communicating with members of the public about progress.[2] Exxon would allow Alyeska to remain responsible for mechanically containing and picking up the oil already in the water, per the contingency plan. However, Iarossi's announcement seemed to contradict the obligations spelled out in the contingency plan on file with the state Department of Environmental Conservation which stated, "Alyeska will maintain full responsibility and control in the event of an oil spill unless a government agency specifically notifies Alyeska that they have assumed responsibility and control."[3]

State approval of the contingency plan was based on the specific guarantees it outlined which included mobilization of pre-identified workers and specified equipment in response to a spill. The plan provided no indication that a parent company of the consortium would step in to assume responsibility. Now Exxon would have to mobilize the cleanup effort and equipment from headquarters thousands of miles away. Iarossi later admitted, "We started from ground zero. There was no logistic system in place."[4]

Reacting to Exxon's assumption of authority, DEC Commissioner Dennis Kelso said, "There is no authority for such a transfer. We expected Alyeska to take care of the spill. In my view, the handoff is inappropriate. We are seeing a pattern of promised activity and broken promises. Alyeska has dropped out of the picture completely, washed their hands of this mess. Exxon says they are assuming responsibility, but there is a lack of organization."[5]

Iarossi seemed equally surprised by Kelso's response stating, "I am very puzzled by Kelso's comments about never being informed of our taking over a large spill. I don't think Dennis Kelso was ever aware of all the correspondence between his department and Exxon. I mean, we clearly stated all the way back in 1982 that in the event of a major spill, we would mobilize the spill response."

Iarossi went on to explain that in a 1982 letter to the DEC, Exxon wrote "for most tanker spills the response outlined in the Alyeska plan will suffice. However, in the event of a major spill by an Exxon owned and operated vessel it is anticipated that Exxon Company U.S.A.'s oil response team would be activated. In 1987, we spelled out our mobilization plan and where the equipment would be coming from. The state came back to us and said, 'Should Exxon vessels be limited to trade with the Trans-Alaska Pipeline Service Company and limited to Prince William Sound traffic, no contingency plan would be necessary.' The Alaska Department of Environmental Conservation never once raised any objection, so we said fine."[6]

Saturday morning dawned as still as the day before it. Nearly eighteen hours after the grounding, the *Exxon Baton Rouge* stood by to relieve the *Valdez* of her remaining cargo. But Bligh Reef was proving to be a precarious perch and bringing the *Baton Rouge* alongside the grounded ship progressed slowly. Divers went below the surface of the water, through a foot of solid oil, to inspect the damage and stability of the *Valdez*. It was eerily dark underneath and they had to wipe the thick oil from their masks and headlamps. What they found was unnerving.

The seven-eighth's-inch steel hull was ripped apart like a soft tin can, and holes large enough to drive a small car through were gushing oil. Eight of the eleven cargo tanks had been compromised and 50 percent of the ribs and hull of the ship's underside was damaged, perhaps from Hazelwood's frenetic attempts to command the ship off the reef. But the most alarming discovery was the narrow pinnacle of rock supporting the enormous weight of the ship. The supertanker continued to flex with the ebb tide and remained in real danger of rolling over or breaking apart as the weight rested more heavily on the reef.

Iarossi would not consider the possibility of abandoning more than a million barrels of oil despite the dangers of transferring the oil to another ship.[7] Engineers proceeded to carefully calculate the order in which tanks should be emptied and replaced with seawater to maintain balance. With four tugs and two Coast Guard vessels standing by, the *Baton Rouge* tied up alongside the *Valdez*. The thirty or forty crewmembers on board were equipped with exposure suits in case the ship capsized in spite of their plan. Until this task was accomplished, tensions would remain high.

The *Valdez* was captained now by Exxon's marine expert, William Deppe. As Captain Deppe deployed the ship's cargo pump, he noticed that oil emerged from the starboard side of the ship. It appeared as though the ship's piping system was too badly damaged to complete the transfer. With only 10,000 barrels transferred, Deppe elected instead to use portable pumps rather than knowingly release additional oil into the Sound. The Coast Guard was able to supply three pumps later that afternoon, and Exxon ordered nine additional pumps from Anchorage, Seattle, and Detroit.

The nearby skimmers remained idle, even as the additional skimming equipment that Exxon ordered from California and England began to arrive. The response crew still lacked an effective way of transferring the oil from the skimmers to a collection barge.

Twenty-four hours later, less than 1,000 barrels of oil had been recovered from the water, representing yet another failed attempt to meet the specifications outlined in the contingency plan. Iarossi was incredulous when he discovered that still no boom surrounded the *Valdez* in an effort to contain the oil hemorrhaging from her underside into waters now completely black and sluggish. He barked to his staff to get it done immediately. The media was crucifying him for it, he said.

Though the oil slick was slowly moving to the southwest, it was mostly still afloat on top of the water. A fire could still burn it off, skimmers could still pick it up, and dispersants were all still viable defenses against uncontrolled spreading. Dispersants were Frank Iarossi's first choice. Yet, he had been informed that the Coast Guard wanted to see tests before granting the go ahead for using the chemicals. On-scene coordinator for the Coast Guard, Commander Steve McCall was feeling the pressure for making such an important decision. Alyeska's contingency plan stated, "…dispersants will be considered as a possible response option only when mechanical containment and recovery response actions are not workable." As a state with one of the most liberal dispersant policies in the entire U.S., the state of Alaska had approved the plan years ago. The contingency plan also stated, "In all cases, the use of dispersants will be based on the determination that their impact will be less harmful than that of non-dispersed oil." Though he was being bombarded with opinions from state regulators, industry experts, fishermen, and environmentalists, McCall had no scientific training that could help him weigh these opinions or provide a basis for his decision. He concluded a test would be the best solution.[8]

This conflicted with what Iarossi understood he had been told earlier, but he agreed to record the results of a test spray on video. It took until early afternoon for Exxon to obtain a plane and load the dispersants. It was nearly dark by the time they got off the ground with 3,700 gallons of dispersants on board. The video crew said the film couldn't positively verify that the targeted area resulted in clearer water than the oily water surrounding its swath. But one thing was becoming clear—the prevailing political wind was not in favor of using chemical dispersants.

A test burn worked well at clearing approximately 15,000 gallons from the water, but the smoke it emitted was intolerable to the tiny nearby Native village of Tatitlek. The smoke had given them all headaches, and a pregnant woman had even miscarried, they said. Plans for another test burn were put on hold.

During a follow-up test on Sunday morning, Exxon dumped 5,100 gallons of dispersant on the slick, and after watching the video, Commander McCall seemed ready to approve the use of dispersants. Dennis Kelso remained very hesitant about an all-out approval, preferring instead that Exxon rely on mechanical recovery, the primary response priority outlined in the contingency plan. By Sunday morning however, Exxon had in fact only recovered 3,000 barrels of oil, while the plan projected that 100,000 barrels should have been recovered by then. As Valdez Mayor Devens noted, "That's 3,000 barrels under ideal [weather] conditions."[9]

In a Sunday press conference at the Civic Center, three days after the spill, Iarossi explained to a skeptical crowd, "We have been limited to mechanical pickup. It's not gonna do the job… It is the slowest and least effective tool. That is why it is so important to get the state's permission to burn, and so important to get the permission of all the authorities to begin to use dispersants."[10]

The meeting heated up as fishermen and environmentalists accused Exxon of caring more about the public relations debacle of the unsightly slick than doing the least long-term damage to the Sound. Using dispersants, they argued, would just be letting Big Oil off easy. Sitting next to Jack Lamb, president of the Cordova District Fishermen United, Riki Ott openly challenged Iarossi. "The contingency plan makes mechanical pickup the number one priority," she said, "So, let's get the stuff out of the water first, before relying on dispersants. Exxon is jumping on dispersants as the cure, but dispersants are just like soap. They just break up oil, the water looks better but the oil is still there."[11]

Iarossi argued, "We'll be here a year from now if we have to use only skimmers."

In exasperation, more to herself than aloud, Ott replied, "Oh, Iarossi. *That* guy. He'd never make it as a fisherman."[12]

Although the DEC argued that Exxon only had enough dispersants to treat 9 percent of the spill even if they were allowed, Commander McCall announced that there was an agreement to use dispersants by Sunday evening. However, experts noted that dispersant effectiveness is dependent upon a number of variables and had only been tested in hypothetical lab models. As Dr. James Butler of Harvard observed, "No one has successfully treated a spill of this size."[13]

Journalists from around the world converged on the small town in flocks, and by Sunday afternoon, outnumbered Exxon's seventy employees in Valdez. For the next few weeks, Prince William Sound would become a familiar landscape on the nightly news—the tanker cast on Bligh Reef, the Alyeska Terminal, and the utilitarian town of Valdez. They were images so horribly vivid, it seemed people could never forget, or fail to learn from such a tragic event. The first pictures were of dead birds of all shapes—small squatty murres, or cormorants with once graceful long necks—now oiled and limp. How helpless and dependent they were on humans to preserve their environment, and how neglectful we have been to allow this to happen, reporters said.

Public anger grew and many American citizens cut up their Exxon gas cards, resolving never to purchase gas at an Exxon station again. Exxon took out full-page ads in major metropolitan cities across the country, apologizing for the spill. Studies have shown that corporate disasters such as the exploding Ford Pinto, Tylenol tampering, and impurities in baby food can take years to overcome. With such information at hand, Exxon made an early offensive play to allay the emotional images of dead animals and pollution. But Americans still became angry with the oil giant. Before Wall Street could open after those first shocking three days, there was speculation oil prices would spike as a result of the spill. Alaskans, in particular, were enraged that the oil industry would rub salt in a fresh wound by profiting from the spill.

The pipeline closed down until further notice immediately after the spill. That would cut the national supply by eight million barrels a day, or one of every four gallons of gas, reporters said. Oil flowed through the Alyeska pipeline at a profit of $400,000 per hour. At that rate, the oil companies would be anxious to resume the supply for an energy hungry nation. In Seattle, a town with a strong emotional bond to Alaska and to the environment in general, Kathi Goertzen of Channel 4 News followed the spill and developing stories closely. She said the pro-oil Bush administration's bill before Congress to open the Arctic National Wildlife Refuge could be in jeopardy. The sudden attention drawn to the environment may have been just enough to thwart drilling in one of the last untouched places in the world.

By Sunday, the third day after the spill, the press conferences had become a twice-daily event. The mood in the Civic Center grew increasingly angry and frustrated as arguments over the lack of progress and use of dispersants erupted. At the start of each meeting, Exxon began with an update on the progress being made. Oil boom and skimmers were on the way, this many dispersants had been marshaled, and equipment was being flown in from all over the world. But these activities seemed to Valdez residents to be merely busy work performed by men in suits. What of the grubby, hands-on activity of actually containing and recovering the oil? What about the oil remaining aboard the stricken tanker? The oil companies seemed to run a highly efficient machine, extracting millions of gallons from the earth, sending it down a pipeline and transporting it to market. But when it came to a crisis like this, they seemed literally helpless to stop the oil now spreading unbridled through their pristine waters.

In the Civic Center, a divider separated the spill meeting from an Easter Sunday church service. Frustrated voices from the meeting permeated the religious gathering. It was a bitterly sad hour for all those inside the center. Some mourned the sacrifice of Christ, that all may be saved, while others mourned the sacrifice of their place on earth, that a nation so dependent on oil might be provided with the energy it needed.

The pocket-sized town of Valdez was being taken by storm. Consultants, contractors, politicians, executives, and journalists all arrived with laptop computers and cameras in hand. There was a sense that sheer activity would somehow help. Three critical days had passed since the spill. All the mobilizing, organizing, approvals, disapprovals, arguing, meetings, and marshaling of equipment had accomplished pitifully little. As the sun began to set in the pearly pale sky that Easter evening, the locals began to acknowledge they had lost the battle.

A breath of wind stirred on the powdery white Chugach Mountains encircling the town. Resembling a perfect Disneyland sculpture, Sugarloaf Mountain stood perhaps not higher, but more distinct than the rest. The fine wispy snow atop Sugarloaf began to swirl, forming a spiky disorganized halo around its peak. The locals called it "smoking" and they all knew that when mountain began to smoke, it was a signal of stormy weather to come.

5

Irreconcilable Views

PRINCE WILLIAM SOUND: APRIL 1, 1989

I T WOULD BE EIGHT DAYS BEFORE BOBBY DAY actually saw the oil for himself. Not through the lens of a CNN camera or described by a reporter, but with the accompanying smell and taste of oil finally confirming the magnitude of the tragedy. In the days past, he'd been inundated with news of the slick spreading throughout Prince William Sound. He thought he was ready.

For the first time that spring, the April day was as soft and warm as a kiss on the cheek. The tiny plane vibrated as Lori wound up the engine. Sun shone hazily through a fine film of clouds and Bobby reached over to open the tiny fold-down window. The air was as smooth as the water and Lori's takeoff was perfect. Bobby hardly noticed they were underway. He watched as the tree-lined beach grew smaller and distant. They were quiet in anticipation of what the day would bring. Their lack of conversation was the comfortable, easy silence of two people who knew each other well.

Both were weary of talking about the spill, speculating, and going over scenarios. Lori had been offered a contract to work on the oil spill, and not knowing whether the herring season would open or not, he encouraged her to take it. She would fly him back to Valdez, only to leave again for Cordova. For two hours they flew quietly but for the drone of the engine, north by west along the edge of the Gulf of Alaska.

As the plane followed the contours of the rugged coastline from Glacier Bay to Yakutat and Cape Yakatanga, Bobby's mind raced from recollections of his own experiences fishing in these waters to the history that had shaped south central Alaska and its residents. With Kayak Island on the left and the Bering Glacier gleaming like a jewel in the Chugach mountain range to the right, the plane would soon cross over the oil-rich marshes where the town of Katalla once stood.

Once the epicenter of oil development in Alaska, the town no longer existed. Bobby reflected on the folklore that locals shared about the once booming oil town.

In September of 1902, golden birch leaves blew frenetically in the autumn breeze, sifting through slender evergreens and settling in the tidal sloughs where the Bering River flows into the Gulf of Alaska. Burnt orange marsh grass concealed trumpeter swans and hundreds of tweed colored ducks. A sudden explosion filled the skies with flapping wings and cries of excitement from the men beneath them. An oil gusher, spewing and steamy, shot eighty-five feet into the air before it could be capped. That fountain of oil, estimated to produce 1,600 barrels per day, symbolized an unbridled greed that would descend upon Alaska in the coming century. The character and politics of the land would forever be changed, for better and for worse, from that day forward.

The site was known as Katalla, meaning "oil."[1] The drill site had been discovered eight years earlier by an Alaskan pioneer named Tom White. According to Alaska folklore, White was chasing a bear he had shot when he fell in an oily pool, smearing himself and his gun with the black stuff. He took some of it back to his camp, and found that it lit his campfire with "great success."[2] He returned to Katalla in 1897 with two friends and an idea that he had perhaps found something of value and substance. As White himself recalled, "We found a little stream of petroleum bubbling out of the ground. I thought this was a fine chance so I lighted another match and threw it down into the oil. Heavens what a surprise! Instantly the oil was aflame, and a flow of natural gas issuing with the oil created a gusher of fire as high as the trees. I was singed about the face before I could get away."[3]

White and his companions collected samples and sent them to Seattle to be tested. The results showed a very high paraffin base, indicating that lubrication and illumination value could be obtained with very little residue from this oil. So along with two of his friends, White lobbied several different oil companies to come and drill the site they had since claimed. The "three greasers," as they came to be known, were finally rewarded on that blustery September day in 1902.

Although it was the first commercially promising well, the notion of oil existing in Alaska was not new. The Eskimos had used it for burning, likely even before the land was purchased from Russia in 1867. In 1836, the Hudson's Bay Company had observed oil seeps along the Arctic Coast. In fact, oil seeps could be found from Oil Bay in Cook Inlet to Icy Bay. Some of the old sourdoughs were convinced there was oil all over Alaska. The first well was drilled inside Cook Inlet on the Iniskin Peninsula in 1898. The well produced fifty barrels of oil at a depth of seven hundred feet, but turned to water at one thousand feet and was abandoned. It wasn't until that September day in Katalla that a well of commercial significance was discovered. Oil speculation would soon reach a fever pitch on the order of a second gold rush.

On September 18, 1902, the *New York Times* ran a full-page story saying, "An immense oil gusher was struck at Cotella (sic) on the south Alaska coast… The gusher took everything away with it, rising nearly 200 feet before it could be capped…. An important new industry is thus added to Alaska's resources." Even though the following winter proved to be unusually harsh, it did not discourage the throngs of speculators coming to stake a claim. By March 17, 1903, the *Seattle Mail & Herald* printed an article stating, "The whole country way out on the mountains and glaciers has been staked on the snow, and recorded, and in many instances several times over, and it is such cases as this in which the grafter and curb broker are now offering at any price on the street, and the myriad of fly-by-night fakes are being organized, and this statement is printed in order that intending investors may take notice." By late spring, the Alaska Petroleum and Coal Company had platted a new town site. It wasn't long before a booming town of ten thousand people and six saloons came into being. By 1904 fifteen more wells were drilled and half promised to deliver commercially viable quantities of oil.[4]

The discovery of oil at Katalla didn't go unnoticed by the mining interests in the interior Wrangell Mountains. Massive deposits of copper had been discovered in an area that would soon be known as Kennicott. During the early 1900s, no less than fifty railroad interests were negotiating to build rails and secure an exclusive contract to transport the copper to a seaport. Valdez, Cordova, and now Katalla were all possible sites.

Valdez was the metropolis of south central Alaska at the turn of the century. The bustling little town was well established and protected by the military base at nearby Fort Liscum. With a protected deep-water port to offer, the people of Valdez felt certain their site would be chosen. Cordova, not yet an official town, was seventy miles to the southeast of Valdez, and Katalla was another fifty miles southeast of Cordova.

Two of the railroad interests began laying track from the town of Valdez, racing for Keystone Canyon, where only one line of tracks would fit through the narrow chasm at the base of the Chugach Mountains. As the tracks neared the mouth of the canyon, a shootout ensued and the Copper River and Northwestern Railway, owned and operated by a Guggenheim Syndicate, was victorious. The operator of the losing railway left in the middle of the night, having spent the hard earned investment contributions of several Valdez residents. But the Guggenheim Syndicate ultimately chose Cordova as the railroad terminus, a defeat that fostered a lasting resentment and rivalry between the people of Valdez and Cordova.

The town of Cordova evolved from a Native village called Eyak, nestled on an evergreen covered ridge between Eyak Lake and Orca Inlet on the southeastern edge of Prince William Sound. Seventy miles to the southeast of Valdez, the village of Eyak was nearer to the Gulf of Alaska yet still offered a protected deep-water port. Though the area was breathtakingly beautiful and rich with natural salmon runs and wild game, it was extremely remote and lacking in infrastructure. During the late 1800s, the Alaska Packers Association established a cannery, wharf, and docks at the village of Eyak. According to visiting Presbyterian Minister Sheldon Jackson in 1894, "the town consisted of 25 white men, 25 native women, and 25 stills capable of producing 2,500 gallons of liquor...."[5] It was a very inconspicuous beginning for a town that would soon be booming.

Michael J. Heney, backed by the Close Brothers Consortium of England, originally filed a claim to run a railway up the Copper River through Abercrombie Canyon, following its natural path into the interior. Heney's consortium purchased the wharf and buildings from the Alaska Packer's Association located at Three Tree Point. A steamer unloaded supplies using the tramline at the old Packer's Association wharf and the building for storage. Seven men pitched tents, and it was in this canvas camp that a telegram arrived on the steamer *Elsie* from Valdez. Heney's telegram instructed his men to form a town and name it Cordova, after the name given to the bay by Spanish explorer, Salvador Fidalgo. So, in the spring of 1906, a wooden sign was carved bearing the town's new name and nailed to a tree.

Katalla, fifty miles to the southeast of Cordova, proved to be a poor location for a seaport. Situated on the edge of the Gulf of Alaska, the area was plagued by violent storms, shallow waters, and crashing tides. Still, the Guggenheims preferred the Katalla site for a railway terminus as its rich deposits of coal could be used as fuel to run the railroad and smelter the copper from the interior mines. Katalla reached a high point in 1906, when it was considered the "Pittsburgh of Alaska." But a devastating storm in the winter of 1906 took most of the wind out of the town's sails, which had adopted the slogan "Katalla—Where the Rails meet the Sails."[6] A late autumn storm collided with the highest tides of the year, scattering the boulders of the newly built breakwater like pebbles in the heavy seas. Only a few random pilings from the pier revealed evidence of development. The railroad trestles built over the nearby sloughs were all but destroyed. Steamships refused to dock at the remnants of the Katalla site. Though the *Katalla Herald* insisted that the Guggenheims had not abandoned the town, it was inevitable. The Guggenheim Syndicate bought out the interests and right of way developed by the Heney Consortium. Cordova would be the railway terminus for the copper mines at Kennicott.

The winter of 1907 again brought harsh storms to the region of Katalla and Cordova—endless downpours of rain and snow, eighty-mile-an-hour winds, and dark clouds of jealousy. The hours of Alaska winter darkness and confinement indoors left plenty of time for bickering and barbs between the two towns. The bantering revealed itself in the towns' rival newspapers. Cordova stole the slogan "Where the Rails meet the Sails." The *Katalla Herald* responded by sniffing at Cordova as a "temporary base of supplies."[7] The *Cordova Alaskan* retorted, "Pity the blind, Katalla should send for a box of Dr. Hill's famous eye salve. With this medicine, Katalla would be able to see its own demise."[8] Little was heard from the Valdez newspapers. The town seemed to be stewing privately in its own pot of resentment over the lost economic opportunities that might have arrived with each train.

In April of 1911, the first steamship of copper ore left Cordova, bound for the Port of Tacoma in Washington State. During World War I, the market prices for copper skyrocketed and the mines at Kennicott accounted for one-fifth of the world's copper production. The town of Cordova was bursting at the seams, sending the prices for real estate soaring. After some negotiating and a good deal of political wrangling, the town folk filled in a salmon stream and small canyon to expand the town's reach and create the site where Cordova sits today.

Katalla's culture became as turbulent as the weather as claim jumpers and drilling skirmishes abounded. Steamships, even the mail, passed the town by. Soon protest meetings were held, castigating the Heney Consortium and the Guggenheims, steamship companies, and of course the town of Cordova. Meanwhile, four different companies drilled for oil, but few wells of commercial significance were ever discovered. On Christmas Eve in 1933, a tremendous fire burned the refinery at Katalla. The people of Katalla could deny it no more—the town had met its demise.

After World War I, demand and prices for copper collapsed and in 1938, the railway to Cordova closed down, having transported $200 million worth of copper. For a few decades at least, Cordova had enjoyed an old-fashioned Alaska boom. As the railroad hauled load after load of copper ore from the interior, the fishing industry in Cordova flourished, creating a diverse economy that would ultimately save the town. By 1938 when the railroad closed down, the number of Cordovans employed in the fishing industry outnumbered railroad workers by a ratio of five to one.

During the 1920s the city had constructed a small wharf to support a robust fleet of small fishing vessels delivering their catch to the canneries. Crab and herring fisheries developed in the late 1920s and early 1930s, adding to the salmon and clam harvests for which Cordova would become increasingly famous. Front Street and the slough south of town were crowded with nine salmon and clam canneries. With the closing of the railroad in 1938, Cordova returned to its roots. Just as the Alaska Packer's Association had once been the only source of economic sustenance for the town, Cordova's economy again became dependent solely upon fishing and salmon canning.

The isolated town of Cordova, accessible only by boat or plane, grew comfortable with its dependence on the abundance of seafood in Prince William Sound. But remnants of the oil and copper boom remained. The old building that had served as a gambling house, a reading room, and church on Sundays, still stood. A massive, ornate, stained-glass and mahogany liquor case, brought over from Katalla, stood majestically behind the bar in the Alaskan Hotel.

The people of Cordova would not soon forget the economic boom that copper had brought to the town, nor the potential consequences the closure of the mines would have wrought had the railway been the sole source of economic activity. In the decades to come, Cordova would cast a wary eye toward extraction of non-renewable resources that could disrupt the stability and comfort of a community dependent upon Prince William Sound.

The plane had traced fifty miles of coastline since they passed over the old town site of Katalla, and the familiar curve of Orca Inlet and the town of Cordova were coming into view. Bobby thought it was little wonder that Cordovans had been wary of oil development, and that rifts between the towns of Valdez and Cordova became chasms at the outset of the latest oil boom.

At the first mention of shipping oil through Prince William Sound, members of the Cordova District Fishermen United gathered at the union hall to oppose a pipeline terminus in Valdez. Bobby would never forget the night his friends and fellow fishermen stood at the doorway of the hall, refusing to let him in. Although he had fished alongside his union brethren and been a card-carrying member for over ten years, they shared different histories and loyalties.

That night the fishermen intended to take a vote on whether the union should file a lawsuit to stop the construction of any oil pipeline that would include tanker traffic through the Sound. Bobby lived in Valdez and it seemed he couldn't be trusted to act in solidarity with the opinion of the majority of the members. Just when the conflict promised to become violent, the weathered face of Chet Chaser,

Bobby's friend and mentor, appeared at the center of the crowd. His soft voice reminded the group that although Bobby was from Valdez, he was one of them. "You ought to let him in," he said. Bobby reflected now how right his union brethren had been.

The soft air coming in through the window of the plane suddenly became pungent and oily, bringing him back to an unwelcome new reality. He looked down at the waters of Prince William Sound and exhaled in disbelief. The once-emerald waters of the the Sound were now fouled with a frothy brown mixture of emulsified oil and seawater. The smell was unbelievably strong, stinging their eyes and seeming to grasp their lungs with a tightening fist. The slick extended across 1,200 square miles of the Sound.

After the three calm days following the spill, the winds that stirred atop Sugarloaf on Easter Sunday delivered on their promise. The halo around Sugarloaf ushered in a spring blizzard replete with seventy-knot winds and twenty-foot whitecaps that raced across the Sound carrying the oil more than forty miles in one night. Planes that were to carry dispersants to the slick were grounded, boats were hemmed in the harbor by heavy seas, and a late spring snow blew across the Sound and town of Valdez. An estimated eleven million gallons of oil had escaped the cargo compartments of the *Exxon Valdez*. Looking down at the water, Bobby realized that his future was now inextricably tied to the will of the currents and winds destined to carry the oil to the most valuable fishing grounds, and to the holding pens of the San Juan hatchery where more than 117 million pink salmon fry were due to be released into the Sound. Out at the entrance to Sawmill Bay in the southwest corner of the Sound, a fleet of Cordova fishermen struggled to hold back the leading edge of the oil surging toward the hatchery on a three-knot current, using a boom that was far too light for the task.

Lori took the plane lower, skimming fifty feet above the foul water, then turned north as they crossed over the northern end of Montague Island. Through the window on the passenger side, they could see the beach was black and thickly matted with oil. A dead deer and her fawn lay bloated and stiff, their bellies full of young tender sea grass covered with crude. Bobby had never felt such anger and desperation. The oil companies had come to Alaska with promises that every possible technology and safeguard would be used. They promised this could never happen. He'd risked his life making a living in these waters. In defending the promises of the oil companies, he had made enemies of friends. He'd been betrayed.

Fist clenched, he stared down at the scene unfolding in front of him: there was oil in a place where it never should have been, in a place the oil industry and government regulators promised would be protected. Bobby wondered about news reports alluding to a drunken oil tanker captain. How had the Coast Guard missed the tanker veering off course on the radar? Where had the rescue tug and harbor captain been? Why had the oil not been contained and recovered as the contingency plans outlined? He knew only that nothing could undo what had been done.

Bobby could not meet Lori's eyes as he glanced out her side of the plane. As each island came onto the horizon—Knight, Eleanor, Smith and Naked Island—he could see that few escaped the reach of the massive oil slick. Once gems among emerald waters, they were now rimmed in black up to forty feet above the tidal rocks where waves from the spring storm had splashed oil and left it behind. Bobby had spent a lifetime in these waters, among these islands, each one evoking a memory.

Carved by glaciers, abrupt rocky island cliffs emerged from the Sound. Sitka spruce covered their steep slopes, shading hidden coves and crystal clear water falls. Bobby remembered pulling his boat onto the beach at high tide, then rigging a funnel and hose to trap the water flowing down through dark shiny boulders and filling the tanks of his boat with the best water he'd ever tasted. He recalled the times he tiptoed through the forest carpeted with thick moss and pine needles, suddenly emerging from the forest at the edge of a beautiful meadow to surprise a deer calmly eating blueberries from a bush. He loved sitting perfectly alone next to their ponds and lakes, the smell of skunk cabbage filling his nostrils. Sometimes he was the only human being on an entire island. It was a soul-filling solitude.

At times, the islands could seem wild and harsh in a winter storm or like a protector as he slipped into a friendly cove to hide from the wrath of a frigid northerly gale and buffeting whitecaps. Other times, they were generous as he dug clams on their beaches, fished at their capes or hunted for food in their forests. Always, they had seemed timeless. Now they seemed fragile and vulnerable. Like a friend in need, the islands seemed to beg him for help. He touched the glass of the window as he looked out. He knew he was powerless to help and his throat tightened in utter frustration and sorrow.

Lori took the plane on a sweeping curve back to the right. They had completed a semicircle and were again heading east. The Narrows, the entrance to Valdez Bay was the view to the left. Straight ahead and just to the right was Bligh Reef. The *Exxon Valdez* remained cast on the rocks with approximately twenty-five million gallons of oil remaining on board. The *Exxon San Francisco* sat alongside, relieving the *Baton Rouge* of the lightening effort. Two fishing boats secured boom around the two ships.

Bobby tried to analyze just how the tanker had come to rest at that angle and direction. He shook his head, failing to find any explanation. They banked and flew directly over the tanker, unable to guess what impact it would have on their lives but knowing they would never forget what they had seen that day.

Straight ahead, the rounded shoulder of Knowles Head extended out into the Sound, just south of Bligh Reef. Three tankers were anchored just off Knowles Head, waiting to enter the Port of Valdez under new restrictions the Coast Guard enacted after opening the port again for tanker traffic in the days following the spill. Tankers now had to be accompanied individually by a tug, and could only enter the port during daylight hours.

Bobby thought of the countless hours he had spent fishing herring in the wintertime just off Knowles Head. He had come to believe the best time to catch herring was on a dark, moonless night and thought back to the nights he had spent there. The winter air coming in through the window tasted as cold as a martini on the rocks. Green and blue hues of the aurora borealis flashed and shimmered in the sky. He heard the sea lions barking and diving down for the same herring he was trying to catch. Their doglike heads with whiskery faces and question mark ears would pop up suddenly next to the boat, dark eyes looking curiously. He heard an occasional whoosh as a whale breached right next to the boat and the air coming in the wheelhouse window would suddenly turn warm and foul. Bobby had the strange feeling the orcas and humpbacks somehow sought the companionship of their fellow human fishers and were trying in some way to communicate. These encounters never ceased to thrill him.

Perhaps that was why he loved the winter "bait" fishery so much. Most of his catch was frozen in giant blocks and sent to zoos all over the west coast and Hawaii. The herring he captured at sea went to feed penguins, otters, dolphins, orcas, and bears in captivity. Other fishermen would use his herring as bait to catch crab, halibut and black cod. It was satisfying to think he had helped to pioneer this fishery. Not many others participated in the wintertime fisheries and he reveled in the solitude. The part-time fishermen who had other jobs, but fished for salmon in the summertime, were gone. Only a hardy few whose entire income depended solely on fishing pursued elusive herring in frigid winter waters.

Whether it was superstition or the wisdom gained from years of experience, Bobby believed the herring had almost supernatural senses. He insisted the boat be kept completely dark, that all lights were turned off. He thought even a tiny beam peeking out from behind the blinds would scare the herring away. If a door or drawer was slammed absentmindedly by a crew member, he would hiss in a loud whisper to be quiet. Stealthily, he would idle the boat back and forth off Knowles Head using a sonar and depth finder to locate them. Herring are only about eight inches long and travel in large schools resembling mobile, swarming spheres. It is uncanny how quickly they can suddenly dart together, several hundred tons of them at once, disappearing in the depths as suddenly as they had come.

Bobby thrived on the challenge of catching them. To him, it was the ultimate game and he had always felt lucky to make a living doing what he loved. On those dark but starry nights, the scent of nearby pines blending with the sea, his heart would quicken as the sonar began to make a pinging sound. Quickly, he would check the depth finder to see how thick they were. It was an art to interpret the signals of the instruments and to judge the size of the school. When he had them wrapped in his net like a drawstring purse, they would panic and dive for the deep bottom of Prince William Sound. Part of the game was placing the boat and skiff strategically to keep them contained until they could be pumped aboard the boat. After so many years of fishing, he still felt a pride and sense of accomplishment when the boat was loaded with fish. It was a lifestyle he wouldn't trade for anything—it was the only thing he had ever known. The markets and prices had been good to him lately. Just last year, the Prince William Sound herring fishery yielded over $12 million to the fishermen. Finally, his years of hard work and sacrifice had been financially rewarding.

As he looked down at the tankers now anchored at Knowles Head, he wondered if nature was powerful enough to overcome the effects of eleven million gallons of crude oil. If the powerful currents of Prince William Sound would eventually scour away the filth and devastation he had seen that day. He wondered if he would ever catch another herring at Knowles Head.

They circled around Bligh Reef then headed through the Narrows toward Valdez Bay. Lori began to lower the altitude of the plane and called ahead to the Valdez tower. Although she wouldn't normally check in for a water landing on the bay, these weren't normal times. She would have to wait for clearance, they told her. With a population of about 3,000, Valdez usually received three flights a day from a local passenger aircraft, and a handful of small planes. In the week following the spill, more than a thousand flights had arrived. The tiny airport nestled next to a buffer of cottonwood trees at the base of the Chugach Mountains was still struggling to coordinate the barrage of air traffic.

"Clearance?" Bobby asked, thinking he had not understood. Lori nodded. For over forty years he'd been flying in and out of Valdez. Never before had he seen so much traffic. Everything he had seen that day, and now that voice from the tower. It was no longer the Valdez he knew.

They were nearing the end of the bay—Valdez on the north side, and the oil terminal to the south across the water from the town. As he looked at the view of the terminal framed by the plane's tiny window, he saw not what was there, but what used to be. In the picture in his mind, there were no cylindrical tanks cut into the rocky hillside. The loading berths, offices, and the ballast water holding pools were all gone. It was the 1950s again, before Alaska revealed the riches she held deep within her, perhaps a simpler time. Before the economics of development had influenced politics, when a sparse population lived in harmony with the land and each other. In his sudden vivid recollection was the picture of an idyllic tiny town.

The memories came flowing back as sharp and fresh as if it were only yesterday. A small peninsula of land reached out in a hook shape, as if extending a protective arm around the small cove it formed. The spit of land about a mile long connected to the mainland with a narrow strip of sand ideal for family picnics. At the point of the peninsula were sturdy buildings his father had helped construct. On the outermost tip, facing in toward the cove they called Swan's Port, was a two-story lumber mill and warehouse. It had the shiny finish of galvanized tin and extended out into the water on pilings.

Next to it was a smaller, false fronted, western-style building. Across the top, neat block letters read "A.S. Day & Sons General Store." A rocky shale cliff fell away in front of it and stubby evergreen trees surrounded it on the other three sides. A weathered wooden boardwalk led to the salmon cannery next door. The cannery building was once part of an army base known as Fort Liscum. The building had been moved down the steep hill in pieces, and out onto the peninsula in the 1930s. Up the hill across from the buildings, the remaining army barracks had been formed into individual houses, as simple and sincere as the black and white photos in his family album. What was once the commander's house sat up the hill above the rest. The Big House, as they called it, was where Bobby's Grandma and Grandpa Day lived. Allison Creek tumbled down the mountain next to the houses, providing them with power and pure glacier water. A simple wooden archway identified the rustic little town as "Dayville, Alaska."

Bobby Day in the skiff, Dayville, Alaska, circa 1953. *Gloria Day collection*

Cannery at Dayville, early 1950s. *Gloria Day collection*

Cookhouse at Dayville. Early 1950s. *Gloria Day collection*

Oma Belle built by Walter and Andy Day at Dayville. Launched in 1931. *Gloria Day collection*

The store was one of the original buildings at Dayville. *Gloria Day collection*

Cannery, store, sawmill, and warehouse at Dayville, early 1950s. *Gloria Day collection*

Bobby Day and his son Ed. Mending net for the upcoming salmon season, 1965. *Author's collection*

The *Theresa Marie*, launched at Delta Marine in Seattle, Washington, in 1983. *Author's collection*

Cordova, Alaska, boat harbor in 2002. *Author's collection*

Bobby Day offering advice on mending a net in the Valdez boat harbor in 2007. *Author's collection*

Construction of the Alyeska Marine Terminal at the Dayville site in 1974. *Author's collection*

Herring set of 240 tons in 1974. Dale Dawson on the flying bridge. *Author's collection*

Seine boats waiting for the spring herring opener in Emerald Cove, near Columbia Glacier in Prince William Sound, 1975. *Author's collection*

Village of Tatitlek, 2007. *Author's collection*

A flotilla of commercial boats protesting the docking of foreign flagged tankers. Oil tanker in the background. Valdez Harbor (Prince William Sound).
ASA-RG348-SR612-AS17959-1917.jpg. Alaska State Archives

Governor Steve Cowper and DEC Commissioner Dennis Kelso tour spill impacted beaches prior to the one-year anniversary of the *Exxon Valdez* oil spill. Sleepy Bay, LaTouche Island (Prince William Sound). March 22, 1990. *Alaska Resources Library & Information Services, www.arlis.org.*

Alaskan Governor Steve Cowper is questioned by the press during the *Exxon Valdez* one-year anniversary press conference. Visual Arts Center, Anchorage, March 23, 1990. *Alaska Resources Library & Information Services, www.arlis.org.*

6

Silver On A Line

THE CHILL OF AN EARLY MORNING AUTUMN FOG seemed to cling to young Bobby's wavy amber hair and eyelashes as he walked down to the cannery. He kept an eye out for black bears, which were particularly brave this time of year. His grandmother regularly chased them off her porch, waving a broom and screeching. Bears weren't known to approach people, but Bobby's pale blue eyes scanned the woods just a little warily.

He stuffed his hands in his pockets, hunching his shoulders against the cold as he made his way a mile down the hill. He wasn't really supposed to go alone but he often found himself there. Though he was only ten, he thought of himself as quite grown up. The nip in the air had seeped through his canvas jacket and the warm humid air inside the cannery felt good. It had a smell all its own, a steamy mixture of machinery grease, cooking salmon, and wet wood. He walked slowly through, fascinated by the machinery, making sure to stay out of the way. At this hour the workers were well into their day. They worked eighty hours a week during the summer, and when the short days of winter came the cannery would again sit silently encased in a tomb of snow before coming to life again the following summer. It was a cycle quite typical in Alaska. It seemed as though everything was boom or bust. As busy as the rapid report of a miner's pickax, or still as fresh fallen snow.

The *Olivia H* was tied to the dock, just below the cannery. She was loaded with pink salmon and sat low in the water like a satisfied bear with a full stomach. Two men stood on her deck with sharp, single-tined forks on a handle known as fish pughs. They would unload the *Olivia H* by hand using the pughs to pluck the deck clean and toss them onto a conveyor belt, fish by fish. The conveyor belt began to turn with a whump, whump, as the paddles on the belt rounded the end and returned the opposite direction. The motor hummed, carrying the fish up inside the cannery. The paddles were placed three feet apart and dumped the fish into sorting bins just inside the cannery.

Several men sorted the fish in the boxes. If an odd silver or chum salmon was mixed in with a batch of pinks, it was set aside. Most of the workers had golden brown skin—they were Aleut or Athabaskan Natives, or Filipino. White-cotton-gloved hands worked quickly as they sorted and pitched the fish. Bright yellow oilskin aprons covered their legs, and booted feet never wasted a step. The process started with a man gently shoving one fish at a time into a machine they called the "Iron Chink."

Invented and named in a time before political correctness was a consideration, the metal machine was first used in Victoria, British Columbia. There on Vancouver Island many of the cannery workers were Chinese. This new gadget, invented during the early 1900s, revolutionized the fish butchering process. It was so named because it did the work of thirty Chinese workers. It stood about the same height as a man and took up nine square feet.

Once a fish was inserted into the grips of the machine, carefully so no fingers were included, it traveled up the chute. A blade removed the head and split the fish down the bloodline of the belly. The fish then traveled around the main circular part of the machine and a spinning brush at the bottom scooped out the innards. The floor was open under the Iron Chink so the heads and innards fell to the water below. Before the tide could carry them away, seagulls gathered in flocks of white and gray, feasting in grand style on the rejected parts. Bobby could hear their loud calls through the opening. The melancholy cries echoed off the steep mountains behind and reverberated throughout the bay.

The trip through the Iron Chink took only a few seconds and the fish were once again traveling on a conveyor toward the "sliming table." Five or six workers would put the finishing touches on each fish. They cleaned inside or trimmed fins the Iron Chink had missed. Bobby watched the quick motions of the slimers as their knives flashed and clicked. The fish were ready to be canned. Once again, they scuttled along a conveyor, this time toward the slicing machine.

The razor-sharp knife was almost soundless as it cut cleanly through each fish, skin, bones, and all. A separate machine took flattened cans, rounded them out, and lined them up just in time to receive the fish from the slicing machine. A worker observed the machine as it packed and weighed each can. Over or under weights were kicked off the conveyer, while the others proceeded to the next step. Another machine measured and dumped salt into each can, set the lid in place, and sealed it. The cans emerged from one last conveyor and lined up in metal racks. Finally the racks were slid into giant retort ovens and cooked for ninety minutes at 240 degrees. The system yielded 200 cans per minute. Bobby remembered a time not so long ago, when the whole process had been done by hand. So many workers, hours, and sleepless nights for so few cans. He would never grow tired of watching the machines tirelessly doing the work human hands had once labored over, progress he had witnessed within his short lifetime.

Wondering where his father might be, Bobby kept walking through to the warehouse section. Racks of cans that had just been wheeled in from the retort were lined up across the warehouse floor. He listened to the pinging sound they made as the cooling cans contracted. It sounded like a band of vibes—a happy melodic sound that echoed off the high ceiling. He knew that sound always made his father happy. It told him the cans had all been properly sealed. It was the sound of profit.

Bobby walked toward the back of the cannery and stuck his head inside the boiler room. It smelled of hot oil and he could hear the roaring oil-fueled fire. He saw his father lying on a narrow wooden bench.

Walter Day lay on his back, thick hands folded over his narrow waist. Emerging from his half-unbuttoned flannel shirt, and tousled upon his head, curly black hair gave him an unruly look. His small wiry body appeared perfectly comfortable. Watching the easy rise and fall of his father's chest, Bobby hesitated to walk into the room. It seemed his father never actually slept—that his kind, gray eyes would instantly flutter open if he sensed anything at all was amiss.

During salmon season, his father rarely came the mile up the hill to the house. The cannery operated nearly as many hours as the Alaska summer days were long. When the workers were there, Walter coordinated and kept everything running as only a dynamic leader could. At night, he methodically took apart, cleaned, sharpened, and oiled all the machinery. Only as the first pale light of early dawn arrived would he lay down on his bench to rest. For the many months of salmon season, he seemed to run on sheer strength and passion for what he did. How many others could have worked so tirelessly, been responsible for so many livelihoods, and remained such a kind and unflappable leader, Bobby would later wonder. Perhaps it was just his unique personality, his deep religious faith, the struggles in his past, or a combination of those factors.

Born in Bradshaw, West Virginia, Walter was the oldest of five children. His formal education ended with the eighth grade, as he joined his father in the coal mines. They shoveled coal by hand and watched as it trundled away on rail cars, leaving them behind in a fine choking dust. Oil lanterns gave off a stingy amount of light, revealing a mountain-side of work to be done. Walter was a quiet, thoughtful boy who could do the work of any man.

It could have been the government pamphlets circulating at that time, advertising free land to homesteaders. Or perhaps it was just the realization that America held many promises for those brave enough to pursue a dream. For whatever reason, the Day family decided to leave the dark and dusty mines for the promise of something better. Walter and his father had worked a year to save the twenty dollars stashed in the glove box as their Model A crossed the West Virginia state line.

It was the early 1920s and odd jobs supported them all the way to the badlands of eastern Montana. A wind squall stirred a cloud of dust and the Days stared with wonder as the barren flat land unfolded around them. As they approached Miles City, Montana, the land became dotted with farmhouses. They were of a sturdy sort, of the same modest and practical build as the European immigrants who had constructed many of them. Some stood eerily vacant—the recent cold and arid weather having chased away their inhabitants.

The family survived a few bitterly cold winters, their flock of sheep growing to a sizeable herd. As the grip of colder weather patterns tightened on the Badlands, a deadly storm would again uproot the Day family. A wicked blizzard drove the sheep to seek shelter in a narrow canyon. They huddled together, then piled up on one another and were smothered. Fighting to keep them apart, Walter lost his way in the blowing snow and nearly died. Everything they had worked for was gone. Like those who came before them, they pushed once again westward, leaving behind their dreams in a vacant house.

Young Walter and his father felled timber in Fort Fraser, British Columbia. His mother Oma drove a horse team, pulling logs down the mountain. The entire family picked apples and potatoes in Washington State and once again worked as loggers in the tiny coastal town of Copalis Beach, Washington. The logging town was nearly bursting with stories of the Alaska gold rush. Though the rest of the country was on the brink of the Great Depression, Alaska seemed to be prospering, at least according to story-tellers. Tales of those who had struck it rich were as tall and wide as the evergreen trees surrounding them. It was irresistible. With all their earthly possessions in worn black suitcases, the Day family boarded a steamer in Seattle, bound for Alaska.

To the appraising eye of Grandfather Day, Port Valdez seemed to hold more promise than did the gold fields of the interior. He fell in love with the raw beauty and noted the opportunities a deepwater port might present. "Pop" Day, as he was called, had finally found a place to plant his restless feet. A handsome man, though short in stature, his personality was as magnanimous as it was strong. He was the persuader, promoter, and deal maker in what was soon to be a thriving family business. Pop Day became friendly with the town magistrate and one day approached her about purchasing the abandoned army base called Fort Liscum, located across the bay from the town of Valdez. For a total of $500—ten percent down, and the rest on a ten-year note—the buildings at Fort Liscum became property of the Day family. Pop filed for a homestead to acquire the land after the Army relinquished all rights to it.

Walter was eighteen years old when they settled in Valdez in 1929. Soft spoken and hardworking, he labored endless hours to help build the community of Dayville. Local fishermen and Natives welcomed the family, teaching them to build boats and weave nets. With their help, the Days built a small cannery and a boat to carry supplies. The family also won a contract to carry mail to the fox farms located throughout the remote islands of Prince William Sound. After only two years in

Alaska, the former coal miners launched their first vessel. The *Oma Belle,* named after Grandmother Day, was a handsome white boat, built to last. She was the first of a fleet of boats—the remainder of the fleet was named for each of Walter's sisters. When the small salmon cannery burned a few years later, the Days refused to be discouraged. They built the bigger, more efficient building which housed the new machinery.

While Pop Day was the leader of the enterprise, Walter was the quiet and steady hand that held the family and operations together. His calm and quiet manner, coupled with an uncommon ability to engineer, build, and maintain nearly anything, earned the respect of his family and employees.

Bobby stood wondering if he should wake his father, when he stirred. Walter stood up and wished him good morning, looking quite refreshed.

"Would you like to have some breakfast with me Bobby?"

"Sure," he said.

With his father's hand on his shoulder, they walked out of the cannery. As they made their way up the boardwalk toward the mess hall, they paused long enough to watch the *Olivia H* as she came to sit just a little taller in the water. Walter grinned and looked at his son. As he stood watching the workers unload the *Olivia H*, Walter sensed the passion Bobby held for the boats, fish, and the cannery. He noted how closely the strength in his son's jaw and the lines of his profile matched his mother's, just as his inquisitiveness and resolve matched her personality. He hoped that Prince William Sound would always offer Bobby the sense of place, happiness, and abundance that his own parents had found.

When the bus pulled off the gravel highway and turned toward Santa Claus Lodge, Alaska, Gloria Denton knew she was a long way from home. And that was just where she wanted to be. The year was 1945 and she figured Alaska was just about as far from Columbus, Ohio, as she could get without leaving the country. She couldn't really say why she was on a bus traveling from Anchorage to Valdez, other than she just got "adventurous." In those days Santa Claus Lodge was the overnight stopping point on the two-day trip. As she settled into her bunk that night, she began to think that Alaska suited her. The rugged mountains just outside of Anchorage, the massive Matanuska Glacier, hardy scrub evergreen trees struggling to survive on the endless tundra, and the way the sky turned a pale shade of sapphire in the spring sunlight, seemed to set her soul free. It was bigger than she could have imagined. Compared to the landscape, the people who inhabited it seemed as insignificant as mere drops of water in a vast ocean. It was the sort of place a young woman could lose herself only to discover her own strength and a passion for something greater than her affluent home in Columbus could provide.

The following day, the view outside the bus windows became nearly surreal. As they approached the Chugach Mountains, Gloria lost her thoughts in the utter beauty of the landscape. Marshy areas left behind by receding glaciers were full of moose and their leggy calves. As the bus struggled to the top of Thompson Pass, she could see the moon in the pale sky, like a cherry hanging just over an ice cream sundae. The mountains were rugged and majestic and seemed close enough to reach out and touch. Once over the pass, the bus slowly descended through Keystone Canyon and arrived at the tiny town of Valdez. Nestled between the mountains and the head of Valdez Bay, it was constructed conveniently on the level tailings of sand and gravel left by the receding Valdez Glacier.

Gloria knew right away she liked this town. It was like a quaint Swiss village, with sharp peaks rising three thousand feet around the bay. Yet the square false-fronted buildings gave it a frontier flair. The people who lived there were just as rugged and tough as the land, but much more warm and forgiving. There weren't many employment opportunities—George Gilson's Grocery Store, John Kelsey's Dock Company, and the Valdez Salmon Cannery. George Gilson couldn't help but admire the spunk of a handsome young woman from the Midwest and soon she was working as a grocery clerk.

It didn't take many days for her to recognize most of the faces in town. But when Walter Day came in, deep in a discussion with another man about salmon prices, she knew she'd never seen him before. He absently laid down his grocery order on the counter, continuing his conversation. Gloria began gathering the boxes of supplies. When she returned to the list, she found the bottom of the list curiously ripped off. She remembered the last item, now missing, was two gallons of whiskey. She glanced up at Walter who now had his entire attention focused on her. She flushed a little and tried to hide an impish smile. Trying to make a good impression, she thought. Walter loaded a month's worth of supplies on his boat and went back across the bay to Dayville.

The next day Pop Day came into Gilson's and leaned his elbows on the counter. Appraisingly, he looked Gloria in the eye and grinned. It seemed he could use a bookkeeper across the bay for the Dayville Cannery. Would she be interested?

Gloria found more than a job across the bay. She discovered the rest of her life. On a chilly spring day less than a year later, she stood in front of a full-length mirror. She turned around and around and decided the secondhand wedding dress she'd found in Valdez was just beautiful. She carefully undressed and rolled the dress up into her backpack. Then she pulled on a thick pair of oversized wool pants and slipped her feet in lined leather boots with rubber soles known as shoe pacs. As she pulled on her parka and backpack, she felt thick and bulky, but her heart was light.

Walter looked equally oversized in his overclothes as they met in front of his cabin. Slate gray skies loomed low overhead and a fine film of ice covered the bay, meaning they would have to walk to Valdez instead of taking the boat. Arm in arm, they waded through the heavy spring snow around the end of the bay and were married that day.

At first her parents had wondered what possessed Gloria to leave and settle in such a remote place. Their family had always been close and Ohio offered so many opportunities, they thought. But any doubts they had about her decision were allayed with their first visit to Dayville. Summer after summer they returned to see their daughter and her growing family. Gloria kept a huge garden that proved to be prolific in the long hours of summer sun. She lined up cans of produce from her garden in the pantry, sewed clothes, and baked bread. She made do with few conveniences, but she created a home for a family of seven that was clean, comfortable, and inviting.

On one of their summer visits years later, Bobby's grandfather, Cromwell Denton, absently walked out onto the dock by the cannery. His gnarled hand held two fishing poles. Overhead, seagulls floated and dipped on the breeze, their loud cries echoing off the steep cliffs rising above. Cromwell had set out to find his grandson but his thoughts distracted him. Every summer wasn't often enough for a visit, he thought. But when they were here, he reveled in every minute of it. He breathed deeply, allowing the unique smell of saltwater and creosote pilings to fill his lungs and soul. The glacial water of Valdez Bay was a brilliant shade of liquid jade in the late summer sun. It seemed a world away from his home in Ohio. The sheer beauty inspired him.

A tug on his sleeve pulled him from his thoughts. Looking down, he saw the small blueberry stained fingers of his oldest grandson. The boy's face squinted up at him, blue lips grinning.

"Grandpa, I thought I heard you calling me," he said.

Cromwell leaned over and looked seriously in the boy's face. "Bobby, would you like to show me how to catch a salmon?"

The boy looked down at the small skiff tied to the dock, waves rocking it gently. It was beckoning him. There was nothing he would rather do than go fishing with his grandpa.

The afternoon breeze carried the first chill of fall air. They pulled on wool sweaters as they rowed along the edge of the bay. Evergreen trees covered the rocky cliffs rising sharply above the water. Further up, scrub alders and fiddlehead ferns covered ground too harsh for trees. The tops of the peaks were gray shale with fine tendrils of last year's snow reaching downward. Another six weeks or so and they would be clothed in white for the duration of winter.

Silver salmon, the last run of the season, were just beginning to come into the bay, searching for their freshwater birthplace where they would spawn and die. Around the boat their fins flickered and dimpled the water. Occasionally one would jump above the surface.

Once they were around the bend and could no longer see the cannery, they decided to cast a line next to the mouth of a small creek. Small, nimble fingers helped grandpa put shiny lures on the end of two lines. Again and again they cast out. They were patient, not knowing that salmon weren't usually caught on lines at that time. Salmon were commercial fish caught in nets that could gather up thousands of pounds like a huge drawstring purse. Few had the time or patience for such foolishness as catching a single salmon on a line.

It was nearly evening when Bobby felt a pull on his line. Instinctively he jerked the pole, then gently but firmly reeled in the line. The silver salmon was willing to battle the line and hook for its freedom, a trait that would ultimately make it a favorite for sport fishermen. As it neared the boat, it erupted from the water with a splash then dove quickly for deeper water. Bobby could see its silver flanks flashing in the green water and he wanted that fish so badly. After a long struggle between fish and determined boy, the salmon finally tired. As it neared the boat, grandpa grabbed a gaff hook and pulled the prize from the water. Bobby admired it as he held it in his outstretched hands.

They rowed eastward back toward the dock. As they came around the point, two black bears were plucking salmon from a creek. Grandpa paused to watch their hapless fellow fishermen lumbering nonchalantly around in the creek. The salmon were plentiful and the bears would merely take a bite out of the tender underside of the belly, leaving the rest to rot on the beach. Sometimes they would set the fish on the edge of the creek, then step strategically on their sides, causing delicate tasty eggs to squish out. Grandpa laughed and said they must be very high-class bears who favored caviar.

When they neared the dock, Gloria and her youngest son were waiting for them. Little Pat was just a toddler and he clung tightly to his mother's hand. Bobby held up the fish in greeting.

Laughing, Gloria said, "I guess even a flat-lander can catch a fish!"

"It wasn't me Gloria. It was Bobby. I don't know, I think the kid has some real talent!"

Bobby's chest swelled a little with the compliment. He held out the ten-pound fish for his mother to inspect. The scales were shiny and bright in the twilight, eyes clear and staring. It felt full and firm in his hands. When Pat put his hands out wanting to hold his brother's fish, Bobby carefully placed the salmon in his arms. He tousled Pat's unruly black hair and told him he could go fishing with him one day.

"Mom, can we go to the cannery and show it to Daddy?" Bobby thought of walking past the Iron Chink with his own fish in his hands. The workers were friendly to him, but now maybe they would see how grown up he was. Like the captains who brought in loads of fish on the cannery-owned boats, he figured he would gain a new respect in their eyes.

Walter was surrounded by pinging cans of cooling fish when his family found him. As they walked through the warehouse, he could see the fish in Bobby's hands, his son grinning from ear to ear. Young Bobby reminded Walter of his own father, with the same mischievous smile, eyes full of enthusiasm and possibility, and quick laugh. Walter grinned as Bobby thrust the salmon towards him.

"That's a beautiful fish son," he said. He was proud and he put his hand gently on the boy's shoulder to show it.

"Daddy, I know now what I want to be when I grow up. I want to be a fisherman, like the men who work on the *Olivia H.*"

Walter's eyes grew serious. He bent over, leaning on one knee so he could look directly into the boy's eyes. "Fishing is a hard life, Bobby. It's hard to have a family when you are always gone. Fishermen have always struggled for their living, and are always at the mercy of Mother Nature. When you grow up, you'll have the opportunity to go back to Ohio with your grandparents and get an education. You're a smart boy and a hard worker. Life will hold many more opportunities for you than fishing."

Bobby stood looking at him, saying nothing. Walter could see defiance in the boy's eyes. What had been meant as a loving admonition had been taken as a challenge.

As it would turn out, Walter's words for his son would be prophetic in his own life. A life dependent on fishing would soon be the end of Dayville, Alaska.

7

Siege at Sawmill Bay

VALDEZ: APRIL 1, 1989

D ROPS OF WATER SPRAYED THE WINDOW as the plane's floats touched down on Valdez Bay, drawing Bobby back from his memories of Dayville. Lori circled the plane around to the boat harbor and cut its engine as she sidled it up to the dock. He gave her a quick hug and wished her luck on her contract to work on the spill. He would let her know as soon as he heard whether the herring season would open, he said, although they both suspected it wouldn't. Then he released the plane's tiny door latch and jumped down lightly onto the floating dock. Grasping the wing strut in his left hand, he pushed the plane away and wondered when he would see her again.

His eyes scanned the boat harbor to see what boats were in as he strode across the dock and up the walkway toward town. Valdez was laid out in an orderly way in front of him—on a grid with the business and industrial district nearest the harbor and the community college and homes extending several blocks north to the base of the Chugach Mountains. The town was fairly new, as it had been moved to this spot four miles down the bay after the 1964 earthquake. Some of the buildings from the "old town" had been moved over to the new town site and now rested atop solid bedrock. The buildings and homes gave an impression of substance over style, designed to withstand the heavy snows and high winds of Valdezean winters. It was a place as comfortable to Bobby as a pair of worn slippers.

Yet today it lacked familiarity. Cars backed up in the business district and a crowd gathered along the sidewalk in front of the Civic Center just ahead of him. Without a single stop light, the town was ill-equipped to handle the throngs of activists, job seekers, journalists, oil company representatives, and government officials that had nearly doubled the town's population.

Walking toward the Civic Center, Bobby decided he might as well stop in on what appeared to be a gathering of folks for one of the twice-daily press conferences that had become notorious for their rancor in the past few days. As he approached the door, he was surprised to discover the building was guarded by Valdez police and state troopers. At the bag check, officials argued with a disheveled looking woman who refused to reveal the contents of her backpack. Apparently, police had received a tip that she represented Greenpeace and planned to throw a dead, oiled bird or sea otter onto the stage during the press conference.

As Bobby glanced through the doors, he could see that this had become an entirely different place than he had once known. The partitions in the auditorium had been removed to accommodate the growing number of people who crowded into these town meetings. He saw his parents sitting toward the front near the makeshift stage, but decided to walk along the outer hallway and enter the doors at the back of the auditorium.

With his arms crossed over his chest, he stood along the back wall and inventoried the people in the room. With the partitions removed, he figured the auditorium could hold about four hundred people, and it was packed. By his count, fishermen outnumbered journalists and others he didn't recognize by about three to one.

Local fishermen and residents were losing their patience, if they ever had any, over the slow pace of the cleanup. At the town meeting held just yesterday, Exxon spokesman Don Cornett had announced that a dozen skimmers were out there working, although he didn't know where. Three hundred workers had been hired to clean beaches, but weren't out there yet. He'd told the crowd, "You have to understand. Something like this doesn't get done quickly. We're taking our time, finding out where the cleanup camps have to be, getting supply lines figured out for keeping these people fed and with enough equipment."[1]

Today, Governor Cowper appeared just as frustrated as the fishermen when he stepped out onto the stage, accompanied by Jack Lamb, the president of Cordova District Fishermen United, and Dennis Kelso. Cowper's quiet and steady demeanor conveyed both confidence and resolve. In his folksy Virginian lilt, the Governor began,

"I just returned from a tour of Prince William Sound. It looks a little different than the tour I took in 1985. And it is clear to me that we've got a real big job to do. There is no question about it. I went over to Cordova this morning and talked with people there. I went over to Tatitlek and then stopped over at Green Island where there is a lot of oil on the beach, and some dead birds and some other things that I didn't want to see. But that is the situation that we are working in here.

"Now, jurisdictionally, there is a federal statute under which we are required to operate. And I'm not going to go into a lot of detail about that. But there is a state statute also that gives us separate jurisdiction, and where the existing management structure of this cleanup is not adequate to the task, then we are going to do it ourselves, independent of that."[2]

No longer willing to put their faith in Exxon's cleanup efforts, the Governor and DEC announced their commitment of funds, the state ferry *Bartlett,* and a forty-man crew to protect the hatcheries. Of particular concern was the San Juan hatchery at Sawmill Bay, which along with the other hatcheries was due to release millions of salmon fry from its holding pens. The Governor went on to say, "We have put together the state and fishermen's strike force. That is what we are going to call it. And it has already been deployed. We've got a lot of volunteers who understand what this country is like and what we have to do to save whatever we can."[3]

Exxon had assumed that the oil would flush out into the Gulf of Alaska south through Hinchinbrook Entrance. Even the computer models used by the Department of Environmental Conservation predicted that the oil would flush out of the Sound much sooner and with less damage than was proving to be the case.

But the fishermen had known differently all along. They made it their business to know which way the currents ran in the Sound and which way eddies pooled around the islands. Because the tides create circular currents in some places, they knew that salmon sometimes swam around Knight Island six or seven times before finding the scent that would lead them up the stream or river from which they originated. When the tides ebbed, the fishermen had watched V-shaped formations emerge on the top of the water as the salmon schooled up in rips in the current. And those who fished crab and shrimp in the

Sound had to know which way the currents ran so that their pots settled in the right place on the bottom when they threw them overboard.

The currents, the fishermen had maintained, would force the oil to move in a counter-clockwise swath right around the western edge of the Sound. It would threaten to oil the bays where most of the hatcheries were located. And when the oil began to move just as the fishermen predicted, a DEC representative commented that the fishermen "advised the agency better than anyone. When a fisherman and a computer model disagreed on where the spill was going, the fisherman turned out to be right, and since then the DEC has relied on local expertise."[4] Their predictions prompted the Governor and DEC to come to the aid of fishermen already working to keep the oil from compromising an entire generation of salmon about to be released from the hatcheries.

The Governor said, "We certainly want to save those hatcheries. We want to be sure that the strike force has the equipment, material, and whatever else they need to get the job done. I want to commend particularly the fishermen out of Valdez and fishermen out of Cordova. I think increasingly we are going to see participation by fishermen from other areas of the state."[5] The Governor admitted it seemed like a very small step in the long process of recovering the Sound. "But," he said, "You have to start somewhere."[6]

Governor Cowper went on to say that the state would not hesitate to shut down the pipeline if the oil companies and Alyeska couldn't comply with requests for an oil spill prevention and response plan that works. "There's going to be a much better plan," Cowper said. "I will demand that the companies hire enough people to handle a major spill, keep them trained, equipped and on hand. Alyeska's existing and woefully inadequate contingency plan will not be tolerated," he said. "If that's all there is, the line's not gonna be open."[7] He paused as the room exploded in applause. The fishermen liked this kind of tough talk, even if it was a little late in coming.

Cowper continued, promising that those who lost money as a result of the spill wouldn't have to wait years for litigation to make them financially whole. He said, "The thing I want to stress here today is that we have just started. This thing is going to last for months and months and months. We want to be sure that those who are damaged by this disaster are properly compensated. We are going to put a representative of the Governor's office, both in Valdez and Cordova—we'll be here tomorrow—and we want for the people of this community to coordinate through those representatives.

"The damages that are caused by this tragedy are going to last for a long time. We don't want anybody to think they have to hire a lawyer and go into federal court and sue the largest corporation in America. We want to put a system together that will allow you who are suffering damages—the fishermen and other people in this area—to bring to us a fairly simple set of proof of whatever you lose and we want you to be paid quickly and expeditiously.

"You don't have to wait until the damages are all proven out here five or six years from now, maybe, in order to collect. As soon as you can show that you have suffered damages by reason of this, we want to be sure that you are paid. We are working out the details of this, and we haven't gotten it together completely yet, but I want to assure you that we are on your side. That the state of Alaska represents *you*. And we want to be sure that, particularly the fishermen, but other people who are damaged by this, get compensated fairly and quickly."[8]

And, he said, the state would see to it that the Sound was cleaned up, regardless of the cost. When someone called out from the crowd asking how much it would cost and how much the state would pay, Cowper responded, "All it takes. We'll take whatever steps we have to take to recover that money. But we're not going to be in a situation where we are haggling over nickels and dimes when the work needs to be done. If we need to advance the money from the state and get it back later, that's what we'll do."[9]

"Now," Cowper said, "I want to say one other thing. It is necessary for the State of Alaska and Exxon, and the U.S. Coast Guard to work together on cleaning up this spill. It is necessary that we work together. We will get a lot more done that way. I've said earlier, that if we happen to disagree with the other two members of that group, that if we believe our stance is correct, we'll do it ourselves. But please bear in mind that this is a cooperative effort. It is going to take a long, long time to clean up this mess."[10]

State officials and local residents now seemed equally frustrated with the slow pace of the cleanup efforts. Already eight days had passed and despite mobilization plans and promises, little progress could be seen. A boat could now start at one end of the slick and not reach the other side in the same day. As Dennis Kelso took center stage, he admitted that the spill area exceeded five hundred square miles, by any calculation. A bird specialist reported over two thousand heavily oiled gulls and several thousand murres, scoters and mergansers between Montague Island and Knight Island.[11]

The lightering of the oil still remaining on the *Valdez* seemed to demand all the resources and expertise on hand, and Exxon announced the effort would be complete in another two days. Valdez citizens protested bringing the ship back to the Port of Valdez, which remained free of oil. They were concerned that it would trail crude oil up the narrow fjord and into the bay. Exxon agreed, saying they would perform rudimentary repairs in an already oiled bay, perhaps at Naked Island.

Jack Lamb, a fisherman from Cordova, stepped forward on the stage and told the crowd, "Prince William Sound was the most beautiful piece of marine environment in the world two weeks ago, and now it's not. We're going to bring it back, but we can't do it in two weeks or two months. I'm extremely skeptical we can do it in two years."[12]

As Bobby stood in the back of the room watching his old friend up on the stage, he thought how difficult this must be for Jack, how he and other long-time members of CDFU had warned of just this kind of catastrophe even before the Trans-Alaska pipeline had been constructed. As the state contemplated how to transport oil from the North Slope to markets after the 1968 strike at Prudhoe Bay, the Cordova fishermen became increasingly concerned by reports assessing the risks of tanker traffic from a pipeline terminus in Prince William Sound. A U.S. Department of Commerce report released in the early 1970s described the potential consequences that incremental leaks and day-to-day spills from tankers would have on "normal marine life processes in both the estuaries and the open sea," and warned of the threat of a major tanker accident in Prince William Sound.[13] A Department of Interior Impact Statement devoted only two pages out of approximately two hundred to the issue of spill prevention and response.[14]

The question of whether and how to transport oil through a pipeline with a terminus in Cook Inlet or Prince William Sound stirred controversy among Alaskans—from the editorial pages of the *Anchorage Times*, to the bars and other community gathering places in small towns across Alaska. Although Alaskans generally acknowledged the *Times* provided an objective reporting of the arguments on both sides of the issue, editorials occasionally revealed the pro-business stance of its publisher and editor, Robert Atwood. One *Times* editorial read, "The fears about damage from oil spills are like the fears of Henny-Penny when she ran to tell the king that the sky was falling."[15]

In early February of 1971, the Department of Interior scheduled "pipeline hearings" in Anchorage to settle the matter of public concern over development. The hearing of public testimony would satisfy the requirements for due process as decision-makers weighed considerations about the potential construction of the Trans-Alaska Pipeline. CDFU representatives led by Ross Mullins urged government officials hosting the hearings to resolve the dispute over oil development in a way that carefully weighed the risks to fisheries in the Sound and didn't sacrifice a renewable resource for a non-renewable resource. At the hearings, Ken Roemhildt, a supervisor for the Royal Pacific cannery in Cordova testified, "What about the long range effects of small spills and loading problems in possibly diminishing the Prince William Sound fisheries? We stand a chance of losing our livelihood either all at once or by slow strangulation. Cordova stands a chance of becoming a ghost town... What recourse would fishermen and processors have against the oil people should a major disaster completely wipe out the Prince William Sound fishery?"[16]

Walter Day also spoke at the pipeline hearings, as the mayor of Valdez. His message resonated with a much different tone. He testified, "The major part of the years I have spent in Valdez, I have earned my living from the fisheries resources of Prince William Sound. My two sons, my brother, and many of the townspeople have continued to earn part, or all, of their livelihood from this source. I believe that the two industries—the oil transportation facilities and the fishing industry—are compatible. They could survive in their joint use of Prince William Sound...The proper protection to prevent human error can be provided. But we must demand such control. Our position on this is clear—we want Alaska protected...

"There are those who ask for no change. They ask the impossible! Nature itself is constantly changing, changing the landscape, changing shorelines, changing the very face of our planet, building in one area, tearing down in another. The human mind grows from nothing to greatness then dies in a single moment of time—constantly changing. Since we know we must change, let us build these changes constructively for the benefit of all mankind."[17]

Standing against the back wall of the Civic Center, looking out across the crowd, Bobby reflected on the irony of the opposing opinions in a debate that had played out nearly two decades ago. His father sat in the crowd, surrounded by fishermen who had opposed his point of view so many years ago. It was no wonder Bobby's union brethren had gathered around him, refusing to let him into the meeting in Cordova just two weeks after the pipeline hearings in 1971. The CDFU was intent on blocking him from attending a meeting at which they were determined to take decisive action to stop construction of the pipeline. They feared Bobby's loyalties fell with the pro-development stance of his father and others in Valdez.

In fact, they were right. Although he would not overtly oppose their actions, Bobby made no effort to conceal his opinion on the matter. He believed the Cordova fishermen failed to acknowledge what he thought to be true. They could not stop the clock, they could not preserve Alaska as they had known it, but must instead focus on adapting to an inevitable future.

In 1971 the small boat harbor in Cordova had served informally as a public forum for the growing consensus among local fishermen about what should be done in light of inevitable oil development. The morning before the union meeting, Bobby had loaded a bucket and clam shovel in his skiff, and motored fifteen minutes along Orca Inlet to dig enough clams for a gathering at the Alaskan Hotel and Bar later that evening. With cold, cramped hands, he tied back up at the dock just as Marty Deville walked down the float.

Bobby called out to him, "Hey Marty. You want to take some clams home with you?" It was common for friends in the small community to share shrimp or clams, or whatever they may have gone out to catch for an evening meal. He tied up the skiff and invited Marty into the cabin of his seine boat. He lit the oil stove and rubbed his hands over it, as if encouraging it to heat up faster. He set a pot of coffee on to heat up. It began to hiss as the tiny galley warmed with the smell of coffee and oil from the stove. Outside a steady rain began to fall, dimpling the waters of the harbor. Overlooking Orca Inlet and Spike Island, the view from the galley window seemed to represent everything worth preserving in the Sound. Inside, the bucket of clams to share symbolized a lifestyle that was worth fighting for.

Bobby poured two cups of coffee and slid onto the bench across the galley table from Marty. As the steam rolled off their cups, they considered the upcoming meeting of the CDFU. He told Marty, "I'm not sure we should take a stance, as a union, to oppose construction of the pipeline. You know, the money the oil companies could pump into the economy could actually help us keep what we have, or even make it better. The fish are running strong now, but it might not always be that way."

Bobby outlined his vision for the future, a future where fishermen could get grants or loans from the state, using some of the money that the oil industry will bring. Then they could build salmon hatcheries that could guarantee salmon returns every year. "I can't understand why others in the union can't see the possibilities," he said.

Marty sipped his coffee and looked thoughtfully out the window. He knew part of the reason Bobby had moved to Cordova was to get away from the political debates and preparations for development of the pipeline terminus in Valdez. Although Alyeska didn't yet have a permit to construct the pipeline, the first shipments of steel pipe were already arriving in Valdez. He knew Bobby felt more comfortable among other fishermen and in a town solely committed to fishing as a way of life. As his roommate in a single-wide trailer during the first winter Bobby spent in Cordova, Marty had gotten to know him well.

"I think it comes down to the fact that they simply don't trust industry to take the precautions they say they will, or the government to make sure that they will," Marty responded after some time. "I think they believe they have a responsibility to save what's best about Alaska and our way of life."

Bobby knew there were a lot of fears and loyalties embedded in this debate, shaped in part by Cordova's history as the terminus for the copper railroad. Naturally, fishermen in Cordova would be wary of risking the seafood that had sustained a way of life for generations, for a non-renewable resource. Though he had fished in Cordova, even taken his first job here one summer in high school at a cannery, he knew he was a newcomer to town, someone from Valdez who would always be seen by others in town as a potential rival, an outsider.

Still, Bobby felt strongly that members of the CDFU had a responsibility to help shape the future of fishing and of the state. He told Marty that trying to fight the pipeline outright probably wouldn't do anything but delay the inevitable. He thought it better, he explained, to try and influence how the pipeline is constructed and regulated. Bobby agreed with his father's vision of citizens setting the standards for protection, as Walter had suggested in his speech at the pipeline hearings, and that regulatory agencies should enforce those standards. Both he and his father believed that locals who depended on the Sound for their livelihood could best ensure that it was protected. This was a central tenet of Alaskan culture that had grown out of its frontier roots, in a remote place where people depended on each other to solve problems, and in some cases, even to survive.

"Bobby, I don't disagree with a lot of your views," Marty offered. At the same time, he also appreciated the values and philosophies of the union members had guided the organization since it formed in 1935. "Our friends in the union probably won't see the value in any point of view that expands the debate beyond the town of Cordova. They are simply focused on what they feel is best for fishermen. That means not putting the fisheries at risk."

At the union meeting later that evening, members spoke in favor of an alternate proposal to build the pipeline across Canada with a terminus in Chicago, or any other route that would promote development in a way that was less likely to compromise their lifestyle. One fisherman stood and made a motion that the CDFU oppose the proposal for a pipeline terminus in Valdez or the Copper River Flats outside of Cordova. The vote was overwhelmingly in favor of taking all action necessary to protect and preserve their economic livelihood. The CDFU office mailed out referendum ballots to formalize the vote, which ultimately supported the motion 476 to 7.[18] Later that evening, the CDFU hosted an open meeting in the high school gymnasium and half the town's citizens came to discuss the future of their town in the face of oil development.

The CDFU conducted a survey of the town's commercial enterprises and found that 84.9 percent of their business depended on fishing. On March 8, 1971, union members met again in the high school library and voted unanimously to dedicate $10,000 to initiating a lawsuit to stop construction of a pipeline terminus in Prince William Sound. The following day, the Copper River and Prince William Sound Cannery Workers Union met and voted to contribute an additional $2,000 toward the effort. CDFU president Knute Johnson reported at the time that letters of support were rolling in from Kodiak, Petersburg, Bristol Bay, and Sitka. "This is much broader than just our area," he said, "Fishermen have a common cause."[19]

The fishermen also found themselves aligned with environmentalists and conservationists from around the country who opposed construction of the pipeline in the context of the nation's nascent environmental consciousness. Groups such as the Wilderness Society, Sierra Club, and Friends of the Earth filed suits along with CDFU. Although the fishermen recognized the position they shared with these groups gave them more power in Washington, D.C., they were concerned their perceived alignment with "birdwatchers, wolf-pamperers, and ivory tower idealists"[20] could hurt their image in Alaska. In a full page *New York Times* ad placed the day before the pipeline hearings commenced, David Brower of Friends of the Earth warned that "If oil is pumped out of Prudhoe Bay and then shipped down the west coast, we will eventually have an oil spill leading to the greatest kill of living things in history."[21] In 1973, the fishermen's lawsuit was ultimately combined with litigation initiated by environmental organizations and their claims were upheld in a U.S. District Court.[22]

Fearing that the suit could stop construction of the pipeline indefinitely, the U.S. Congress introduced an amendment to legislation known as "the pipeline bill" which would preempt further court appeals and exempt the Trans-Alaska Pipeline from requirements outlined in the recently enacted National Environmental Policy Act of 1969. Perhaps recognizing that the amendment could set a precedent to weaken the relatively new and untested legislation, the Senate vote on the amendment resulted in a 49–49 tie. On July 17, 1973,

Vice President Spiro Agnew cast the deciding "yes" vote to break the impasse.[23] The amendment effectively undercut the basis for the lawsuits filed by fishermen and environmentalists, as well as the possibility of appeal.

Some claim the matter might have languished at an impasse for years were it not for Congressional action taken perhaps in response to events taking place half a world away from Washington, D.C. The Organization of the Petroleum Exporting Countries (OPEC) imposed an oil embargo on the United States in 1973, reportedly in retaliation for aiding Israel during the Yom Kippur War. As Americans waited in gas lines and paid record high prices for gasoline, some doubted that the crisis was real. "I felt it was a contrived oil shortage," said David Brower, President of Friends of the Earth. "It was contrived to get Congressional approval for the pipeline."[24]

Whatever the cause, legislators were compelled to action by their constituencies. The Trans-Alaska pipeline amendment reflected the economic and political context of the early 1970s and the urgency of getting fuel to market. The legislation stated, "The purpose of this title is to insure that, because of the extensive governmental studies already made of this project and the national interest in early delivery of North Slope oil to domestic markets, the Trans-Alaska oil pipeline be constructed promptly without further administrative or judicial delay or impediment."[25] Before the close of the 1973 Congressional session, the Senate passed the entire bill 80–5 and the House approved the bill with a 361–14 vote. President Nixon signed the Trans-Alaska Pipeline Authorization Act into law on November 16, 1973, and Interior Secretary Morton issued the construction permit in early 1974.

After Congressional action to approve the pipeline, Alaska Senator Ted Stevens reportedly told the Cordova fishermen, "Werner von Braun, you know, the spaceman, assured me that all of the technology of the space program will be put into the doggone tankers and there will not be one drop of oil in Prince William Sound."[26] This assurance offered little comfort. The issue of tanker traffic was not forgotten by Cordova fishermen and Ross Mullins, who continued to serve as a cautionary voice on their behalf. Mullins said, "The fishermen were seen by the state and industry as pariahs."[27] Although Mullins was ultimately able to convene regulators and industry officials to discuss their concerns, the fishermen lacked the ability to compel or even influence oil spill prevention and response policies.

Just as construction on the pipeline commenced in 1974, Alaskans elected a fisherman, Jay Hammond, as their new governor. The Alaska legislature passed the Hatchery Act, which allowed for private, nonprofit development of salmon hatcheries. Governor Hammond issued orders to Alaska Department of Fish and Game to "make the hatchery system work."[28]

The Cordova fishermen worked together to establish the Prince William Sound Aquaculture Corporation which would be governed by a forty-five-member board representing fishermen, Natives, processors, and local municipalities. The fishermen secured the services of Dr. Wally Noerenberg, a biologist from the University of Washington, and selected Sawmill Bay as the site for the first hatchery.

As Bobby stood in the back of the Civic Center listening to the plan for diverting the leading edge of the oil slick away from the San Juan hatchery at Sawmill Bay, he could remember the excitement that he and his fellow members of the aquaculture board had shared. He remembered the days and weeks they had worked together to catch the initial brood stock for the hatchery in the summer of 1976.

It seemed as though rain poured down every day for a month that summer as the group of fishermen and graduate students rounded up pink salmon returning to Ewan Bay. Their faces and slickers glistened as they hauled their nets, dripping and flapping with fish, onto the rocky beach. Makeshift tents of tarps draped over lashed poles sheltered the workers as they stripped eggs from the female salmon and sperm from the males, and mixed them together in buckets. They were consumed by the smell of saltwater, fish, and the wet wool of their sweaters. With cold, cramped fingers, they ate Spam and canned sardines for lunch and downed gulps of whiskey in the hopes it would warm them up. They were perpetually wet, but it didn't dampen their spirits.

The tedious work was a step toward the self-determination fishermen had sought since the turn of the century. As a territory of the United States until 1959, Alaska fisheries had been regulated by the Federal Fish and Wildlife agency. Federal regulators permitted the use of fish traps that extended across the mouths of rivers and streams, allowing very little fish escapement. The fish traps had been developed by the largest canneries in response to a strike by a loosely organized fishermen's union in 1912. The traps effectively eliminated the need to hire fishermen to run the cannery-owned boats. Despite appeals by Natives, small local cannery owners and fishermen, federal regulators continued to allow fish traps even in the face of drastically declining fish runs.

The largest cannery operations wielded the most significant influence with federal regulators. In 1920, there were more than a hundred canneries operating in Alaska. By 1939, the Federal Trade Commission reported that nine companies controlled 58 percent of the total pack. These companies were largely owned by out-of-state interests and the combination of absentee owners and federal oversight came to drive much of the political impetus for statehood in Alaska.

In 1948 the largest canneries recognized that state governance, if it were achieved, could mean the end to fish traps and the relative monopoly that a few cannery interests enjoyed. They engaged in a no-holds-barred effort to seek Congressional support for fifteen-year terms for leases on the fish trap sites they currently operated.

At a U.S. Senate hearing in 1948, an Alaska fisherman testified, "We Alaskans charge emphatically and can prove that the fish trap is a menace to a continued successful operation of fisheries in Alaska. By this measure you would legalize the destruction of the major industry of Alaska and jeopardize the livelihood of the many resident workers, of the many small businesses; in whole, the entire economic structure of Alaska. For what? The continued exploitation of Alaskan resources by an absentee monopoly that must have a profit far in excess of that of any other business."[29]

Fearing that the canneries could use their influence over federal regulators to secure long-term leases, the Alaska territorial government responded with a referendum seeking to ban fish traps. With the largest voter turnout on record at that time, Alaskans voted in 1948 to support the abolition of fish traps by a margin of eight to one.[30] Although this show of support did not prompt federal regulators to ban fish traps, Congress did refuse to pass the leasing measure requested by the canneries.

Salmon stocks continued to decline and forced closure of the entire salmon season in Prince William Sound in 1954, 1955, and 1959. Alaskans were convinced that local knowledge and commitment to the land and waters would result in more sustainable management of the fisheries, and persisted in their quest for statehood. Congress finally granted Alaska statehood in 1959 in part due to the promising oil discoveries in Cook Inlet, which seemed to provide assurance that Alaska could sustain itself financially.

Trap nets were banned at the time of statehood and the fishermen's lot improved throughout the 1960s. By then, most fishermen owned their own boats rather than working as paid skippers on cannery-owned boats. As independent operators, they personified the same rugged individualism that the old "sourdoughs" who settled Alaska had instilled into its culture. Yet the Cordova fishermen's union preserved a sense of solidarity among those who had once worked as employees rather than entrepreneurs, and who sold their catch on the open market.

This sense of shared history and struggle served to foster a strong sense of community among the Cordova fishermen. When fish stocks again flagged during the early 1970s, forcing the closure of seasons in 1972 and 1974, the fishermen rallied around the question of sustainability with common purpose. They resolved to meet a growing demand for seafood by developing fish hatcheries modeled after those in Japan and the Soviet Union. And that resolve sustained them through the wet summer of 1976 as they caught brood stock and produced the first generation of hatchery-bred salmon. Recognizing that the salmon market was changing with the emergence of fish farms in Norway, the fishermen acknowledged that they might have to increase the volume of fish caught to maintain their current income levels if worldwide prices declined as some economists predicted they would.[31] The fishermen would essentially be dependent on themselves to manage the reproduction and harvest of salmon returning to the Sound, and their efforts could guarantee steady, predictable fish runs in perpetuity.

In a presentation to the new aquaculture corporation, Dr. Noerenberg predicted that hatcheries could increase the reproduction of existing stocks tenfold. With agreement to tax themselves to support the operational costs of the hatchery, and an $18 million loan from the state, the fishermen had agreed to commence operations as soon as possible.

The fishermen selected Sawmill Bay for the first hatchery because it offered the old San Juan cannery buildings and a steady supply of fresh water from the lake above. They'd worked at their own expense to catch the brood stock, to strip the eggs and milk the sperm, and to hastily transport the buckets of fertilized eggs by boat or plane to Sawmill Bay where they could be placed in fresh-water incubation trays. In the spring of 1977, the hatchery manager sent word that salmon fry were beginning to appear in the trays. The fishermen climbed in float planes and flew under a graphite gray layer of clouds to the remote site. They stood there in the old San Juan cannery, champagne bubbling across the wooden plank floor, admiring the tiny salmon darting about in the trays. As they raised a toast to the salmon fry, it was with an undeniable sense of satisfaction. Their collective work had transcended any prior differences in opinion and old rivalries, and strengthened their sense of solidarity. The tiny fry represented a promise of success, independence, and prosperity for the future.

The hatchery ultimately surpassed their expectations. By 1982, the San Juan hatchery had returns of 2.5 million salmon—the largest in the western world at the time. In 1988, salmon from the San Juan hatchery helped to prop up an otherwise disappointing salmon run, yielding a record price of a dollar a pound for a total of $20 million worth of pink salmon. Now the leading edge of the oil threatened the 117 million salmon fry waiting in holding pens to be released into the ocean. Even more importantly, it threatened the sense of community and common purpose that the tiny fish had instilled among the fishermen.

While Bobby had once believed that creating and operating the hatcheries had healed the acrimony over the issue of oil development, he now sensed the rending of old wounds. Everything his fellow Cordovans had feared and fought against for nearly two decades had proven prescient. Though he had moved to Seattle in 1982 after more than ten years of living in Cordova, he still fished in the Sound among his old friends. Watching his fellow fishermen gathered on the stage and crowded into the Civic Center auditorium, he reflected back on his support for oil development during the early 1970s. He felt like an accomplice to this catastrophe that threatened the Sound and the way of life they shared. Perhaps for the first time he felt he didn't belong among them. He could watch them no longer. As the town meeting continued on, Bobby slipped silently away from his position against the back wall and out the door.

8

"You Have My Word on That"

Naked Island: April 1, 1989

A FTER LEAVING THE MEETING AT THE CIVIC CENTER Bobby found refuge in the shroud of shadows and smoke at the Pipeline Club bar. It was nearly deserted at this hour in the late afternoon. He settled onto a stool at the end of the bar next to the dart board. A chunk of original pipeline steel hung behind the bar, cut open and laid out into the shape of the state of Alaska. The sculptor had etched rivers into the steel and welded mountain ranges and a miniature replica of the pipeline across the state.

Bobby knew the bartender well and was cheered when Louis offered a grin as he came to take Bobby's order. Miller Light in a bottle. He told Louie he'd just come from the town meeting. Louie said there'd been a bunch of yahoos in town lately for those meetings. Lots of folks seem pretty upset over this deal, he'd said.

Rumpled sections of the *Anchorage Daily News* lay scattered on the bar. Seeing the headline "Valdez Folks Feel Cheated," Bobby picked up the section dated just two days earlier. It read, "Valdez is holding its breath, expecting to change because of the *Exxon Valdez* oil spill, but still wondering how much. The town will still be kept by oil, but like a betrayed lover, is unlikely to maintain blind trust anymore. 'Valdez has always been one of the most pro-development communities in Alaska,' said Valdez City Councilman Lynn Chrystal. 'We probably still will be. But we feel very let down, and very cheated. It's almost like you found out your wife is cheating on you.'

"The marriage of Valdez to oil, although betrayed, will survive. Valdez lives on oil. Except for the fishermen. They're not talking about marriage, they're talking about rape. Fishermen say the spill was a violation and a loss of innocence...."[1]

Bobby's concentration was interrupted by a slap on the back and a nasal chuckle he would recognize anywhere. Dale Dawson slid onto a stool next to him, a goofy grin on his face. Bobby knew he was about to get a hard time over something from his best friend and crewmember.

"What are you doin' here, Bobby? You hanging out at Captain Hazelwood's favorite spot?"

"What do you mean?"

"Oh Jesus, Bobby, you haven't heard? Turns out the guy's blood alcohol content was over six times the legal limit when he ran the ship onto Bligh Reef."

"You're kidding me."

"Nope. That's all they're talking about on the marine radio. I had to wash all the son-of-a-bitch's oil off the *Lady Lynne* when I pulled into the harbor today. Jesus, Bobby, you can't believe the mess out there in the Sound."

"You made good time getting through it," he said, pausing to order Dale a beer. "I ended up staying in Sitka a couple days after you left. Lori and I just flew in earlier today."

"Before I forget, someone down in the harbor's looking for you."

"Who is it?"

"Don't know. Some guy from a company called Ocean Tech or something like that."

Bobby leaned on his elbow and swirled his beer in the bottle. He'd heard that Exxon and its cleanup contractors were trying to hire boats and crews for cleanup efforts—good offers for thousands of dollars a day. But he didn't want to have his boat tied up in case they were able to fish salmon in some parts of the Sound this summer, even though it was hard to imagine fishing for anything out there in that mess. He figured the herring fishery would be closed for sure, since it was due to open in less than a week.

The springtime herring return from the ocean to lay their eggs right in the near-shore saltwater, on kelp or at the edges of the beaches. He remembered what he'd learned at Knowles Head, that herring come up to the surface when it is completely dark and wondered what would happen to them if they swam underneath the heaviest parts of the slick. He shook his head, listening now to Dale's account of the state of the Sound. Neither could imagine what the days and weeks would bring and how long the Sound would take to recover.

"Well, let's go see what the guy down at the dock wants," he told Dale. He tossed a twenty dollar bill on the counter to cover their beers and followed Dale out the door into the waning afternoon sunlight. The two men were polar opposites in many ways, as any observer could note watching them cut across town on their way to the harbor. Dale was as tall, loose-jointed, and easy going as Bobby was short and tightly wound. Their physical appearances served as nearly perfect metaphors for their personality types.

A logger from Northport, Washington, Dale had come to Valdez looking for construction work just after the 1964 earthquake. They'd played city league basketball, cards, and pool together and it wasn't long before Bobby took Dale fishing with him. When the *Dotty G* and her permit came up for sale a few years later, Bobby insisted that Dale could make more money owning his own boat than working as a crew-member, and he talked him into buying it. Dale sold the *Dotty G* and his salmon permit just last year and Bobby thought now that might not have been a bad financial move given the disaster they now faced.

They found the guy from Ocean Tech leaning up against the harbor railing, surveying the boats or the scenery, they weren't sure which. As it turned out, his company had a contract to select a spot at Naked Island suitable for anchoring the *Exxon Valdez* while repairs could be made before towing her south. Their company would supply the sonar and technical equipment, so their main interest was in finding a newer boat with comfortable amenities to contract for a two-week time period. They needed to get out to Naked Island right away, he said. Bobby didn't need much time to think about it. He could live with a short-term contract and besides, he was ready to get out of town.

As they idled out of the harbor, Bobby wondered what the people of Valdez had done to deserve two disasters of epic proportions on Good Friday exactly twenty-five years apart. The hair on his neck and arms stood straight on end as he recalled the day that rocked Alaska. It was an ironic coincidence that the spill fell on the 25th anniversary of the 1964 earthquake.

On March 27, 1964, the steamship *Chena* sidled up to one of the two wharves in Valdez with the first shipment of goods and fresh fruit of the year. The ship's arrival was greeted by enthusiastic town folk, excited not just for the goods the ship carried, but for the new faces of the crew and a break in the daily routine of small town life. In the cottony pale light of an early spring evening, the square-fronted buildings of the bustling frontier town sprawled invitingly in front of the ships' crew. The town's cozy residences stood slightly up hill behind the waterfront and downtown area. Tall cottonwood trees provided a partial buffer between the houses and Valdez glacier directly behind town, and they swayed gently in the late afternoon breeze coming off the bay. The crew looked overboard at the happy faces of about thirty adults and children who had come to greet the ship, and tossed candy and fresh oranges down to the children who filled their arms with goodies.

The Dock Company warehouses were conveniently located on the wharves that were connected to town by a raised gravel road built across the tide flats. The longshoremen grabbed hold of the lines and tied the ship securely to the dock. Inside the warehouse, the forklift operator warmed up the machine he would use to go inside the *Chena's* hold and retrieve the freight she carried. It had been Bobby's job until a few short weeks before.

Walt and Gloria had just finished printing and folding the latest edition of the town's local newspaper, the *Valdez Breeze,* and delivered it to the post office. Their girls came through the front door, giggling and clutching fresh oranges in their arms when the house began to shake. The sound was faint at first but it grew alarmingly louder, like the sound of a freight train approaching. Glass jars that Gloria used for preserving vegetables from her garden and cans of fish crashed to the floor. The sound of breaking dishes and rattling filled the room. Small earthquakes were common in Valdez, but the family began to realize this was no small tremor. The piano seemed to take on a life of its own as it raced across the room on its rollers and slammed against the far wall. The old house rolled and shook violently. The piano turned and bore down on Gloria who was struggling to stay on her feet. Walter somehow gathered Gloria and his girls up in his arms and guided them out onto the front porch.

The second-story porch shook and swayed, creaking with every shift in direction and Gloria feared it would surely tear loose from the house, leaving them clinging to the rails of an unsupported tall tower. Walter pointed in the direction of the bay and his face turned ashen. Normally, they could not see the docks from the house. Suddenly they could see the *Chena* rising up above the warehouses. One of the petroleum tanks by the boat harbor exploded into a column of flames. Down the street, the Morgue Bar rose and fell from view. A wall of water swept over the docks toward town, then returned just as suddenly toward the bay carrying buildings and bodies along with it. With a terrifying, apocalyptic feeling the Days realized the town was being destroyed before their eyes.

The shaking lasted for four minutes and the earthquake registered between 8.4 and 8.6 on the Richter Scale, the largest ever recorded in the northern hemisphere. The epicenter was fifty-six miles west of Valdez, seventy-five miles south of Anchorage and approximately fourteen miles deep. The force of the quake was equal to ten million times that of an atomic bomb and the shaking caused an underwater landslide in the glacial silt of Valdez Bay. Underneath the harbor, ninety-seven million cubic yards of earth shifted violently, generating a thirty-foot wave that had partially inundated the town. Three crewmembers died on the *Chena,* which rolled with the giant wave but somehow stayed afloat. Her remaining crewmembers looked on in horror as people tried in vain to outrun the tsunami. The Dock Company wharves and warehouses were knocked apart in the giant wave. The crewmembers who lived through it would be forever haunted by the sight of bodies carried back out into the bay on a giant wave. Some, they said, were still clutching their oranges.

Thirty-three people were killed that day in Valdez. The body of the young man who had replaced Bobby as the forklift operator was never found. The wave moved down the bay and out toward the Sound, gaining momentum as it rolled down Valdez Arm. Harry Henderson owned a cabin on the left just before the Narrows. As the wave funneled into the narrower channel, it reached a height of 230 feet. Harry was never seen again. Only the footing of his cabin remained, and the small indent in the coastline is known as Henderson Bay today.

As darkness settled in earnest on that Good Friday in 1964, nothing remained of the docks or warehouses and the entire waterfront area of Valdez was a total loss. More than 40 percent of the homes were destroyed, sewer lines were broken in over 150 places, and the roads were cracked and crumpled. Nearly every family in the town of

2,000 would mourn the loss of loved ones. Night fell over the scene of destruction, and the captain of the *Chena* cried out over the marine radio, "Mayday, mayday, Valdez is gone!"

For all the world knew, the Good Friday earthquake had indeed taken Valdez off the map. The last communication from Valdez was the ship captain's mayday. Then silence. Bobby was in Anchorage at the time of the quake and the silence terrified him. He was frantic to get home but knew that this time of chaos required control of his emotions. He reached inside to find the strength and sense of calm that would be required again and again in his life.

The six-hour drive back to Valdez took him three days. Bridges had been compromised and engineers allowed only one car to cross at a time. Wide chasms yawned in the two-lane highway and in some places they were freshly filled with gravel by the time he reached them. When he finally arrived in Valdez, his sense of awe at the magnitude of destruction was diminished only by the shock of seeing his father.

Walter's thick hand twisted the whiskey glass in front of him. His thin, wiry body hunched over the old wooden counter of the Glacier Bar. He looked like someone who had just witnessed a ghost. Bobby had never seen his father drink and he quietly slid onto the stool beside him.

A few structures still stood in town. The Glacier Bar, downstairs from Bob Brown's living quarters, was in the residential area slightly up hill from downtown. The freight docks, fuel terminals, and much of downtown had been lost either to the violent tremors, underwater landslide and resulting tsunami, or fires. The prophetically-named Morgue Bar had washed into the bay. Built in 1898, it was one of the original buildings in town. For five years before the electrical grid was established, it had served as an icehouse, and doubled as a temporary morgue for those who perished in the wintertime. Bodies were stored in the back room until the ground thawed enough for a proper burial in the springtime. When electricity was established in the frontier town, it became a bar, named in remembrance of its beginnings. Now it would forever serve as an underwater morgue somewhere at the bottom of Valdez Bay for those patrons and employees who were washed away with it.

Walter quietly recounted to Bobby all the town folks who were missing. For three days and nights Walter and the other men in town had searched for survivors. They found neither survivors nor bodies. They drank late into the night, sharing sorrows and grieving for the friends and family who had been lost.

When Valdez was founded as the starting point for the trek to the interior gold fields, it made sense to build at the trailhead at the base of the Valdez Glacier. But the mostly level town site was built atop glacial moraine comprised of gravel and silt. It was especially damp from the spring glacial melt that made it susceptible to "liquefaction" during an earthquake. The unstable ground magnified the effects of the powerful earthquake. The early settlers had not considered the stability of the ground beneath their buildings—nobody had until that tragic Good Friday in 1964. The U.S. Geological Survey ultimately condemned the town, declaring the site unsafe to rebuild.

The people of Valdez had a choice. They could simply write the town off and abandon it or they could band together in an effort to rebuild the town on solid ground. Bobby pondered the similarities between the catastrophic oil spill they now faced with that of the earthquake a quarter century ago. Faced with the nearly complete destruction of their town, Valdez residents had embraced each other in sorrow and grief, and resolved to remain a community. Their shared experiences prompted them to rally together with common purpose to recover and rebuild four miles away from the old town, atop a solid rock foundation. Their community had become stronger in the face of this adversity.

Cruising into the bay, Bobby glanced back at the breakwater and seawall that separated the harbor from the town sitting just above it. He remembered hauling the boulders to build it after the quake. Strapping himself inside the cab of a dump truck, he would steel himself with the knowledge that dumping his load might tip the entire truck over, as it did on occasion. The crane would right him and he would set off to retrieve yet another load. Boulder by boulder, brick by brick, and timber by timber the town folk had worked tirelessly to design and rebuild a new town. If the individual boulders represented his own efforts, he thought, the completed seawall and breakwater represented the collective efforts of the community and what they had accomplished together.

As he turned his attention back to the captain's wheel and Valdez Bay unfolding in front of him, he pushed the throttle forward and wondered what lay ahead for the Sound, for fishermen, for the oil industry, and for the residents of Valdez. Already this disaster proved to be a divisive rather than uniting force. If there was a common sense of purpose, it seemed to be that of assigning blame. He recognized that such a focus could only detract from efforts to recover the health of the Sound, and ultimately to reconsider prevention and response regulations. But he couldn't help but feel angry himself.

This was a preventable disaster. It was one that fishermen and other local residents had feared for years, but lacked the power to prevent. Citizen concerns had been no match against powerful oil industry representatives who lobbied state legislators and the DEC to ease regulations or compromise on compliance. Yet Exxon representative Don Cornett had told the Cordova fishermen just a few days before, "You have had some good luck and you don't realize it... You have Exxon. And we do business straight."[2]

Cornett had stood before an angry crowd in the Cordova High School gymnasium four days after the spill. Many of the residents in attendance were the very same who had gathered there in 1971—nearly twenty years prior—to voice their concerns over the proposed construction of an oil pipeline terminating in Prince William Sound or Cook Inlet. The same citizens and Don Cornett, along with DEC representatives and scientists, gathered there again in 1977, just two months before the pipeline construction was complete. On that day in 1977, nearly thirteen years before the spill, they gathered to discuss tanker safety and oil pollution liability. Now four days after the spill, they convened again to discuss the spill they hoped would never happen. Four days of anger had built upon nearly two decades of fear, which the audience was primed to direct at Cornett. As he stepped toward the podium, a fisherman yelled out, "Prince William Sound was beautiful a week ago and now it's full of shit!!"

Another called out suggesting it would take twenty years for Exxon to make it right with the fishermen. Cornett responded, "Is it going to take twenty years to settle these claims? I have a great deal of knowledge of how Exxon settles their claims. And unless you are a very difficult person to satisfy, it shouldn't take anywhere near twenty years. I guarantee you, we have never had a claim go twenty years. The answer to the question is no, the claims will be settled promptly. We have no interest in haggling. People with reasonable claims don't have a thing to worry about."

Another voice in the audience called out, "I guess as far as compensation for when this gets in the food chain, just tough luck, huh?" Cornett responded, "We- I- I believe the research data that I have seen indicates that if the fish do go through the oil, they will take it up, it will get in their system and then it will go out of their system. But if you get them too soon, they taste a little like diesel." This response was met with angry murmurs from a crowd in no mood to joke about the damage done or the future of their livelihoods.

Cornett spoke up with resolve, as if he hoped his words could quell the ire that seemed to be literally thickening the air in the gymnasium. "You don't remember this, but I was here thirteen years ago in this very room, we had this same conversation. And I told you the same thing then I'm telling you now. We will consider whatever it takes to keep you whole."

Another Cordovan countered with a question about the long-term effects on the sea life in the Sound, noting, "We don't have the ability to assess what the financial loss would be for a period of up to ten years." The crowd grew increasingly restive and belligerent as Cornett responded. "That's right. We don't have any idea. We're afraid of what might happen. Were I in your shoes, I would be very afraid. You see, if you can't fish, or you don't do the herring fishery this year, bring it to the table. But standing and yelling at each other about it isn't going to get us there. Show us what you're talking about. Now that's…you have *my* word on that. Don Cornett. I told you that." With that, some members of the audience laughed out loud.

These reassurances did little to build trust between Exxon and the fishermen who rightly figured Exxon's offers to "make whole" were for 1989 only. In exchange for accepting a settlement for lost income due to closure of the herring season which seemed imminent, Exxon sought a full release of all claims. They had no interest in speculating about harm to fisheries in the years to come. Fishermen are usually most in need of cash at the end of a long winter and it appeared as though Exxon hoped to capitalize on the short-term need for cash by compensating fishermen for what they would have made on herring and salmon that year, in exchange for full exoneration of any claims in the future. The day after Cornett made an appearance at the Cordova High School gymnasium, two fishermen filed the first in a spate of lawsuits to come.

The suit filed by Martin and James Goreson in Anchorage Superior Court sought class action status and alleged gross negligence on the part of Exxon Corporation, Alyeska Pipeline Service Company and the Department of Environmental Conservation in the spill and ensuing cleanup efforts. The suit also named Captain Joseph Hazelwood as a defendant, noting his failure "to operate the *Exxon Valdez* in a safe and prudent manner in accordance with accepted navigational practices."[3] Although the suit accused Hazelwood of leaving the helm to an unqualified crewmember, it did not address Hazelwood's blood alcohol content and the reports from the Coast Guard and harbor pilot Ed Murphy that said they smelled alcohol on his breath, or his recent drunken driving convictions.

The suit alleged that Exxon, Alyeska, and DEC had an obligation to fishermen "to respond to the oil spill as quickly and responsibly as possible to minimize damage" but failed to do so. It accused DEC of failing to declare an emergency and take charge of the cleanup as allowed by state statue, when it became clear in the hours and days that followed the spill that cleanup efforts were faltering at the hands of Alyeska and Exxon. DEC, the suit alleged, could have ordered "a person or persons to take action if the department believes necessary to meet the emergency, and protect the public health, welfare, or environment."[4]

As the *Lady Lynne* crept through the Narrows, Bobby thought how much he hated the idea of a lawsuit. The depositions, paperwork, and searching for records all added up to the kind of hassles he hated most. He'd much rather spend all night mending a net, pulling fish from a gill net until his hands bled, contending with wind and waves and elusive fish, or convincing a faltering engine to keep going so he could avoid crashing onto a rocky beach. He felt much more comfortable dealing with challenges he could touch, that required mechanical skill, or a trained eye. These things he could control.

As the tanker came into sight, still stranded on Bligh Reef, Bobby thought about the many repercussions it would have on his life that were far beyond his control. Before he left Sitka, he'd been on the phone with Pat McKay, his attorney in Anchorage. Pat had told him, no matter what, don't sign anything or accept any money from Exxon until he could review the contract or settlement documents. Everything in his life had once seemed certain. He'd taken for granted that spring tides would carry herring he would catch up in his net in a frenzied season opener, that he would awaken to the sound of salmon jumping around his boat as the summer sun rose over Unakwik Inlet, and that money for his boat and house payments would be secured in his Seafirst bank account as the days shortened into winter. Now these things seemed anything but certain.

Yet those simple certainties had supported a lifestyle and relationships that meant everything to him. He'd sought to secure these parts of his life ever since the family had been forced to shut down the cannery and leave Dayville with the closure of the salmon seasons in the late 1950s. His livelihood was interwoven with his relationships and sense of identity, which were built by helping others learn to set or mend a net, or when others shared a spare part he desperately needed. These challenges and experiences brought an interdependence and closeness with his crew, with Lori and other pilots, with his brother and son, and with other fishermen that he knew he needed in his life. These relationships were all built on the bond they shared with the waters and the landscape of the Sound.

As he looked out now on what had once been a flawless picture of emerald green swells and talus island cliffs, he saw tarballs floating in the tide rips and black crude coating the rocky beaches of Naked Island. He realized that this place was completely interwoven with every other aspect of his life, and that realization frightened him. Without Prince William Sound as he had known it, would he have anything left that he really cared about? Would those other pieces of his life come to be as tenuous as the Sound's future?

As he guided the boat into Outside Bay on the south side of Naked Island, he heard a sound that startled him. It sounded like a baby crying. He pulled back on the throttle to quiet the engine. Another cry. This time louder.

He leapt out of the captain's chair and scrambled down the ladder to the deck. As he leaned over the side and looked down into the water still filmy with the sheen of oil he saw what had surely made the noise. A sea otter struggled to stay afloat. Its once mischievous eyes were mere bloody holes where its strong paws had clawed them out. No doubt the oil blackening its whiskers had stung its eyes, driving it mad with pain. Bobby's hands gripped the side of the boat and hot tears streamed down his face. Nothing deserved to suffer like that. He wanted to scoop it out of the water and hold it to his chest, although he knew shooting it would probably be more humane. Like it was yesterday, he recalled the first time he'd ever seen a sea otter up close as a boy at Dayville.

It was one of the first days of fall when a soft snow fell from clouds that looked pregnant with moisture. Wearing a wool cap pulled down to his eyebrows and a red-checkered flannel shirt, Bobby's Uncle Doug carried his shotgun in the crook of his arm. He found Bobby chopping wood and asked him if he would like to join him on a duck hunt. The two walked down onto the peninsula and down the steps, to the dock where fishing boats tied up at the cannery in the summer. A small wooden skiff rocked gently, squeaking against the dock with each gentle wave. At ten years of age, Bobby had never shot a duck and he would have been a little nervous with anyone but his father or favorite uncle. Doug rowed the skiff out of Swan's Port and around the tip of the peninsula. His red-checkered flannel had turned mostly white in the falling snow.

The smell of wood smoke drifted on the air. The water was dark gray under the clouds and he could hear a quiet splash each time the oars plunged below the surface. The deep green of spruce and hemlock peeked out from under a heavy dusting of snow. Not a house or building was in sight. There was a silence only a snowy day could deliver.

Bobby heard the splash of the otter before he saw it. His mittened hands grabbed the edge of the skiff as he looked down into the water, just as he was doing now. But the otter looking back at him in his memory was bright-eyed and its eyebrows seemed to lift in curiosity. The light-colored whiskers against its dark fur gave Bobby the impression the furry little creature was grinning. It floated on its back, clutching a tiny crab on its chest. The otter worked at the crab shell with its strong front paws. Then it quickly rolled face down in the water and popped back up again. The otter seemed to be showing off, enjoying the companionship. Uncle Doug told Bobby they roll over like that to rinse the shells away from their meal.

Doug kept rowing quietly. They spotted a small flock of black ducks with white patterned wings and yellowish eyes. Goldeneyes, Doug explained, are very good eating. But they will be hard to sneak up on. Even on a snowy day when sounds are muted, the ducks sensed the presence of their pursuers. In a sudden eruption of splashing water, honking and flapping, the Goldeneye ducks left the water in unison. Bobby couldn't remember seeing anything so beautiful, so magical, as black and white blurred in front of him and blended into the falling snow. The sharp report of the shotgun startled him and he squeezed his eyes shut. Again and again, the force of the shotgun rocked the boat. Three ducks fell lifelessly back to the water.

Bobby felt a twinge of regret, suddenly wishing he hadn't come. As Uncle Doug rowed and scooped their limp bodies from the water, Bobby tried to force back the lump in his throat. His uncle knew how much he loved all animals. Doug glanced at the boy out of the corner of his eye.

Doug was a rawboned sort of fellow with warm, kind eyes that endeared him to all the children who lived at Dayville. He was typical of the kind of person who settled in Alaska, a person who seemed naturally in tune to the rhythms of nature and attentive to the need to sustain it as their way of life depended upon it.

As he rowed toward the ducks he'd shot, Doug explained softly, "Hunting is a way of life for us Alaskans, Bobby. It's a rich land, and it's okay to take a few animals for ourselves to eat if we do it wisely. Same with fish. And timber. We're going to be here for a while." There was a lesson in his words that Bobby would later recognize as a principle of balancing their own needs against that of the sustaining the land and animals.

The ducks simmered in brown gravy for the rest of the day. Bobby was invited to dinner at Uncle Doug and Aunt Glenna's. A simple candle burned in the middle of the table covered in a blue-and-white-checkered cloth. The soft light and flickering shadows made the simple room feel elegant. It made Bobby feel all grown up to be invited to dinner by himself, without his brother and three sisters. The breast of duck on his plate was tender and savory and he could remember the heavenly taste and compliments to the hunters.

He remembered this day as he stared down at the oil-soaked otter. The earthquake had taken Uncle Doug's life twenty-five years ago. Bobby realized that everything Doug had cared about and the philosophies he embraced were dying, too. Oil development had brought people to Alaska who weren't dependent on the land and water to survive. They were driven instead by corporate profits and accountability to shareholders, not to the land or local communities. The promises and agreements industry representatives made with the people of Alaska over two decades ago had initially been codified with little more than a handshake, which was typical of the culture of trust and interdependence that a harsh landscape and small communities had fostered.

Now, Bobby had to have his attorney look at any document he signed. Fishermen, their union representatives, processors, Natives, and municipalities lined up to file lawsuits. Local residents wrung their hands as Exxon, Alyeska, and DEC sought to assign blame and argued about how to stem the damage from eleven million gallons of oil, and prevent further suffering and dying of fish, otters, birds, and whales.

It was no longer a handshake culture where people got together to govern themselves in small boroughs. They were forced instead to rely on government officials to balance their interests against industry. The rational side of him knew that things had certainly changed gradually since his childhood at Dayville. But standing there on the deck of his boat now at the entrance to Outside Bay, it seemed that everything had changed in an instant.

9

"Hang On, We're Going Around a Curve"

JUNEAU: APRIL 4, 1989

A S THE LAST OF THE OIL REMAINING ONBOARD the *Exxon Valdez* settled into the cargo tanks of the *Exxon San Francisco*, the Alaska Department of Fish and Game announced the official closure of the Prince William Sound herring season over the marine radio. It came as no surprise to any of the Sound's fishermen, or to Bobby and Dale as they sat inside the wheelhouse in Outside Bay. They could see the herring schooling up on the *Lady Lynne's* sonar and moving toward the surface of the water, which was still covered with an oily sheen, thick in places. The herring harvest usually averaged about ten thousand tons and last year, fishermen had received $700 to $800 per ton. This announcement followed the official closure of the Sound's pot shrimp and black cod fisheries a few days earlier, which altogether, meant a loss of jobs for hundreds of fishermen and cannery workers.

Apparently on recommendation by the Ocean Tech consultants aboard the *Lady Lynne*, the *Exxon Valdez* would be towed to Naked Island's Outside Bay for minimal repairs before being towed south. But the final offloading now seemed merely a small victory for Exxon. Efforts to contain the negative wave of sentiment against the oil company were proving as futile as containing the millions of gallons of oil that now coated the islands and coastline on the western side of Prince William Sound from Naked Island to the Kenai Peninsula.

In Juneau, fishermen and environmentalists marched in front of the capitol with signs proclaiming, "Oil companies break promises; break lives; break hearts," and "Exxon stashes the cash and passes the buck."[1]

State legislators were considering a bill to eliminate the Economic Limit Factor, a tax break for oil companies. In the past few days, the bill had gained momentum even amongst the most conservative, pro-development legislators. Representative Ron Larson, a Democrat from Anchorage and co-chairman of the House Finance Committee, had voted against raising taxes on oil companies in the prior month. But in the days following the spill, Larsen announced the Finance committee would consider raising additional money to establish a $50 million emergency relief fund for oil spill cleanup by increasing real estate taxes on the Trans-Alaska pipeline. Senate President Tim Kelly, a Republican from Anchorage said, "There is going to be a different attitude toward the industry in the legislature following this last act of negligence."[2]

At an April 1 press conference, DEC Commissioner Dennis Kelso announced, "The senate on Friday voted in favor of a bill the Governor submitted that would increase the oil and hazardous substance release response fund by $20 million. The Governor two years ago asked me to evaluate where the agency stood and what we needed to do our job. And we looked at what we already had assigned to us by statute, nothing new, no frills, nothing extra. And, essentially it came down to the good news being we knew what the shortfall was. The bad news was, it was about $10 million. And that didn't include anything like strengthening our oil and hazardous substance spill response, it just meant getting up to a basic minimum."

Kelso went on to say, "Last year, the legislature increased [our budget] somewhat, but didn't appropriate all the money the Governor had requested. One of the items that didn't get appropriated was the money for oil spill contingency planning and inspections. This year the Governor again asked for additional funding…I don't want to give you the impression that we are out of the woods. But we are hoping people are listening this time around."[3]

The legislature did indeed seem to be responding to an increasingly cynical Alaska citizenry. By a wide margin, the House approved a resolution to ask President George H.W. Bush to cancel an oil lease sale at Bristol Bay that would open up exploratory drilling in a sensitive, high-value fishing area. And the Senate Special Committee on Oil and Gas unanimously passed a resolution to establish an arbitration commission to help settle claims against Exxon. Reflecting on the vote, Chairwoman Pearce acknowledged the influence of the spill and public opinion on the legislative process. "I think the backlash is going to be on Big Oil as an industry," she said. "They have real public relations problems and a credibility gap."[4] This changing public sentiment was pervasive. It hung over the boat harbors, Native villages, and small towns that ringed the coastlines from the Aleutian Islands to southeastern Alaska. And as Bobby listened to the herring closure announcement coming over the marine radio, the sense of irrevocable change clung to him as persistently as the smell of oil still rising off the waters of the bay.

Port Valdez was closed to tanker traffic in the days following the spill. When the Coast Guard reopened it for oil shipments, traffic was limited to daylight hours and each tanker was to have two rescue tugs escorting them through the Sound. Before the *Exxon Valdez* had even been hauled off Bligh Reef, oil shippers sought to renegotiate the new regulations with the Coast Guard. They had only been able to get five tankers loaded and out of the port in the four days since it had reopened. Before the spill, three to four tankers would leave the port each day. Chairman and chief executive officer of ARCO, Lodwick Cook, argued that the Coast Guard should develop an alternate safety plan to expedite Alaska crude shipments. An estimated twelve million barrels of ARCO oil had gone undelivered as a result of the new restrictions. "We share the Coast Guard's concern for a safe and conservative operation of the port," Cook said. "But reasonable action is needed now."[5]

In 1989, Alaska crude supplied 50 percent of the oil refined and consumed on the West Coast. Refiners kept an estimated four-day supply on hand and already people Outside were rushing to fill their tanks and paying higher prices at the pump. Both BP and Exxon estimated 15 to 20 percent reductions in the amount of oil they would be able to deliver in April. Before the spill, these economic considerations and resulting political pressures would likely have persuaded regulators to bend to the requests of the oil industry. But the Coast Guard said it would not consider easing restrictions, according to spokesman Ken Freeze. He said, "These measures were not undertaken lightly but were mandated by our responsibility to the public."[6]

Refusing to bend to the requests of Chairman Cook was a dramatic turnaround for the state of Alaska, which had long revered ARCO. It was yet another confirmation that Alaskan culture had changed since it welcomed the oil industry with open arms in the 1950s. Then, Anchorage had been an economically depressed frontier town with bars and burlesque houses that stayed open all night, and rampant underground crime. The need for a stronger and more diverse economy was obvious to all who lived there. The gold rush was all but over, the copper mines at Kennicott long shuttered, the timber industry was still in need of subsidies, and the salmon industry had slumped nearly to the point of extinction under federal regulation.

Excitement about oil development was percolating during the 1950s despite the fact that since Katalla, no promising wells had been found. Over a hundred holes had been drilled throughout Alaska, producing only enough oil to fill one medium-sized tanker.[7] Prices of only $1.00 to $1.50 a barrel in the first half of the century made the challenges in Alaska costly compared to other places in the world. But global events of the early 50s revived oil fever in Alaska.

In 1951, Iran nationalized all oil operations. Egyptian president Nasser allied himself with the Soviet Union and attempted to close down the Suez Canal. As international politics chilled with the increasing intensity of the Cold War, suddenly Alaska looked like a friendlier place.

By 1953, Chevron was conducting exploration on the Kenai Peninsula. Phillips Petroleum obtained drilling rights in the Katalla and Yakataga districts. Standard Oil of California sent geologists to Icy Bay, between Cordova and Yakutat, and Humble Oil (later Exxon) explored near Yakutat.

It wasn't just the oil companies who could profit from oil exploration and speculation. State regulations allowed, even encouraged, average citizens to participate. For a ten dollar filing fee and twenty-five cents per acre, anyone could obtain an exclusive ten-year lease that could later be optioned for cash, or earn a royalty if oil was discovered. The oil companies themselves were restricted then to 100,000 acres leases throughout the state. So the big companies rarely filed leases unless they were relatively certain the site would be commercially lucrative. Any "little guy" could earn a 5 percent royalty from his lease if oil was discovered.

By the end of 1955, oil companies and individual speculators had filed for more than five million acres of land. Irene Ryan, the first woman to fly solo in Alaska and to serve in both the territorial and state legislatures, kept her colleagues in an extended session one day in 1955. Ryan believed that an oil strike was imminent. With her perseverance, the legislature passed a 1 percent tax on the gross value at the well of all oil and gas produced in Alaska.

Richfield Oil (later ARCO) and their young geologist Bill Bishop hardly seemed to be the dynamic team that would make it big in Alaska. Only thirty-six years old, Bishop had been hired before he finished his master's thesis at UCLA. Formed in 1911, Richfield Oil had no foreign holdings, was operating under bankruptcy reorganization, and had shown four straight years of declining earnings.

The Richfield holdings were located inside the Kenai National Moose Range, which after two years of hearings Congress had threatened to close—along with other wildlife preserves—to exploratory drilling. Fortunately for Richfield, Eisenhower's Secretary of Interior Douglas McKay had declared in 1954 that oil exploration on public lands was in the public's best interest. In fact, McKay allowed so much exploration on public lands he became known as "Giveaway McKay" and eventually faced a congressional investigation. Still, Richfield had to abide by the new rules of a country just beginning to acquire a collective environmental conscience. They had to follow new regulations when crossing streams, not use dynamite or seismic equipment for testing as was customary, and repair and restore a site before abandoning it.

So instead of dynamite, Bishop used a less conclusive hydrophone sounding to try and determine if the site held a cache of promising oil reserves. After only thirty-three soundings and a couple of flybys in a helicopter, Bishop set his sights on a dome-like structure near the Swanson River in the fall of 1956. According to Alaskan legend, Bishop dug his boot heel into the ground next to a lone hemlock twenty-three miles from the nearest road and instructed his crew to "drill here." It was the 166th hole drilled in Alaska, but the first for Richfield.

By July of 1957 the drill had cut through ten thousand feet, at which point the crew was instructed to abandon the effort. But Bishop's assistant, G. Ray Arnett, instructed the roughnecks to "drill just a few feet more."[8] The drill bit barely caught the northern edge of a sizable oil field and the gusher promised nine hundred barrels per day. The *Anchorage Times* trumpeted "Richfield Hits Oil." A front-page editorial proclaimed, "The best advice for Alaskans today is that of a San Francisco cable car conductor to his passengers, 'Hang on, we're going around a curve.' Alaska is turning a sharp curve and is starting down a new road of development such as never has been seen before."[9]

With the Swanson River discovery, Alaska suddenly jumped sides on the national balance sheet. It was no longer seen as a territory requiring federal subsidies, but a source of revenue for federal coffers. Congress passed the Statehood Act of 1958 and the new state of Alaska was awarded 103 million acres of federal land of its choosing. State officials eyed the North Slope, and based on the advice of the U.S. Geological Survey, selected the easternmost portion of the Slope known as the Arctic National Wildlife Refuge. When the U.S. Department of Defense refused to release it, the state instead chose Prudhoe Bay, a 4.2-million-acre site between the Arctic Refuge to the east and the U.S. Naval Petroleum Reserve to the west. No longer considered the nation's "icebox" or "Seward's folly" (for the former Secretary of State who purchased the land from Russia), Alaska was finally coming into its own. Nothing could stop it now, or so it seemed.

In the steep, spruce-covered forests of Cook Inlet, a group of Athabaskan Natives from the village of Tyonek made a discovery that nearly stopped Alaska's oil boom dead in its tracks. While hunting for lynx or moose, what the Natives instead found was an oil rig. The hunters returned to their village with the unhappy news.

In 1915, President Harding had created a 24,000-acre reservation called Moquawkie, one of the few in Alaska. A federal organization known as the Bureau of Indian Affairs (BIA) was entrusted with overseeing the reservation. The BIA, a division of the Department of Interior, built a school and operated a grocery store in reservation village of Tyonek. The Natives felt it was important to retain their culture and subsistence way of life. But fur-bearing animals were becoming scarce and restrictions on hunting grew proportionally. The declining salmon runs of the 1950s had shortened the commercial salmon seasons that provided both a source of food and cash income. The village of Tyonek had become one of the poorest in Alaska with families of ten or twelve living in tar-paper shacks. The only flush toilet in town was at the BIA school. The Tyonek people had become increasingly bitter about their dependence on, and intervention of, the Bureau of Indian Affairs.

With the discovery of the oil rig, the leaders of the Tyonek Village Council contacted their friend Stanley McCutcheon, a pilot and attorney in Anchorage. In the past, McCutcheon had initiated food drives at the Anchorage grocery stores and flown the supplies himself to the people of the Moquawkie Reservation. McCutcheon discovered that in 1962 the BIA had leased part of the reservation to the Pan American Oil Company (later Amoco) for $1 million and placed the money into a government fund. He filed suit against the Department of Interior and the Bureau of Indian Affairs on behalf of the Tyonek people. The Natives won in court, negating the lease negotiated by the BIA and allowing the Tyonek Village Council to negotiate their own leases in the future.

One of the council members said, "All of us on the council went to Anchorage and rented rooms in the old hotel on Fourth Street. Then we all got drunk and toasted our victory over the BIA—Bastards Inflicted on Alaska."[10] The Tyonek Village Council then leased the same land for $12.5 million.

Their victory energized what had been a nascent and scattered stirring among the Native people all over Alaska. With their revenues from the new lease, the Tyonek people funded a delegation of three hundred Natives who would gather in solidarity to evaluate their rights to land that had originally been theirs, and for which they had never been compensated. From the Arctic tundra to Kodiak Island, they convened in Anchorage in October 1966 and established the Alaska Federation of Natives (AFN). In an empty storeroom above Miller's Furs on Fourth Street, delegates of different cultures and dialects from across Alaska came together for a common purpose.

With elections just around the corner, the Native delegation found itself courted by a number of candidates seeking the votes of Alaska's 55,000 Natives.

Against a backdrop of heightened awareness of civil rights and notions of fairness during the Johnson era, the claims of the Natives gained national attention. In the nearly hundred years since Alaska was acquired by America, the issue of aboriginal rights had been largely ignored. Stanley McCutcheon helped the Natives form legitimate entities for claiming lands surrounding their villages. Those on the North Slope laid claim to the same lands the state was trying to claim for itself. Uncertain of the rightful owner, oil companies were hesitant to sign leases and proceed with exploration. Tension between whites and Natives grew as white people claimed the "greedy Natives"[11] were halting progress. The mood was exacerbated by a statewide radio address by Governor Hickel who claimed, "Just because somebody's grandfather chased a moose across the land, doesn't mean he owns it."[12]

By 1967, Natives had laid claim to more land than was in the entire state of Alaska.[13] Secretary of Interior Stuart Udall declared a halt to any further land leasing, asserting that the question of aboriginal rights would have to be settled prior to further development. The land freeze was imposed in 1967, coincidentally the same year that annual royalties from oil production displaced fisheries as the state's leading source of income for the first time in Alaskan history.[14]

Springtime in the Arctic comes late, but it is so magnificent it is almost possible to forget the realities of harsh, hard bitten winter months. The permafrost melts into a spongy plain of brilliant wildflowers and golden plovers lay their speckled eggs in woven grass nests on the ground. Every July, the well-known "Porcupine Herd" of about 25,000 caribou crosses the coastal plain, home to foxes, swans, and hundreds of species of birds. Mostly treeless tundra stretches across millions of acres as far as the eye can see.

During World War II, the government considered this area north of the Brooks Range a war zone where no oil exploration was allowed, all travel was restricted, and even the mail was censored. This policy continued well into the Cold War years. But like a spring thaw, the government softened under pressure from the oil companies after the major strike at the Swanson River. In the mid-1960s the North Slope area between the Naval Reserve to the west and the Arctic National Wildlife Refuge to the east was opened for exploration.

Richfield Oil sent two young geologists to map and study the North Slope. With data from the U.S. Geological survey in hand, novice explorers Gar Passel and Gil Mull worked along the banks of the Sagavanirktok River where they noticed oil-soaked sand just above the water line. Thinking the surrounding rock structures looked promising, they sent a note to their supervisor in Anchorage on the next supply plane. Reportedly, Passel claimed in his note, "if we can't find an oil field in this stuff, I give up."[15] The note made its way to Harry Jamison, Richfield's Alaska exploration chief.

Lacking the cash to fund an operation on the North Slope Richfield's Jamison walked into the office of Humble Oil (now ExxonMobil) and sat down at the desk of J.R. Jackson, the West Coast exploration chief. They struck a deal to share half the costs of leasing, exploration and wildcatting, ultimately a $40 million proposition for each company.

In July of 1965, Richfield surprised everyone with a successful—and precedent-setting—bid of $93.78 per acre for the lease of what was known as the Sadlerochit Formation. A third of the formation around the skirt remained unclaimed and BP picked it up for $47.60 an acre. Hauling three thousand tons of equipment into Fairbanks and then by plane to the drill site, Richfield was suddenly faced with an antitrust suit from the Justice Department. In order to satisfy the Feds, Richfield agreed to a merger with Atlantic Refining. The merger was completed September 16, 1965 creating Atlantic-Richfield (ARCO).

On February 27, 1966, the new company's drill bit into the foothills of the Brooks Range. For all the effort, dollars, and enthusiasm put into this well named "Susie," it turned out to be a dry hole. Over the previous eighteen months BP had drilled six holes and found equally disappointing results. Most of the other companies had pulled out of the North Slope. BP considered selling their interest to Atlantic Richfield since they seemed to be the only ones left on the slope.

Thornton Bradshaw, the president of the newly merged company stood before the board. He had been impressed with Jamison's confidence in the lease and persuaded the board to approve one more drill. The gear and equipment are there now, he said. One way or another, we'll have to dismantle it and take it off the slope. The board agreed to one last attempt.

The rig was moved sixty-five miles north, almost to the edge of the Arctic Ocean. On the day after Christmas in 1967, Gil Mull was taking a turn at "sitting on the well" monitoring the samples of rock and moisture during the drill. When he opened the pipe, a fifty-foot burst of flame erupted and blazed sideways in the stiff wind. Mull knew the flame was no guarantee of oil beneath the surface, but he thought it held the possibility of a major reservoir.[16] Harry Jamison, then the general manager for Alaska operations, waited two months before he was confident enough to call the press on February 16, 1968. They had a major strike!

A test drill seven miles away, very near the river where Passel and Mull originally discovered sand-soaked oil, confirmed the size of the field. In 1969, BP also stuck oil in what would ultimately be the largest find on the slope. Five smaller companies also announced significant strikes. The companies estimated that a 350-square-mile area at Prudhoe Bay contained twenty-two billion barrels of oil and thirty trillion cubic feet of natural gas—by far the largest oil field in North America.[17]

On Wall Street oil stocks went crazy. Atlantic Richfield's stock rose from $90 a share to $162 over a five-month span. But Wall Street was a world away from the remote plain of the North Slope. The strike was hundreds of miles from the nearest sea port, and even further from the major oil-consuming markets. On July 10, 1968, Robert Wright emphasized in his "Marketplace" column of the *Wall Street Journal*, "Fantastic reserve figures [in the Alaska discovery] are making the rounds of Wall Street...but even if the North Slope discovery turns out to be a major source of oil, many problems and many years would be required to get the petroleum to market."[18]

But there was no shortage of proposals for getting the oil to market. Governor Hickel proposed that the railway from Fairbanks extend to Prudhoe Bay. Oil could then be loaded into tank cars and shipped to the port city of Seward, he said. From there, the oil could be loaded into ocean going tankers.

With a major stake in the oil fields, Exxon (then Humble Oil) favored an all water route around the northern coast of Alaska. They commissioned an ice-breaking tanker, the *Manhattan,* to explore a direct shipping route through the Arctic Ocean. Fifty million dollars and two troublesome attempts later, they abandoned this idea. Some proposed a pipeline through Canada, delivering oil to the major markets in the Midwest through Chicago. Other raised concerns about what the Canadians might charge for the right-of-way.

Labor unions in Alaska lobbied for an all-Alaska route, ensuring more jobs for Alaskans. Natives opposed the idea of an Alaska pipeline route out of concern for caribou migration and the potential for spills in inland rivers and streams. Their concerns ratcheted up the debate about aboriginal land claims, as any proposed pipeline would cross lands they claimed were rightfully theirs.

The issue of land claims had languished in stalemate for the past two years, met with hostility by the majority of Alaskans and inaction by Congress. Governor Hickel had unsuccessfully sued Stuart Udall, Secretary of the Interior, and appealed to Congress to release the land freeze. With the discovery at Prudhoe Bay, the oil industry would become a powerful, if unlikely ally for Natives struggling to resolve the issue of aboriginal rights. Without a resolution, a permit to construct the pipeline would not be issued.

Walter Hickel had a change of heart on the issue of Native land claims. When Richard Nixon nominated him to be Secretary of the Interior after the election in 1968, environmentalists protested his appointment, figuring that installing him into such a position would be like "appointing a fox to watch the henhouse."[19] Hickel needed the support of Alaska's Natives to offset this opposition. Under the watchful eye of the Alaska Federation of Natives (AFN), he began work in Washington to break the impasse. After much political maneuvering, a series of Congressional hearings and some 120 AFN visits to Washington, D.C., President Nixon signed the Alaska Native Claims Settlement Act into law on December 18, 1971.

The settlement was unprecedented in the history of the United States, ultimately awarding Alaska Natives $962 million and 44 million acres of land. The assets were to be distributed to shareholders through thirteen newly formed Native "corporations." To be a shareholder required a person to prove that at least one grandparent had been an Alaska Native. Shares would pass down from generation to generation. Some Natives were dissatisfied with the terms, believing that they should have been awarded more specific subsistence hunting and fishing rights in perpetuity. Others felt they should have been awarded mineral rights at Prudhoe Bay. And some believed that making decisions about the use of the resources awarded to them by shareholder vote would prove unworkable. Not least, some felt that awarding rights to resources through shares akin to corporate ownership was dehumanizing and degrading. While many Alaskans generally believed that the settlement was too much, few could argue with the infusion of wealth the settlement would bring to the Alaskan economy.

Even before the land claims had been resolved, or the suits by fishermen and environmentalists had been dispensed with through Congressional action, the first delivery of $100 million worth of Japanese pipe was delivered to Valdez in 1969. The Alyeska Pipeline Service Company was formally incorporated on August 14, 1970, with BP Pipeline Alaska, Exxon Pipeline Company, and ARCO Pipeline Company controlling 90 percent of the shares in the seven-member consortium.

The oil companies estimated that North Slope crude would yield 660,000 barrels per day. At a price of ten dollars per barrel, they figured any construction delays would cost them $6.6 million per day in lost revenues. Although they did not yet have a permit to begin construction, Alyeska Pipeline Company contracted with San Francisco-based Bechtel Corporation for construction of the pipeline itself and with Fluor Corporation to construct the twelve pump stations and a terminal at Valdez Bay.

Behind the scenes, oil company representatives and lobbyists felt the urgency to begin construction. Hugh Gallagher, a lobbyist for BP, later recalled a dinner conversation shared among members of the Alyeska consortium. As BP's Gallagher later recalled, Exxon's Ken Fountain reported on the approval from the heads of the owner corporations, saying something like, "The big boys have approved the schedule, we are ready to roll, and you guys have two weeks to get the pipeline permits approved."

Gallagher responded by telling him he didn't think that was possible, explaining that the issue of the Native claims hadn't yet been resolved, an Environmental Impact Statement had yet to be issued by the Department of Interior, and no provisions yet existed to hire and employ Alaskan workers on the project. To the best of Gallagher's recollection, Fountain retorted, "I didn't ask you what you think. This is an order from the top."

Others at the table pointed out some of the complexities that would take time to resolve, saying something like, "You can't ask Interior to approve the permit before you know anything at all about the impact oil shipments might have on the fisheries in Prince William Sound." The Exxon representative's response made an impression on Gallagher as he would later claim Fountain said, "I don't care if every goddamn fish dies, get that permit in two weeks."[20]

10

Fortune Seekers

As Bobby sat just off Naked Island watching the herring school on his sonar, the pieces began to fall together in his mind. He realized now that he hadn't recognized the implications of oil discovery as the sharp curve described in the *Anchorage Times*. Of course he knew of the sizable discoveries the oil companies had made, but from his vantage point in the tiny fishing village of Valdez, it wasn't at all clear to him that oil development in the state would affect his life. If there had been a sharp curve, he thought, it had not been the day that Richfield struck oil, but rather the night the tanker struck Bligh Reef.

On the other hand, thinking that a single event had changed Alaska's course may not accurately capture the subtleties of all that had taken place. Perhaps the initial oil strike, controversy over the construction of the pipeline, and cutbacks in regulatory oversight had all come together to complete the turn that Alaska had taken. While the discovery of oil in Alaska was at the forefront of the state's political and economic consciousness in the 1960s, it was just a backdrop to Bobby. He simply struggled to make a living fishing in the summertime and hauling semi-loads of jet fuel to Fairbanks to supply the military base in the winter. He remembered the day he came in from working his trap-line in the late fall of 1963 when he noticed a crowd gathered in front of the telegraph station in old Valdez. With shoulders hunched against a stiff wind, some of the folks in the crowd told him that President Kennedy had been shot.

But even this news, while disheartening and shocking at that instant, seemed distant and remote. People who lived in Valdez simply lived a hardscrabble life, struggling to dig out from thirty feet of snow each winter and bracing against the gale force winds blowing down the Chugach Mountains over the Valdez Glacier. Daily tasks associated with living in that kind of environment consumed him and most other Alaskans.

After the 1964 earthquake, the town's population dwindled and unemployment reached nearly 40 percent.[1] Few of the town's citizens were wealthy and nearly all made a living from fishing, construction, or selling and transporting supplies. John Kelsey and his brother Bob restored the Dock Company from the ruins and lost lives, but were reportedly $500,000 in debt. Such a liability could have proven overwhelming to a small family-owned enterprise, but the discovery of oil at Prudhoe Bay in 1968 promised to be just the boon that Kelsey, the town of Valdez, and the state needed. Kelsey called George Gilson, who had since rebuilt his grocery store in the new town and served as the town's current mayor. And he called Bill Wyatt whose newly built hotel, the Wyatt House, would eventually become the Westmark Hotel. They sat down with a map spread in front of them and traced the shortest overland route from Prudhoe Bay to an ice-free deepwater port, which of course was Valdez. Then they sketched a route that could make the most use of federal lands, which would lower the costs of acquiring rights-of-way and land settlements. They also noted that, unlike other port towns such as Whittier, Valdez had a paved road—the Richardson Highway—connecting it to Fairbanks.

As far as these three men were concerned, all the proposals for getting oil to markets in the lower forty-eight following the 1968 discovery made little sense. Kelsey dismissed Hickel's idea of a rail line, calling it "pie in the sky." He said, "All I could think of was a line of tank cars from Prudhoe Bay to Seward. The Canadian land route was bad because we wouldn't have control of our own pipeline. And Natives who were concerned about the caribou and fish were not aware that stiff environmental controls were certain to be imposed on the oil companies."[2]

Certain they could convince the oil companies of the merits of a pipeline terminus in Valdez, they got on the phone. Kelsey said, "We tried to reach the Humble Oil president. We called Atlantic Richfield and British Petroleum. At first they wouldn't talk to us because they thought we were a couple of characters out of the night. We kept badgering and only asked that they listen to us. Finally, they gave in and told us about a study group working in Alaska."[3] Kelsey tracked the group, which was looking at options for getting North Slope crude out of Alaska, to the Captain Cook hotel in Anchorage. They called the study group's suite, saying that the mayor of Valdez would like to talk with them and was on his way there. The group agreed to give Mayor Gilson fifteen minutes of their time.

When Kelsey and Gilson stepped into the elevator at the Captain Cook, the study group emerged from the bar and got on the same elevator. As Kelsey would later recall "They took one look at us with all the maps under our arms and said 'you must be from Valdez.' And they reminded us we had only fifteen minutes."[4] As Gilson and Kelsey laid their maps out and made their case, the fifteen-minute limit was all but forgotten. "They invited us out to dinner, and before the night was over," Kelsey said, "I knew they were falling in love with our harbor."[5]

The phone rang just as Walt and Gloria Day finished printing the latest edition of their new paper, the *Valdez and Copper Basin News,* in their basement. The voice on the line said he represented a construction company. His company was interested in purchasing the abandoned town site of Dayville, he said.

Walter was a member of the Valdez City Council and knew that Kelsey and others had been lobbying the oil companies to build a terminal in Valdez. He also knew that the old Dayville site was the only place on Valdez Bay, perhaps with the exception of Anderson Bay, on which such a facility could feasibly be built. Steep rocky cliffs ring the bay except where the milky glacial waters of the Lowe River enter the head of the bay after journeying through Keystone Canyon.

The caller was waiting on the line. Walter mulled the idea of selling the 160-acre town site, not knowing whether it might command a higher price in the coming months or years if the oil industry ultimately committed to routing a pipeline to Valdez. He favored waiting to see which proposal for transporting oil would emerge from among the dozens on the table. But he knew the decision wasn't entirely his to make. Other family members had an ownership stake in the old town site and he suspected they would be interested in selling. After all, if the pipeline wasn't routed to Valdez, this might be the best opportunity for the family to liquidate the property. The Day family ultimately agreed to sell for a price of $1 million. In addition, the sale contract stipulated that the Days would split the profits with the land speculator if the site was ultimately chosen as the terminus for the pipeline.

Speculators initially estimated the total cost of an all-Alaska pipeline route to be about $900 million. According to the *New York Times,* building the infrastructure to move oil from the North Slope would entail "possibly the largest single private construction project and private capital investment in history." By floating bonds through a state or local government, the oil industry could raise capital tax-free. Governor William Egan agreed to float the bonds until an advisor pointed out to him the significance of saving the industry three to four points on the cost of financing. When Egan suggested the oil companies share half the savings with the state, they hesitated.[6]

An attorney and friend of John Kelsey's offered that the town of Valdez could float the construction bonds instead. Fearing that such an arrangement might harm long-term relationships with the state, Atlantic Richfield initially declined the offer. That is, until John Kelsey secured an agreement that likely helped seal the deal to route the pipeline to Valdez. Kelsey flew to Juneau where he met with Governor Egan, a friend and a native of Valdez. Egan promised no retaliation on the part of the state if Valdez floated the bonds, and the two men shook hands as Kelsey left his office.

The Valdez City Council considered additional arrangements they might need to make in anticipation of the arrival of oil in their town. Walter Day, John Kelsey, Bill Wyatt, and George Gilson all agreed to expand the city limits to increase their taxing authority. They voted to extend the boundaries up Keystone Canyon nearly to the top of Thompson Pass, across the bay to include the old Dayville site, and even to include the waters extending from Valdez Bay out into Prince William Sound. Today the city limits encompass 566,737 square kilometers of land and 141,453 square kilometers of surface water. These enormous limits ultimately generated a windfall of tax revenue for the tiny port town.

The city of Valdez floated $1.5 of the $2 billion in bonds, which in 1969, was the largest tax-free municipal bond issue to date. The city received a one percent dividend, and continues to receive an additional one percent each time the bonds are refinanced.[7] The financing arrangement, coupled with the property taxes on the expanded city limits, allowed the town of Valdez to establish a permanent fund for city improvements.

After six years of political wrangling, court appeals, and an act of Congress, the first section of pipe was finally laid in March of 1975 near Tonsina River, eighty miles north of Valdez. The final and most difficult sections of pipe were laid in the spring of 1977 on a near vertical drop over the Chugach Mountains, not far from the final destination of Valdez Bay. The last weld was ceremoniously completed on May 31, 1977, a little over two years since the first section of pipe was laid. After thirty-eight days of travel time from pump station number one at Prudhoe Bay to Valdez, the first barrels of North Slope crude settled into the *ARCO Juneau* tied at its berth at the Alyeska Terminal on August 1, 1977.

By any account, the Trans-Alaska pipeline is an engineering marvel—its design and endurance is evidence of human ingenuity and determination. Because 75 percent of the pipeline crossed permafrost, burying the pipe was infeasible. North Slope oil comes out of the ground at a temperatures ranging from 158 to 176 degrees Fahrenheit, warm enough to melt the permafrost and create an unstable mix of silt, muskeg, and peat around a buried pipe. So engineers developed H shaped structures that would support the pipe above the ground in most places, and allow it to flex with the cycle of freezing and thawing, or in the event of an earthquake. Working with naturalists, engineers designed animal crossings by raising the elevation of the pipe in 554 places and burying it in twenty-three places along the route. The pipeline traverses thirty-four major rivers and eight hundred smaller streams, on bridges or buried beneath the waterways.

In all, the construction of the pipeline cost $8 billion. A total of three million tons of material were shipped to Alaska. The 800-mile pipeline is comprised of 100,000 sections of welded pipe and 78,000 structures to support 420 miles of raised pipe. The remaining 320 miles of pipe are buried three to twelve feet below ground. In one avalanche-prone area, four miles of buried pipe are refrigerated to protect the permafrost. If it is full, the pipeline holds nine million barrels of oil.

Outsiders rushed to Alaska seeking construction jobs, just as miners had sought their fortunes on the Klondike. The pipeline construction employed more than seventy thousand people, and many who had come from Outside stayed and made their home in Alaska once the project was complete. World prices for crude oil had quadrupled from $3 to $12 per barrel between the time Congress passed the pipeline bill and the time the pipeline construction was complete in 1977. When the first oil flowed down the pipeline to Port Valdez, the price for a barrel equaled the approximate price fishermen received for a single Copper River sockeye. The state's coffers began to fill with petrodollars, thanks in part to the foresight of the territorial legislators who passed the 1 percent tax in 1955. By 1982, OPEC fixed oil prices at $34 a barrel, more than triple the price of oil since the pipeline was completed. That year, Alaska's revenues totaled a heady $4,108,400,000.

The state of Alaska grew rich in the two decades following Richfield's strike at Prudhoe Bay. As Alaskans planned, built, and completed the single largest privately funded construction project of the times, Bobby Day sought his fortune in the depths of Prince William Sound. Now he sat in the wheelhouse of the *Lady Lynne* bitterly watching the herring rise to the surface of the water on his sonar, right into the thick black slick he could see out the wheelhouse window. He'd caught these fish every spring for over twenty years and this fishery represented a significant part of his income.

Alyeska and its parent companies were still profiting from oil flowing through the pipeline, even if that flow was temporarily slowed. The state of Alaska would still collect royalties. The Native Corporations would still generate dividends and their assets, for the most part, would not devalue as a result of this spill. Yet the herring on his screen, prompted by the darkness of the floating oil slick, were heading for the surface to certain death. He reckoned the loss of a significant portion of an entire generation might close this fishery forever.

He heard the clinking of ice in a glass and turned around to find Dale slipping his big frame through the wheelhouse door, cupping two glasses of Crown Royal in the palm of his hand. Dale had chiseled the ice off the boulder-sized chunk of the Columbia Glacier they'd fished out of the Sound and kept on deck for just such an occasion.

"You look like you could use a drink," he told Bobby.

"Yeah, I suppose I could."

They sat quietly for a few moments, sipping. Bobby looked again out the wheelhouse window as if he somehow hoped the view would be free of the crude oil surrounding the boat. He asked Dale if he remembered when they first discovered that they could see a school of herring from the window of a plane.

It was a day in the late 1960s when Tom Parker flew some parts out to Bobby in Chamberlain Bay. Flying at less than a thousand feet, he called Bobby on the radio, his voice barely concealing his excitement. Parker told Bobby he could see a school in a lagoon just around the corner from where the boat was.

"You can *see* them?" Bobby had said. "From the air?"

"I think so," Tom said. "Let me land and drop these parts off for you. Then I'll take off and lead you over the spot." He wanted to confirm for himself what he thought he had just seen.

Tom Parker's observations proved accurate and his discovery revolutionized the spring herring fishery. It didn't take other boat captains long to figure out what Bobby was up to, climbing the mast to see if he could spot the schools from the air and later building a "crow's nest" wired with controls to guide the boat from his higher vantage point. Within the next few seasons, nearly every herring boat had a spotter pilot and herring season openers became dangerous derbies as hundreds of boats crowded the waters and dozens of planes careened in the skies above the boats.

Alaska's commercial herring fishery dates back to 1878, when early European settlers caught fifteen tons of herring, salted, and preserved them in wooden barrels. Herring were later processed in "reduction plants," rendering the oily fish into valuable oil and meal. But competition from lower priced Peruvian Anchoveta (a member of the Anchovy fish family) during the 1950s reduced the market for Alaska herring, and in 1966, the last reduction plant in Alaska closed.[8]

But the last plant closed just as Bobby discovered an emerging market for herring. The oily fish made excellent crab bait, and only a few fishermen supplied the bait market. One spring morning, he'd been docked outside the St. Elias cannery Jim Poor owned in Cordova, when a Japanese technician emerged from the wooden building, summoning Bobby inside. He could speak very little English, but as he split the bloodline of a herring, he revealed the translucent sac of roe, or eggs, the female fish held inside her. "Ichiban," he told Bobby, showing him. Number one. Herring roe, considered a specialty in Japan, could bring a much higher price than herring used for bait. The following spring, St. Elias offered a price of forty dollars per ton for roe herring.

Figuring this could be his big break, Bobby walked into the First Bank of Cordova early in the winter of 1971. Stamping the snow off his boots on the mat at the door, he stopped at the front desk to see if his friend Dick Borer, owner of the bank since 1953, was available. Bobby told Dick he needed $24,000 to buy a boat, and had his eye on the *Demetra M*, a thirty-six-foot wooden boat built in 1947. Dick grinned. "How you gonna pay it back, Bobby?" he asked.

"You'll see," he said. He was young and full of himself. His reputation, he figured, should be reason enough for Dick to loan him the money.

Dick leaned back in his chair and crossed his hands over his ample belly. He knew that the older fishermen in town all recognized and gossiped about local up-and-coming fishermen over drinks in the bar of the Alaskan Hotel. Dick knew that they gossiped about Day and he trusted their judgment. The kid had fish savvy.

He leaned forward in his chair and agreed to loan him the money. He would put it in Bobby's account, he said. Nearly before the ink had dried on the loan papers, the price for roe herring quadrupled to $160 per ton. On his first set in the spring of 1971, Bobby caught 1,000 tons, grossing $160,000. He walked back into Dick's office and wrote him a check for the principle and bit of interest he owed.

Dick had protested, "Are you sure you don't want to make payments, Bobby? I won't make much money this way!"

As Bobby and Dale reminisced, rattling the ice in their near-empty cocktail glasses, Bobby told Dale he would never have succeeded without the help of Dick Borer and others who had faith in him when he needed it most.

Their conversation moved on to a memory of a sunny morning at Green Island in 1974. Tom Parker had radioed that he couldn't believe the size of the earthy colored mass he'd just flown over. Bobby could feel his pulse quickening at the memory, as if he were hearing Tom Parker's voice in real time. In the years since their discovery that herring could be seen from the air, they had equipped the aircraft channel radio with scramblers to ensure no other boats could hear what Tom was about to tell him.

"Bobby," Tom had said. "Get moving toward the southwest corner of Green Island. You can get there along the west side, through the channel to the south of you. It's a real rock-pile but I'll guide you through."

"Roger," Bobby replied, holding down the button on the radio speaker. He grabbed one of the handles on the captain's wheel and turned the *Demetra M* to the south, watching for other boats that might follow him, and listening to three other channels simultaneously squawking and echoing against the walls of the wheelhouse. Then he called out to the crew, alerting them to get ready. He'd barely completed the turn when he thrust the throttle forward, urging the *Demetra M* up to her maximum speed of eleven knots.

As the other boats headed out into the channels where the currents were more likely to push the herring right into their nets, Bobby slowed and picked his way through the rocky channel with Tom guiding him from above. Then he turned and ducked into a shallow cove at Tom's direction.

Mike Phillips jumped into the jitney, a smaller powerboat most fishermen usually refer to as a skiff, ready to secure the end of the net. Then Bobby began to lay out the 150 fathoms (900 feet) of net out around the school of fish. He held the boat steady as the net unfurled off the deck and settled into the water in a semi-circle as large as three football fields. The net hung between a cork-line equipped with heavy-duty corks to hold the top edge at the surface of the water, and a lead-line, which would sink the bottom of the net to a depth of ten fathoms.

Bobby's seine net—a term used to describe the package of net and lead lines—had 60 percent more webbing strung between the cork and lead lines than the seines most other fishermen used. The net cost him $5,000 when he had it custom made after his first one hundred ton set in 1971, hoping the additional webbing would allow him to catch and hold more fish. Catching three hundred tons of spring herring as they crowded into the inter-tidal waters of Prince William Sound to spawn was one thing. But it was another thing altogether to keep hold of them, especially in the Sound's deep channels where the strong tides can work for a fisherman to catch the fish, and against him to keep them. Holding several hundred tons of herring, pulling in unison against the net and diving for the depths, could prove an elusive feat even among the best of fishermen. Sometimes a set required three or four boats, all towing against the mass of herring wrapped in a single seine, to hold them long enough to pump them into a larger tender boat which would transport them to the processing plant.

Sensing he had laid the net around a sizable school in the shallow cove, Bobby kept his hand on the throttle until he had almost circled back to where Mike held steady the other end of the seine. Then he eased back and called out to Mike on the radio. "I think we've got them wrapped up," he said. "Just come around nice and easy." Mike guided the skiff toward the *Demetra M*, gently closing the seine around the school of herring like a drawstring purse.

As they recalled what happened next, Dale's voice picked up tempo. "Jesus Christ, I'll never forget Mike bringing that net around. Herring jumping over the cork line like popcorn. I remember you reaching down into the net, pulling out a herring and biting its head off for good luck! If we hadn't been in that shallow cove where they hit bottom when they dove down, they would have all escaped."

Bobby grinned at the memory. "We might still have lost them if Swend Asp hadn't brought the *Ptarmigan* around real quick so we could start pumping them out of the net. I can't remember…did we fit them all on his tender?"

Dale thought for a minute. "I don't think so." He could still remember the sight of them as he stood up on the flying bridge, watching the water alive with what he figured was the biggest set of silvery fish packed into a single net he'd ever seen. "I think we must have filled more than one tender. Jesus, Bobby, we caught 240 tons of herring that day. More fish than anyone had ever caught and held in a single set! And we had a hell of a lot of fun doing it."

"Can you imagine what it would have been like if we had to brail all those fish out by hand onto the tender?" Bobby said. Up until just a few years ago, the tenders weren't equipped with fish pumps, considered new technology in the early 1970s. Before fish pumps, the crew had to dip small nets with long handles inside the seine, and brail the flailing fish—dip by dip—into the tender's hold.

Now it all seemed like a long time ago. The beach in that cove was now covered in oil. The whiskey encouraged them to live in the past if only for a few more moments, rather than think about an uncertain future. Dale said, "Who was with us on that trip anyway?"

"Well, Mike Phillips ran the skiff, and Louie Albers must have been there too." This was the crew that Bobby would later remember as his "dream team."

Both crewmembers were younger than Bobby and he thought of them almost as second sons. He'd taught them how to work hard, to read the tides and currents, and his favorite hot spots where salmon or herring were most likely to be in the Sound on any given date during the fishing season. He'd been proud when they got older and purchased their own boats. Now they were the best in the fleet—"highliners" in their own right.

Dale laughed out loud. "I'll never forget how Mike Phillips threw the dishes out the window after you flew to town that night. You know, he was always stuck washing dishes, which he damn well hated. He tossed them out one by one, enjoying the hell out of every one that sailed out the window. Mike yelled, 'Bobby Day just made the biggest set in history. He can afford to buy new dishes!'"

Bobby laughed but grew serious again. He said, "What do you think will happen to those guys now that the Sound is full of oil? I'm not quite fifty, but those two have their whole careers in front of them."

Dale nodded. It was hard to imagine the future of the Sound. Maybe it wouldn't be long before the tides would wash away the crude. Or maybe it would take generations to recover. Who could tell?

"Quit worrying about it," Dale said, taking Bobby's whiskey glass from him. "Let's have another drink."

Dale left the wheelhouse with the highball glasses in hand and Bobby could hear him chiseling ice from the chunk of glacier on deck. In thirty years of fishing, he had collected a lifetime of memories of big sets, mending net as the midnight sun cast a buttery glow across the boat's deck. He'd spent a lifetime setting the first net on Monday mornings and getting very little sleep until fishing closed on Friday evenings. He wouldn't have traded it for anything, even a marriage.

Donna had been his high school sweetheart. Tall and willowy, quiet and sassy, she was four years younger than Bobby. It was hard to say which relationship grew first or stronger—his feelings for Donna or his friendship with her father Bob Ditman. The tall Norwegian worked hard and took pride in his accomplishments. Though he worked as a fisherman and a truck driver, he retained an air of class that Bobby admired and aspired to achieve for himself. Ditman also served as a member of the Alaska House of Representatives for their district. For several years they had fished together and they shared a closeness that only hard work and the close quarters of a fishing boat could provide. Since salmon traps had been outlawed at statehood in 1959, the salmon runs were recovering. The promising returns of the early 1960s and low interest business loans from the federal government after the 1964 earthquake persuaded Ditman to purchase the *Arctic Sea* during that spring. Bobby planned to help Ditman bring the boat up from Martinolich Shipbuilding in Tacoma, Washington. He remembered telling Donna he would be gone for an extra two months that season. Her face wrenched and she began to cry softly. "How is your son ever going to know you?" she pleaded. Isn't there a job you can do in town? Bobby knew he would leave in the spring and see very little of her until the fall. It was all he knew how to do. It was all he wanted to do and it called him with a force he couldn't fully understand nor deny.

When the frigid north wind turned to a chilly westerly, Ditman and Bobby left for Tacoma. For a few weeks, they watched as the shipyard put the finishing touches on the new fifty-eight-foot steel boat. They frequented Seattle Marine and Fishing Supply and Doc Freeman's, gathering the rigging and supplies they would need to head north. On the deck, they tied down the new wooden skiff with a 180-horsepower engine they would use to close the purse seine net around a school of fish. They awoke early the morning of their departure, cracked a bottle of champagne across the bow of the *Arctic Sea* and cheered as the bubbles cascaded down into the water. The four-man crew, Ditman and his partner George Hillar, Bobby, and the electrician they dubbed "Kilowatt," set off across Commencement Bay, bound for Alaska.

The calm waters of the Inside Passage and coastal waters of southeast Alaska lulled them into thinking their luck would last across the open waters of the Gulf of Alaska. They knew the extreme tides and turbulent weather of the season could turn on them like a mother bear with cubs. But the *Arctic Sea* handled nicely and she was bigger than most other seine boats. The weather report called for moderate winds. As they passed though Juneau and angled west through Indian Passage they felt certain a trip across the open waters of the Gulf was a fine decision. Salmon season was due to open soon, and they were in a hurry to make it on time. The *Arctic Sea* could handle moderate winds with ease.

Halfway across, at the point of no return, the seas turned ugly. The radio crackled with the most recent weather service update, a warning that gale winds could reach eighty miles per hour. Within a few short hours, wind howled around the cabin and the horizon turned into rolling mountains of whitecaps. The *Arctic Sea* groaned and grunted up every wave only to be hurled down the backside at a reckless rate. Her bow plowed the troughs of the waves while the next rolled over her bow with a shuddering crash. Each threatened to take out the windows of the wheelhouse. The captain of an ocean-going tug sounded a Mayday and gave its coordinates. It was within miles of the *Arctic Sea*. Ditman picked up the radio to respond, but he no sooner opened his mouth to reply than a rogue wave peeled off the radio and radar antennas from the top of the wheelhouse. They would later learn that the tug and its entire crew were lost.

As the skiff tied on deck filled with water, the *Arctic Sea* listed and rolled more ominously with each wave. George Hillar and Kilowatt tied themselves in their bunks and screamed with each wave as if it were their last breath. Ditman and Bobby took turns at the wheel, straining and fighting the force of the water to keep her bow pointed into the waves. They both knew the weight of the skiff could cause the *Arctic Sea* to roll too far over to recover.

With a rope tied around his waist and an axe in hand, Bobby turned the doorknob of the galley. It exploded open with the force of water and wind. He struggled to stay on his feet long enough to get to the skiff. As waves splashed wall after wall of water against the boat and across the deck, he was knocked off his feet again and again and he knew he was tiring. Saltwater stung his eyes and ran down his face.

Gripping the axe, he managed to lunge and grab the side of the skiff. With three decisive blows he gouged out a gaping hole. Water again rushed across the deck and over the side, this time emptying the weighted skiff. Another wave crashed across the deck and slammed him into the railing. His years of fishing, hunting, and working traplines had hardened him, but it took every ounce of his strength to keep from being washed overboard. He wrestled his way across the deck and back into the cabin, his body battered. Tomorrow he would be bruised all over, but the boat was still afloat and that was all that mattered. For the next thirty-six hours he and Ditman wrestled the wheel against the wind and waves until the fury of the storm subsided.

They limped quietly up Valdez Bay. The sun shone down on them almost apologetically and the gentle ripples of the bay were soothing against the side of the boat. Bobby accepted the apology Mother Nature seemed to offer. Quitting never crossed his mind.

Now as he heard Dale's footsteps on the ladder to the wheelhouse, Bobby wondered if the oil spill would become the first challenge he couldn't overcome. He didn't know how much longer he could sit on this boat. Although Exxon had made the decision to tow the *Valdez* over here to Outside Bay, the Ocean Tech consultants had several days left on their contract. They still had final preparations to make and charts to create. There was little for Bobby to do while they worked, and the idleness left him too much time to think.

As Dale sat down across from him in the other captain's chair, Bobby heard Lori's voice on the marine radio. "Bobby, are you there? Over."

"Yeah, Pop Tart. Dale and I are sitting here in the wheelhouse having a couple toddies. How are those oil guys treating you? You getting lots of work?"

"You can't believe it," she said. "Everyone wants to go up and take a look at the spill. I've been busy all right. Anyway, I heard they closed the herring fishery in Prince William Sound. No big surprise there I guess."

Hearing her voice, Bobby made up his mind, if he hadn't already, that he needed to get out of there. He turned to Dale and asked his best friend if he planned to stay in Valdez after their contract was up. If he did, would he be willing to bring the boat in for him?

Dale nodded.

Bobby called back into the radio. "Lori, what are your plans for the rest of the day? I need a change of scenery. Something that doesn't include an oil slick. Want to come pick me up?"

11

"We Can Have Our Cake and Eat It Too"

Prince William Sound: May 7, 1989

D AN LAWN OF ALASKA'S DEPARTMENT of Environmental Conservation stood aside as two journalists climbed into the rear seat of the helicopter. Then he hopped up into the front seat, pulled the door shut, and nodded a greeting to the pilot. The reporters were in town for the Congressional field hearings, chaired by California Congressman George Miller. At the Valdez Civic Center, members of the Congressional House Subcommittee on Water, Power, and Offshore Energy Resources heard the testimony of Mayor Devens, Exxon and Alyeska officials, a representative from the Department of Fish and Game, and Jack Lamb and Riki Ott representing the Cordova District Fisherman United.

The hearing had concluded earlier that day—May 7, 1989—with testimony from a panel of Alyeska employees. The hearing undoubtedly left the reporters with even more questions than answers and they likely looked forward to Lawn's interpretation of the facts presented to the members of Congress.

Since the spill, Lawn had been monitoring and documenting the spread of the oil slick and he often had occasion to include reporters or state and federal legislators on his aerial observations of the Sound.[1] By his own admission, Lawn is frank about what he has seen and heard as a regulator, and in expressing his concerns regardless of the politics. As the chopper made its way down the bay, he shared his concern with the journalists that the oil companies seemed to have little regard for the environment and even less for the promises they made to the people of the United States prior to Congressional approval to build the pipeline. The reporters were about to hear the facts from Lawn's point of view.

As the chopper emerged through the Valdez Narrows riding atop a stiff wind, a view of the Sound opened up in front of them. Pointing in the direction of Bligh Reef, where the tanker had gone aground, and in a voice meant to carry over the rhythm of the helicopter motor, Lawn told them the *Exxon Valdez* accident had been ten years in the making.

He then pointed south to Knowles Head, where the tanker *Prince William Sound* lost power in a storm in 1980. He swept his hand in an arc from east to west across the Sound in front of them, showing them the path the tanker had taken, dead in the water, pushed by 100 knot winds and twenty foot waves.

"The *Prince William Sound* had just about run up on the rocks on Naked Island, when the wind changed and pushed her north toward Glacier Island," he said, gesturing toward his right.

"By that time, we had three tugs trailing her," he said, recounting the events of the day, "one of which was taking on water. None of them had local charts. We got a one-thousand-foot line and loaded it on a helicopter in Valdez to take it out there, but then we got a call at the last minute. The problem was a circuit breaker and the crew was able to replace it and start the engines before the ship ran aground. The line would have been a last ditch effort, especially given the weather conditions."

The *Prince William Sound* tanker incident alarmed both the Coast Guard and DEC. Loaded with some thirty-five million gallons of North Slope crude, the tanker had floated powerless in the Sound for more than seventeen hours. The supertanker was just minutes away from running onto Fairmount Reef when the crew restarted the engines. As a result, Lawn explained, DEC attempted to require towing bridles on every ship and a heavier tug to escort ships out of the Sound. DEC also requested an update to the oil spill contingency plan. Alyeska responded by producing an addendum to their contingency plan in 1982. In the revised plan, Alyeska informed DEC that the estimated time to clean up a 100,000 barrel spill would be less than forty-eight hours, assuming it was thirty miles from port and in calm weather.

One of the reporters asked Lawn to pause. How much had actually been recovered from the *Exxon Valdez* in the first forty-eight hours?

Lawn responded that the actual amount cleaned up in the first sev-enty-two hours after the grounding of the *Valdez* was three thousand barrels—a scant 3 percent of the amount outlined in the contingency plan. "But," he added, "we knew their estimates were too high. After a towing exercise and oil spill drill in 1982, we became even more concerned about Alyeska's ability to meet its obligations under the contingency plan."

On July 13, 1982, Lawn had written to his supervisor, expressing his concerns that the contingency plan was "superficial at best." In his report, Lawn had stated, "Technically, their response probably satis-fies the regulation requirements on paper, however, Alyeska has never been able to demonstrate that the recovery rates listed in Appendix B are possible to obtain. In fact, all our experience with Alyeska oil spill recovery projections indicates that the recovery rates listed are 80 percent too high."[2]

As Lawn described the letter to the reporters, they responded with a flurry of questions. Did Lawn ever receive a response? Was any action taken?

Lawn responded carefully and thoughtfully in an effort to try and recreate for the reporters the political context and circumstances of the 1980s. As an appointee of the Governor, the Commissioner of DEC often faces countervailing pressures between the agency's mandate to protect the environment and political pressure to ensure that oil keeps flowing through the pipeline. As a result, Lawn explained, top man-agement at DEC simply didn't want to hear about problems reported by employees who worked in the field offices such as himself. It was easier for DEC management simply to rely on the assurances and promises that the oil companies made to operate safely. Even though tankers had spilled oil in the Sound at least four hundred times in the past dozen years, DEC leadership never moved to halt operation of the pipeline as a means of compelling Alyeska and its owner compa-nies into compliance with state and federal laws.[3]

Lawn looked out the window of the chopper before continuing on. "It is hard to imagine now, with eleven million gallons of oil spreading down as far as Kodiak Island and into Cook Inlet, that we as citizens and regulators could have become so complacent," he said. And then he began to explain some of the facts and complex circumstances that had lulled Alaskans into complacency.

The oil companies had come to Alaska at a time when the state's economy desperately needed a boost and most Alaskans viewed the prospect of an oil pipeline to be the lifeline the Alaskan economy needed. State elected officials were just as anxious to proceed with development as oil industry executives were. In the excitement after the oil strike at Prudhoe Bay, the executive assistant to Governor Keith Miller had proclaimed, "Hell, this country's so goddamn big that even if industry ran wild we could never wreck it. We can have our cake and eat it too."[4]

Despite such exuberance, the freeze on oil leasing, Native claims, and environmental requirements all became enmeshed in the gears of Congress, significantly slowing the pace of development. Hoping to expedite the resolution of each of the issues in Washington, the oil industry made a number of promises and commitments. The industry provided assurances about the quality, standards, and ethics that would be employed in the development and operation of a pipeline and terminal at Valdez. In their testimony before state and federal legislators, and in full-page advertisements in the *Anchorage Times*, the oil industry made it easy to believe and trust their assertions.

For the fishermen and others who remained concerned about the marine operations of transporting oil, L. R. Beyton of British Petroleum stated in a 1971 Anchorage hearing, "From my own experience and the studies of many other workers in the pollution field, I am satisfied that the tanker traffic to and from Port Valdez, and operation of an oil port there, will not cause any significant damage to the marine environment or to fisheries interests. The contingency plan which will be drawn up will detail methods for dealing promptly and effectively with any oil spill which may occur, so that its effect on the environment will be minimal. We have adequate knowledge for dealing with oil spills and improvements in technologies and equipment are continuing to become available through world-wide research. The best equipment, materials, and expertise, which will be made available as part of the oil spill contingency plan, will make operations in Port Valdez and in Prince William Sound the safest in the world."[5]

In his 1971 speech, Beyton also explained, "When the maximum has been done to prevent the spread of oil, the main cleanup activity of the spill should always be physical retrieval of the spillage. In Port Valdez, this may be accomplished in several ways. There are oil pickup and skimming vessels available which have been proven to work well, and such devices have also been successful in removing floating oil. The problems of oil retrieval are often reduced by the use of floating absorbents, such as straw. It is not proposed to use dispersants for cleanup in Alaskan waters."[6]

But just as oil industry leaders offered assurances they hoped would secure Congressional approval, they also sought to set forth clear boundaries—never failing to remind Alaskans that Canada and other locations had promising oil prospects and they would go where local governments welcomed them. In his 1972 testimony before a joint Congressional hearing, Charles Spahr, CEO of Standard Oil Company of Ohio (Sohio, which later merged with BP) cautioned, "It is understandable to me that there can be a real and continued temptation to solve all the state's financial problems with one or more revenue measures directed at Prudhoe Bay and/or TAPS [the Trans-Alaska Pipeline]. The business and industrial community in all the lower forty-eight states as well as Alaska is watching to see how Alaska will act. I think it is fair to say that industry generally expects to pay for the privilege of doing business here, and that, in the case of the oil industry, it expects to contribute a relatively substantial part of Alaska's revenues. The members of the oil industry are willing to pay their fair share, but if they are required to pay an unduly large and burdensome share, to take huge risks with little prospect of adequate reward for doing so, then Alaska's future development may be slowed..."[7]

In a 1972 address to elected officials in Juneau, E. L. Patton, Alyeska's first president, thanked legislators for their assistance in helping to push the pipeline project forward. Despite the complexities that continued to thwart the industry from obtaining the pipeline permit from Congress, Alaska's legislators, agencies and universities had been a great help, he said. However, he also sent a clear message about how Alyeska would view the regulatory agencies that would oversee the construction and operation of the pipeline.

In what was likely a reference to DEC and the Environmental Protection Agency, both of which were formally established in 1970, Patton said, "What this project badly needs is less—not more—regulation. Because of the great frustrations generated in the past two years, it has already become very difficult to recruit and keep the high quality people we need in this project. To provide still another group of agencies looking over our shoulder just gets that much closer to an intolerable situation, and it inevitably raises costs and creates delays."[8]

Yet as the completion of the pipeline drew near in 1976, Alyeska's president Patton reaffirmed the industry's commitment to those promises in an Alyeska report. Patton said, "Alyeska is determined not to duck any of its problems or obligations. This pipeline is being built to the highest standards for quality and safety, thus ensuring both its environmental and operational integrity."[9]

"You see," Lawn told the reporters as the chopper banked toward the south, "industry promised it could be trusted to ensure that the environment was protected. And these weren't just verbal commitments. Promises made by industry, Congress and the Nixon Administration were codified in the 1973 Congressional approval of the Trans-Alaska Pipeline Authorization Act."

Alaskan oil would be transported in double-hulled tankers and would be for domestic consumption only. Oil companies would be strictly liable, without regard to fault, for damages incurred as a result of an oil spill.[10] The Alyeska terminal would have a state-of-the-art system for recovering vapors from crude oil storage tanks, and for treating the ballast water that empty tankers returning to port carry to balance the ship. Harbor pilots would guide the tankers from Port Valdez all the way to Hinchinbrook Island on the edge of the Gulf of Alaska, and tankers plying the waters of the Sound would be monitored by an updated radar system.

Lawn told the reporters that most of the promises made to Congress, to Alaskans, and to the American people had never been fulfilled. Then he proceeded to summarize those shortcomings, documented and corroborated by Alyeska employees in written internal communications, as well as EPA investigations and reports.

Only three of the four incinerators in the design proposed to Congress to control vapors at the Alyeska terminal were constructed, and they were operated at temperatures lower than design specifications called for in order to save costs. In another cost saving move, fixtures intended to remove the maximum amount of vapors were simply disconnected. In 1981 the entire vapor recovery system was shut down for repairs for a period of nine months.

From 1980 to 1985, internal Alyeska documents show that the vapor recovery system only operated 80 percent of the time.[11] Air pollution worsened when the pipeline began carrying high levels of liquid natural gas in 1987, resulting in estimated annual releases of a million tons of benzene[12] and over 50,000 tons of hydrocarbons[13] into the Valdez airshed. Just before the *Valdez* oil spill in 1989, Alyeska finally undertook a $15 million upgrade on the vapor control system to reduce pollution levels.[14]

In their proposal to Congress, Alyeska and its owner companies also agreed to comply with all state and federal clean water and discharge laws in the treatment of ballast water. Their designs included a facility for treating sludge and ballast water that would meet the needs of a 600,000-barrel per day throughput.[15] Once the ballast water was treated, it would be pumped back into Valdez Bay and a continuous monitoring system would sound an alarm if the effluent did not meet water quality standards.[16] But EPA reports showed, and Alyeska employees confirmed, that the continuous monitoring alarm system was never installed. Employees blowing the whistle on lax environmental practices also claimed heaters designed to separate oil from the ballast water were disconnected to save costs.[17]

The volume and purity of effluent released into Valdez Bay is regulated by federal law. Yet an Alyeska technician said that during his time as an employee from 1977 to 1980, these standards were simply ignored. "The way around it was to shut off the mechanism for gauging how much we dumped," he said. "There was no other way for the regulators to check it."[18]

When James Woodle retired from his post as Coast Guard Commander in 1982 and joined Alyeska to oversee their marine operations, Alyeska management informed him that the treatment facility probably wouldn't meet EPA standards. Woodle and other employees later explained that another way Alyeska got around this was to send the test samples to Seattle and by the time tests were complete, the pollutants had decayed to a point where the results usually came up within legal limits. Woodle said, "Had we tested them in Valdez, they would have been off the scale. In any case, Alyeska dumped the water into the harbor long before the test results came back from Seattle."[19]

These allegations of environmental wrongdoing came to the attention of DEC and EPA in part due to the efforts of Charles Hamel, an oil broker who purchased crude from Alyeska. Hamel believed that crude he purchased from the terminal contained an unusually high percentage of water, which subsequently resulted in rejections of shipments by his customers. This cost him, both in terms of credibility in the industry and a significant amount of money. Hamel began investigating Alyeska's operations. Through his contact with whistleblowers who worked at the terminal, Hamel began to document serious environmental violations at the terminal.

Hamel threatened to sue both the DEC and EPA for failing to take action against Alyeska to enforce environmental regulations. In 1984, Dan Lawn got a call from Anchorage headquarters, asking him to serve as Hamel's point of contact at DEC. It was through Hamel that Lawn would ultimately gain access to internal Alyeska documents and whistleblowers.

As the allegations of environmental wrongdoing emerged in the media, environmentalists, oil industry watchdogs, and Cordova fishermen tried unsuccessfully to establish a formal entity for citizen oversight. Riki Ott expressed her concerns writing, "Alyeska itself reported that it was in noncompliance with its permit limits 100 times from August 1977 through December 1983." She pointed to a Government Accountability Report that stated, "EPA admitted it knew of these violations, but for a variety of reasons (budget cuts, lack of data on ballast water treatment facilities, higher priority problems etc.), EPA was unable to effectively monitor Alyeska and enforce compliance with the permit."[20]

The discharge permit during that period of time was, by today's standards, not very stringent. Prior to 1983, Alyeska had a permit to discharge effluent which contained "concentrations of highly toxic aromatic hydrocarbons, mainly benzene, toluene and xylene, as high as nine parts per million."[21] When the permit expired in 1983, EPA required an 85 percent reduction in the level of pollutants discharged. But Alyeska continued dumping at much higher levels than both DEC and EPA believed was safe, and delayed implementing the proposed new standards by appealing through EPA's administrative process.

By 1985, EPA had documented evidence that Alyeska was disposing of sludge by processing it in the ballast water treatment plant—a violation of the Clean Water Act. When EPA issued a subpoena to investigate water quality associated with the terminal operations, Alyeska refused to comply and EPA was forced to sue to gain access to internal documents. At the time of the *Exxon Valdez* accident in March, 1989, Alyeska was still fighting the water quality standards set forth by EPA in 1983.[22]

The journalists scribbled on their notepads as Lawn described the latest in the tug-of-war between regulators and Alyeska. Lawn explained that in addition to the new standards outlined in the EPA permit application, DEC required that they reduce their daily discharge of hydrocarbons from nine parts per million to 1.3 parts per million. Lawn paused, waiting for them to catch up.

"Just last week, Alyeska filed suit to overturn this change. Given that Exxon just spilled eleven million gallons of crude, it is simply unbelievable they would take this action."

Lawn went on to explain that although Alyeska is in charge of operating the Trans-Alaska Pipeline, including response to spills, the consortium is just a "front man" for the owner companies. Alyeska's operations are overseen by a committee representing the seven owner companies. The owner's committee operates much like a board of directors. Operations subcommittees report to the owner's committee, which meets quarterly.

"And it isn't like there is no money available to them to comply with state and federal standards," Lawn said.

Just before the *Exxon Valdez* ran aground, the Alaska Department of Revenue received a contracted report from a professor and expert in oil industry accounting.

The report estimated that Alyeska's parent companies earned profits of $42.6 billion between 1969 and 1987. The estimated profits, the report said, took into account all expenses including exploration, lease acquisition, income taxes, and depreciation. Underscoring the enormous profits, the report estimated that the oil companies earn $463,144 per hour, twenty-four hours a day, seven days a week.[23]

During the same period of time, the report estimated that the State of Alaska earned $29.3 billion in taxes and royalties. The state set up a permanent fund, which would distribute earnings on the principal to every Alaskan. At the time of the *Valdez* spill, Alaska residents received $400 million annually, equaling about $800 for every man, woman, and child. In 1987, the oil industry budgeted $759,000 for lobbying legislators and regulators—less than two hours' worth of profit from operations.

"But the industry's lobbying budget is greater than the state's budget for overseeing oil industry operations," Lawn said wryly.

The chopper dipped down so the reporters could get a closer look at the *Exxon Valdez,* still anchored for repairs in Naked Island's Outside Bay. It would be another month before technicians could ensure the ship was stable and buoyant and could be towed to the National Steel and Shipbuilding Company in San Diego, which had completed her construction just three years earlier. As they regained altitude and flew south toward Knight Island, Lawn explained that in addition to the cost-cutting measures at the terminal itself, the oil companies lobbied to reduce the harbor pilotage requirements outlined in the Trans-Alaska Pipeline Authorization Act.

Citing concerns about cost and the difficulty of transferring a pilot from a tanker to the pilot boat in the rougher waters further out in the Sound, the oil companies successfully whittled the requirements back from Hinchinbrook Entrance to Knowles Head, and finally to Rocky Point where pilots disembarked in 1989. "If a harbor pilot had been aboard the *Exxon Valdez* as initially required," Lawn told the reporters, "the accident would likely never have happened."

Yet the oil industry hadn't been alone in trying to cut costs, Lawn explained. The state-of-the-art Coast Guard radar system that was to be installed near Bligh Reef never happened. An improved radar system and equipment to accurately monitor ice in the shipping lanes were never implemented. Instead, a cost-saving, 50,000-watt radar system replaced the existing 100,000-watt system. "This is not an upgrade of an existing system, but a downgrade with a new system," a radar technician warned a Congressional delegation in 1984. "I can't help but feel that this is a tremendous waste of taxpayers' money and is also bringing an oil tanker disaster closer to reality."[24] An accurate ice report may also have prevented the *Exxon Valdez* spill.

The chopper swooped low over the eastern edge of Knight Island, its beach still black with crude. Lawn took out his sketchbook and made some notes about the location and appearance of the oil. He pointed out the window to the left, where Applegate Rocks jutted out of the Sound.

He told the reporters about a Congressional delegation that had come to Valdez just a few days after the spill. "We flew everyone out here in a Huey 212 helicopter and landed there on Applegate Rocks. It was low tide, just like it is now. Seals and otters congregate around these rocks, and on that day, Ken Hill was there with his boat and a group of fishermen. Ken fishes out of Cordova and is also a veterinarian. They had about a dozen oiled otters in portable dog crates," he said.

"Even the fishermen, who've been known to shoot otters that were beginning to overpopulate in the Sound, couldn't stand to see them suffering that way. Ken said to me, 'Dan, can you help us out here? These otters are going to die if they don't get back to Valdez quickly.' The Congressmen looked at each other, and we all agreed the chopper should take the otters back to Valdez, then come back for us. Well, it had only taken us a half hour to fly out there. But the chopper didn't get back for nearly four hours. I knew the rocks wouldn't totally submerge because there was no oil on top of them. But as the tide crept up on the rocks, their eyes got bigger. I'm not sure we made the best decision, but we were able to save a few otters," Lawn said, chuckling at the memory.

The chopper turned north up the western side of Montague Island, heading back for the Narrows and town. The reporters wanted to know what had taken place in the years since Lawn wrote the memo to his supervisor in 1982 warning him about Alyeska's lack of preparedness? Lawn explained that in 1984, he had written another memo.

In his 1984 memo, Lawn said, "There has taken place a general disemboweling of the Alyeska Valdez terminal operational plan. Most knowledgeable and competently trained individuals have either quit, been terminated, or transferred up the line. This has left inadequately trained people to maintain the facility and an insufficient number of people to operate it. As you know, we have been under-budgeted and under-staffed to adequately inspect the terminal and keep in touch with Alyeska's day-to-day operations. Unfortunately, this has been a signal to Alyeska that the state is no longer interested in the Trans-Alaska pipeline project. Alyeska has consistently broken promises made to the state of Alaska and the federal government prior to our granting permission to build the terminal. We can no longer ignore the routine monitoring of Alyeska unless we do not care whether a major catastrophic event occurs."[25]

Lawn believed that it was common practice at Alyeska to fire those who questioned practices within the company, or who blew the whistle to regulators and the media. In fact, Lawn wrote his 1984 memo just weeks after James Woodle was fired from Alyeska for "insubordination." Shortly after he was fired, Woodle wrote one last memo to Alyeska president George Nelson. He told Nelson, "due to reduction in manning, age of equipment, limited training opportunities, and lack of experienced coordination personnel, serious doubt exists that Alyeska would be able to contain and clean up effectively a medium or large size oil spill... Response to any spill beyond the limits of Valdez narrows should not be attempted with present equipment and personnel."[26]

Perhaps in response to the concerns Lawn continued to raise, DEC asked Alyeska in 1986 for a plan to address a 200,000-barrel spill. They responded with a letter estimating that such a spill was highly unlikely. In fact, Alyeska had estimated the odds of such a spill occurring in Prince William Sound would be a once-in-241-years event.[27] Despite these long odds, Alyeska agreed to amend its contingency plan in 1987 to include provisions for a 200,000-barrel spill. The new contingency plan estimated that 35 percent of a spill that size would be recovered from the water (70,000 barrels), 30 percent from shoreline cleanup (60,000 barrels), 30 percent would disperse naturally or evaporate, and 5 percent would remain in the environment. Use of chemical dispersants was not included in the plan.

"As of now, Exxon and their contractor VECO estimate that they have cleaned a little over one mile of beach," Lawn told the reporters. "They are operating on a cost-plus basis, so VECO has more incentive to spend money than actually clean up oil. A fisherman claimed that he picked up more oil with his fishing boat and a five-gallon bucket than all of Exxon's skimming equipment."

As the chopper slipped back through the Narrows and past Anderson Bay, one of the reporters asked Lawn what was behind the Alyeska official's testimony that day, when he stated that the plan was to hold the oil in deeper water and then use dispersants on it. Lawn shook his head, recalling that just a few days earlier, Exxon CEO Lawrence Rawl told *Fortune* magazine that if Exxon had been allowed to use dispersants, they could have kept 50 percent of the oil off the beaches. Rawl blamed DEC for listening to environmentalists who expressed concern about toxicity, and the Coast Guard for not giving them the go-ahead.[28]

"I don't really know why they banked on using dispersants," Lawn said. "Other than it was a way to sink the oil to the bottom of the Sound and get it out of sight." As the helicopter approached the head of the bay—the Alyeska terminal out the window to the right, town to the left—it seemed in retrospect that a lot of questions had been left unanswered during the day's Congressional hearings.

In response to tough questions from congressmen that afternoon, Alyeska's vice president of operations testified that "We have not broken our promises to the people of this state." He explained that the contingency plan didn't really claim that it could recover one hundred thousand barrels in forty-eight hours.

Illinois Congressman Richard Durbin retorted, "Well, sir, let me tell you something, you made a promise to a lot of people with this document," he said, waving a copy of the contingency plan in the air. "And without that promise I don't think you'd have been in business. And quite honestly, I believe you abused the basic trust which was given to the company."[29]

The testimony provided at the field hearing held in the Civic Center in Valdez that day led Chairman George Miller to conclude that the failure of Alyeska's cleanup response in the first seventy-two hours significantly contributed to the ultimate environmental impacts of the spill. He said, "We're going to shine a very, very intense light of scrutiny on this system." "I'll be damned if we're going to accept the assurances of the past."[30]

12

Relying on Assurances

SEATTLE, WASHINGTON: MAY 1989

THERE IS NOTHING LIKE THE FIRST WARM AND SUNNY Seattle spring day to set a soul free. And the boat harbor at Fishermen's Terminal was certainly full of high-spirited, free souls on this Saturday in early May. The harbor was a hive of activity as the seine boats, lined hull to hull with their bow lines securing them to the docks, were outfitted for the trip north. It was a gamble this year, as nobody could really say for certain that salmon season would open with the oily sheen still lurking in the tide rips and a thick coating of crude on the beaches in the southwestern parts of Prince William Sound. But it was no secret that this year's salmon run had been predicted to set records based on harvests of the most recent odd-year returns.

Along the west wall dock, seine nets hung on racks as men in T-shirts and Levi's worked to hang new web for the season, joshing each other and betting beers on who would get the first dance with that good-looking waitress at the Salty Dog bar in Homer. Others scuttled packages of hamburgers and steaks, frozen vegetables, eggs, toilet paper, and cases of beer from the backs of pickups into the boat galleys. The Rolling Stones' "Brown Sugar" blared on the deck loudspeaker of a big tender boat tied along the west wall.

A few young men roamed the docks and it was obvious to the skippers and most deckhands that this seemingly aimless wandering belied a very purposeful aim to get hired on one of these boats for the summer. With record-high prices for salmon throughout most of the 1980s, it wasn't uncommon for a crewmember to take home $40,000 to $80,000 for the season. The Alaska fishing fleet had put many a young man, and a few young women through college. And more than a few stayed in Alaska, drawn to the freedom, adventure, risk, and sense of community.

As he walked along the west wall watching the seine boats readying for the trip north, Bobby Day felt like an outsider for the first time in his life. His soul hardly felt free. He'd left the *Lady Lynne* at Outside Bay in Dale's capable hands. After Lori flew out and picked him up, he decided it best to come back to Seattle for a few weeks until he heard whether the salmon season would open or not. He'd tried to busy himself working at his ranch north of Seattle. He bucked bales of alfalfa and built cattle pens, as if the physical work might somehow right the direction he feared his finances might soon take. He rode his horse, hoping that the feel of the gelding's muscles working beneath him and the smell of his sweat could blot out the visceral memories of oil in Prince William Sound.

Yet over the past few weeks, he often found himself here at Fishermen's Terminal, drinking in the smell of water and creosote pilings, listening to the mournful cries of the gulls overhead and feeling the pull of the ocean and points north. He had lived by this ritual of readying the boat and setting off through Puget Sound for the Inside Passage since the first trip he took with Ditman in the *Arctic Sea*. After standing and watching two young guys hanging web for a while, he turned and walked back along the west wall toward Chinooks restaurant.

He walked down past the terminal's hallmark—a statue of a fisherman standing atop a concrete column overlooking the harbor—which served as a memorial to fishermen lost at sea. At the base of the column, the names of some seventy fishermen were engraved in bronze. Seattle was built upon its heritage as a fishing port and had long served as a second home to Alaskan fishermen. Although the fishermen's memorial and harbor evoked that heritage, Bobby thought how the harbor had changed from the first time he'd come to Seattle during the early 1960s.

Chinooks restaurant had replaced the old Fishermen's café, where men in flannel shirts and rubber boots gathered in the dark before dawn to drink their coffee and swap stories. Yachters now frequented Seattle Marine and Lummi Marine Supply along with the fishermen who came to purchase net webbing, rolls of thick cotton rope, and parts for the hydraulic lifts that hoisted the seines on deck. Yuppies had moved to the surrounding enclaves of Ballard and Magnolia, and now outnumbered fishermen in the new Chinooks restaurant over-looking the harbor.

Bobby had no doubt that the salmon fleet would have to adapt to changing world market conditions and consumer tastes—oil spill or not. While canned pink salmon had once been a consumer staple and the lifeline of the salmon fleet, many consumers now preferred fresh fillets or fillets flash-frozen at sea, ready to bake or grill.

The fish farms in Norway and Chile that raised salmon in giant underwater pens from fry until harvest time had prompted the Cordova fishermen to build hatcheries in the 1970s. The Cordova fishermen had rightly anticipated—even feared—that farm-raised salmon might someday meet the increasing demand for fresh fillets at a cheaper price. They could be harvested daily and delivered fresh to market. And now fish farms were just beginning to wrest market share away from wild Alaskan salmon.

For years Bobby iced his salmon in the hold and later invested in refrigeration. He sold his catch to Ray Cesarini at Sea Hawk Seafoods, who demanded this careful care and quality from all of his fishermen. Cesarini was just beginning to carve out a niche to compete with the anticipated supply of farmed fish when the *Valdez* ran aground on Bligh Reef.

From the early 1900s when canneries dotted Alaska's shorelines until the near decimation of Alaska salmon runs by fish traps, prices always adjusted to a new equilibrium based on supply and demand. As Bobby stood there looking north across the harbor and ship canal beyond, he feared that perhaps the oil spill might be an artificial punctuation in markets that would otherwise slowly adjust to global competition, new technologies for preserving and processing fish, and marketing to consumers. Since the spill, scores of seine boat owners had signed lucrative contracts to aid in the oil spill cleanup rather than wait for an uncertain salmon catch that summer. Prices for salmon permits had plummeted and the seine boat market was soft if a willing buyer could be found at all. He'd talked to Cesarini just a few days ago and learned that all the seasonal employees who usually worked in his processing plant were instead taking jobs on the spill. The workers could earn about seventeen dollars per hour scrubbing oil from rocks—and more with overtime—which was twice what Sea Hawk Seafoods could afford to pay in wages.

"Hey Bobby," a voice called out from one of the seine boats tied a few boats up the float. "What're you doin' here? I thought you'd be up in Prince William Sound getting fat on an oil spill contract!" "Nah," Bobby called back, grinning at a skipper whose name he couldn't recall. "I'm a fisherman, not an oil company lackey," he said, walking down the float toward the skipper. "I don't think I could stand being up there, shuttling toilet paper back and forth for cleanup workers. I'll head back up when they say we're clear to catch fish."

"I agree," the skipper told him. "It's a real joke. Some of the guys say they just sit out there in the Sound on call, waiting to do something. Thousands of dollars a day to do nothing. I'm with you Bobby, I don't think I can take their dirty money."

"Well, have a good trip north," Bobby called back. "Watch yourself in Johnstone Straits—I hear the tides are running at a big minus now."

"Yean, I heard that. Will do Bobby. Take care."

As the skipper disappeared into the wheelhouse, Bobby thought about all the times he'd made the trip north in the spring. It felt strange to be here in Seattle, as if the life he had once known was gone. The months and years on the water, the familiar pattern of a fisherman's life, was part of his essence—a life he'd wanted since his earliest years. But it was also a life that wreaked havoc on life at home with his family. Months of separation eroded relationships.

Bobby thought back to his marriage to Phyllis, a lively, intelligent woman. It was his second foray into marriage. Phyllis had inherited long flowing black hair and a petite build from a blend of Norwegian and Native ancestry not uncommon among many Alaskans. Something about the way she rolled and pulled back her hair, and her ease in either heels or rubber clam-digging boots made her seem classy in an understated way that drew people to her. Bobby had been no exception.

Yet he faced the same temptations that all lusty young fishermen face in days and weeks upon end away from home. Their wives, too, for that matter. And succumbing to these temptations was not usually a private event, given the close-knit community and loose tongues of fishermen that combine to take away any sense of inhibition.

But the circumstances that ultimately drove a wedge between him and Phyllis had been much more complex than the usual set of temptations that lonely fishermen and their wives face. It was instead a brewing dispute with the fishermen's union that came to disrupt their lives and ultimately their relationship.

In the early 1980s the Cordova District Fishermen United voted to strike for a higher salmon price. Season after season, despite an analysis of the market by the union's board of directors that suggested otherwise, a majority of the union membership insisted their catch was worth more than what they were getting from the fish processors.

Whether it hearkened back to the days when canneries owned the boats and the CDFU's predecessor represented fishermen in a more adversarial way, or whether his fellow fishermen were simply ignoring the facts related to competition in the seafood market, Bobby was never certain. He couldn't understand why they would vote to strike for twenty-six cents a pound at the beginning of the season, only to agree to twenty-four cents deep into the season after most of the salmon had lost the luster and firmness of fish just returning from the deeper ocean.

Many of the fishermen who spoke out most loudly in favor of striking had been the same voices most vociferously opposed to oil development a decade before. For Bobby, the controversy brought back shallowly buried memories of deep divisions and mistrust. The differences of opinion over prices and striking caused Bobby to resign from the CDFU board of directors and drove him to distance himself from others who lived in Cordova.

Nothing was secret or sacred in the small community and the very sense of closeness that had once fostered fond memories and friendships in the decade he lived there began to close in on him. He and other Cordova fishermen had hunted deer on the islands of the Sound together and built airboats to shoot moose on the Copper River Delta. They'd hunted ducks in the rich tide flats and tributaries of the Delta, cleaned them and drank whiskey together while the ducks simmered in brown gravy. And they'd danced with each others wives and girlfriends at the Reluctant Fisherman bar on Friday nights.

But his differences with the union began to fray the strong ties he'd built in Cordova. The heated disagreements over whether to fish or strike overrode the sense of common purpose he felt they'd all shared when they worked to build the hatcheries. And just as he had been in the minority during the union debates over oil development, he perceived that the differences of opinion over striking once again cast him as an outsider from Valdez. He came to believe that the antagonistic history between the two towns haunted their ability to work together to find solutions that would benefit them all.

And so the tension over fish prices and strikes between Bobby and the other union fishermen pervaded every aspect of his life, as tensions will do in small communities. It crept within the walls of his home and hovered over him in his fitful sleep. It ate at him when he should be enjoying a steak dinner at the Elks Club. It was impossible to go anywhere in town without running into someone who favored striking.

The closeness that had drawn him to the community became oppressive and he wanted nothing more than to leave. But it was the home his wife had always known and she thrived in her position at the cannery, in her work on the board of the Prince William Sound Aquaculture Corporation, and in her friendships. Phyllis had no intention of leaving Cordova.

The rift between Bobby and other Cordova fishermen finally culminated in a violent act of retaliation for breaking solidarity with the union and fishing with other fishermen from different parts of the Sound during a CDFU strike. A group of CDFU fishermen burned down his warehouse on the outskirts of Cordova and they flew out to tell him about it—landing in a float plane next to his boat just as he was hauling in his seine filled with salmon.

But as far as Bobby was concerned, the fire-burnt wood and tin was the least of the damage. The part of him that had once given priority to his affinity and oneness with the people of Cordova went up in smoke—replaced with a steely resolve to be financially successful. By the time they burnt his warehouse, he had already left his wife and Cordova behind. Although he would remember his time on the shores of Orca Inlet and the Copper River Delta as some of the best in his life, he knew he could never go back and reclaim what had been lost.

Now as he stood on one of the floating docks at Fishermen's Terminal on a glorious spring day, he suspected he might soon be divorced for the fourth time. The oil spill called into question his financial stability, even though he figured he would do what he always did—work harder if he had to. He could make up for a bad season or two. The weight of increasing financial uncertainty seemed to grow with every edition of Seattle's evening news that revealed increasingly grim pictures of Prince William Sound. Financial pressures stemming from this manmade disaster created fissures out of fractures in partnerships and marriages.

Bobby thought of his parents' strong and supportive relationship—the kind he had always hoped to share with someone. Now at forty-six years of age, he figured he might never share his life in the happy way that his parents worked together as friends and partners. Their strong commitment and shared passion for life spilled over into the community of Valdez as they took troubled teens into their home, held public office, or volunteered to revitalize the local cemetery.

He wondered if perhaps his father's admonition to him as a young boy had been right on the mark. It *was* hard to have a close family and a fulfilling relationship when you were always gone. But with the same optimism that made him believe—year after year—that the Seattle Seahawks would make it to the Super Bowl this time around, he figured he would work through it all somehow. He would do the only thing he knew to do and that was to work harder. He would work his way out of this thing and someday happiness would find him.

He glanced down at the gold nugget watch on his wrist that looked undeniably Alaskan. He figured he better make his way back to his Cadillac parked on the other side of the net sheds. He didn't want to be late to meet Stuart Lutton.

He drove around to the other side of the Ballard bridge and down Nickerson Street to Ocean Beauty Seafoods' central office and warehouse. As he stepped out of the car, Stuart greeted him and shook his hand. Originally from a wheat farming family in Kansas, Lutton had worked his way up into the upper management of the seafood company and was the main buyer in Alaska. He was tall and trim with a wholesome handsomeness that matched his personality. Bobby knew him as a principled person—one of the few fish buyers you could count on to make good on his word.

Stuart introduced him to his parents and younger sister who had come out from the Midwest to visit. It embarrassed him a little as Stuart slapped him on the back, saying, "Bobby is a real highliner—one of the best fishermen in Alaska. He's sold fish to Ocean Beauty for twenty some-odd years. And he's a darn good friend, too."

With that, Lutton nodded across the parking lot in the direction of the ship canal that connected the Ballard locks to the fresh water bodies of Fishermen's Terminal, Lake Union, and Lake Washington. Tied along the seawall was the *Ocean Pride*, a brand new Ocean Beauty processing ship that would soon embark upon her maiden voyage. "Ready for the tour?" Stuart asked them.

The inside of the processor was like none Bobby had ever seen before. He'd been on several older Japanese processing vessels converted for use in Alaska, but the ceilings in the companionways, galley, and sleeping quarters had been low and narrow in comparison to this ship. The 225-foot-long *Ocean Pride* was roomy, inviting, and immaculate. It was equipped to comfortably house 140 crewmembers and built primarily for processing king and opilio crab (snow crab) in the Bering Sea, although it would be used for other fisheries in Alaska.

This vessel seemed a manifestation of Ocean Beauty's financial success in recent years. Originally established as Washington Fish and Oyster Company in Seattle in 1910, Ocean Beauty first forayed into Alaska in the 1930s. In 1954, it was the first seafood company to vacuum pack and freeze fresh fillets and steaks, and the *Ocean Pride* would further the company's ability to deliver individually portioned fish to market and compete with increasingly popular farmed fish.

Ten years prior—in 1979—Ocean Beauty had been sold to Sealaska Corporation, one of the Native Corporations established by the 1971 Native Claims Settlement Act. With $93 million and 220,000 acres of timber land, Sealaska represented Tlingit, Haida, and Tsimshian Natives. After some initial setbacks following the acquisition, Ocean Beauty thrived in the latter part of the 1980s. By 1989, it operated twelve processing plants in Alaska and marketed more than one hundred million pounds of seafood, earning it the Governor's Alaskan Exporter of the Year award. With more than $200 million in annual sales, Ocean Beauty accounted for three quarters of Sealaska's annual revenues.

After a complete tour of the galley sleeping quarters, fish hold and freezers, they disembarked the ship, emerging back into the warm glow of the May afternoon. Stuart's pride in this new ship, and in working for this company was evident. They all stood in the sunshine, chatting about fishing and farming, the Midwest and Alaska. As they stood there trading stories and soaking up a welcome spring warmth, Bobby felt honored to have been invited to meet Stuart's family. He felt humbled to have been invited to join them on a tour of this company's multi-million-dollar investment of which Stuart was so obviously proud.

When he finally turned to leave, Stuart held out his hand. "Bobby," he said. "Don't worry about the oil spill. We'll work something out—cosign your loans or give you an advance at the beginning of next season. Whatever you need, we'll make it work."

It shouldn't have surprised him, coming from Stuart, but it did. He reached out to shake Stuart's hand. "Thank you my friend."

Staffers for Congressman George Miller delved into their investigation of the *Exxon Valdez* spill in the spirit promised at the field hearings in Valdez held earlier that month. They interviewed employees and obtained internal Alyeska documents that were previously unknown to regulators or others outside the company. What they found would ultimately prompt Congressman Miller to urge the Department of Justice to pursue criminal claims, as well as civil claims, against Alyeska and its parent companies.

The paper trail that would reveal incriminating evidence began with a memo from Alyeska's Marine Terminal Superintendent, W. D. Howitt, to a subcommittee of the consortium's owner companies. Howitt informed the Marine Services Subcommittee that the agenda for their May 18, 1988, meeting in Bellingham, Washington, would include a discussion about oil spill response equipment. He followed up with a packet of materials on April 28.

In his cover letter, Howitt explained, "The first part of the information package contains the T.L. Polasek [Alyeska's Vice President of Operations] briefing that was presented to the Operations

Subcommittee on April 6-7, 1988, at the quarterly meeting. The briefing is the result of an action item from January's [owner's] meeting during which a concern was raised by ARCO on Alyeska's capability to respond to oil spills at midpoint of Prince William Sound."[1]

Polasek, who insisted in his testimony at the Congressional field hearings that Alyeska had not broken its promises to the people of Alaska, had privately expressed serious concerns about Alyeska's ability to respond to a spill to members of the consortium. In his presentation to the Operations Subcommittee, he drew comparisons between equipment available to the Clean Sound cooperative in Washington State's Puget Sound and Alyeska's equipment for responding to a spill in Prince William Sound.

Polasek asserted that Clean Sound's spill cleanup methodology and equipment stood ready to provide "immediate, fast response to spill, at any location, with boom to contain, exclude, and/or divert oil." In contrast, he noted that in Prince William Sound, cleanup equipment was clearly deficient compared to Clean Sound, and that there had been "no new skimming vessels purchased since 1977." In short, he concluded, "Immediate, fast response to mid-point of Prince William Sound not possible with present equipment complement."[2]

The Marine Services subcommittee of the owner companies apparently found the written presentation compelling. It implied that Alyeska could not meet the requirements outlined in the spill response plan approved by DEC.

According to an internal document, the subcommittee voted at the May meeting to recommend improving spill response equipment readiness at the Alyeska terminal, and acquisition of additional equipment to respond to spills in Prince William Sound of the "type best suited for near shore and beach operations."

The Marine Services subcommittee also recommended the purchase of a large barge (fifty- to one-hundred-thousand barrel capacity) to be equipped with ocean boom and skimmers. Finally, they recommended that the owner companies press for pre-approval to use dispersants as a means for cleaning up an oil spill.

The heightened awareness about spill response may have been partly in response to the 159,000-gallon oil spill by the tanker *Glacier Bay* in Cook Inlet in the previous year. The British Petroleum tanker accident happened in July 1987, at the peak of the sockeye salmon run. The lawsuit between the fishermen and BP still languished in the courts.

On the other hand, the concern may simply have been that Alyeska's peak throughput of two million barrels per day (far in excess of the six-hundred-thousand barrel capacity of the ballast water treatment plant) simply increased the chances for a spill to occur.

Or it may have been the added pressure from the loosely organized citizens group in Valdez, which sought to spend municipal funds for the city of Valdez to purchase spill response equipment. For whatever reason, ARCO had raised the concern with foresight.

However, an internal communication dated July 8, 1988, revealed that the owner's committee vetoed the recommendations of the Marine Services subcommittee. The owner's committee was chaired at that time by Darrell Warner, President of Exxon Pipeline Company. The document read, "At the owner's committee meeting in Phoenix, it was decided that Alyeska would provide immediate response to oil spills in Valdez Arm and Valdez Narrows only. Further efforts in Prince William Sound would be limited to the use of dispersants and any additional effort would be the responsibility of the spiller."[3]

The owner companies, under Exxon's leadership, acted more as a cabal than a consortium, clandestinely agreeing not to comply with the provisions set forth in the contingency plan on file with Alaska's DEC. Exxon and the six other members of the consortium never intended for Alyeska to marshal an immediate response to contain or recover oil in the Sound, should such an event occur. Instead, Exxon and the other oil companies planned to simply spray chemical dispersants on a spill and then wipe their hands of it.

These findings would ultimately prompt Congressman George Miller to declare that anything short of criminal penalties would not be sufficient to deter similar corporate behavior in the future.[4] In his efforts to hold the responsible corporate officials accountable, Miller said, "The oil industry betrayed its own promises and deceived the Congress with respect to operations of Alyeska and the *Exxon Valdez* oil spill. Without a commitment by the Department of Justice to prosecute this intentional deception, how is it that Congress and the people of the State of Alaska can rely on such assurances in the future?"

13

The Heart of the Sound

UNAKWIK INLET: JULY 1989

B OBBY THOUGHT THE SPLASHING HE HEARD all around the boat had been part of a vivid dream. As he lay in the bunk of his stateroom, a wool blanket tangled around his leg, he slowly realized the sound was that of pink salmon jumping around his boat. One thudded dully against the hull of the *Lady Lynne*. He pulled on a well-worn pair of Levi's and made his way out to the boat's deck, finally remembering where they'd anchored up the night before.

The Department of Fish and Game had in late June opened up the northern parts of the Sound that had been spared the swath of oil—Unakwik, Esther and Cogill—for salmon fishing. Bobby and his crew had left Valdez in the evening, headed for Esther Island in the north-western corner of the Sound and what promised to be good fishing. But he'd gotten sleepy and turned north up Unakwik Inlet instead of pushing on to Esther. Anchored there in a small indent in the coastline of Unakwik known as Siwash Bay, it seemed they'd happened upon a sizable school of pink salmon. There were no other boats in sight and he marveled this good fortune.

He stood there on deck, bare-chested and bare-footed, absently running his fingers through untamed hair. Judging by the surreal, pale light glowing off the deep green waters and steep wooded forest surrounding the bay, it was about three in the morning. It wouldn't be long before he woke the crew and set about catching these fish, but for the moment, he drank in the cool salty air and relished the feel of it on his chest.

He wanted a minute to study the "jumpers," as fishermen called them, to observe the level of the tide, and to judge how dense this school of fish might be. He stood watching them leap inches above the surface, dripping and shimmering with an almost iridescent glow in the summer twilight, only to disappear again into the clear depths of the bay. Their firm flesh showed no sign of the slight hump that would emerge on their backs as time drew near for them to retreat up the streams to spawn, earning pink salmon the nickname "humpies." The jumpers left only ripples as evidence that they were more than just an apparition.

A pair of red-necked grebes landed and settled on a rock off the boat's bow, waiting for the morning sun to awaken their prey. Their russet neck and chest feathers glowed against the muted colors of deep green water and spruce covering the talus slopes. Off the boat's stern, a half dozen murres floated in the placid water. The crow-sized black and white seabirds usually gathered on the water in large rafts and Bobby feared that this small flock may be evidence of their demise in the wake of the oil spill.

Other fishermen had taken note of the eerie quiet in the Sound since the spill. On the marine radio, the fishermen compared notes about the scant numbers of the seabirds that usually accompanied them on the water. Murres, cormorants, red-necked grebes, green-winged teals, pigeon guillemots, puffins and harlequin ducks that had once filled the Sound with color and calls now seemed hauntingly scarce. These birds dive anywhere from five to seventy feet to feed on small fish, mollusks, and worms, and the fishermen feared that the scarcity of their winged companions was a sign of the Sound's future.

Standing on deck, Bobby could recall the rafts of puffins that normally gathered on the waters when they made a set, looking to lift a salmon out of the net. The puffins, which Bobby thought looked like parrots dressed up in tuxedoes, were fun to watch as they sprang above the water before diving below. He remembered seeing pigeon guillemots playing tag during mating season—their black bodies and white-splashed wings like shadows as they danced underwater in a spring ritual.

His favorite bird though, was the fork-tailed storm petrel. He didn't see them much when he fished salmon in the summer, but they flocked to his boat during the fall bait herring season and in the wintertime when he'd caught king crab in Port Wells. They would gather on the boat's mast and on the railing outside the wheelhouse. Some said they were attracted to the lights of the fishing vessel, but Bobby had always been convinced they sought human companionship in the short, gray days of winter.

He remembered watching a pair of petrels out the wheelhouse window as they hunkered on the rail, snow falling heavily from pregnant clouds, admiring their dark faces and the way their smoky colored feathers blended into the white and gray of the day. He opened the door and talked to them, offered them milk and leftover muffins, and to his surprise, they joined him in the wheelhouse. One of them perched on his shoulder while he drove the boat.

Bobby believed the birds were a part of the natural system and they made a living on the same ecosystem he did. He didn't object to oil development—he recognized the same need to fuel his boat and the nation's economy that the Congress had when they approved the pipeline. But he knew in hindsight that Alaskans hadn't demanded the protections that his father had outlined in his speech in the Pipeline Hearings. Citizens, politicians, and regulators had grown complacent as the pipeline pumped cash into the economy. As the birds now lay dying on island beaches or sunk in the depths of the Sound, Bobby felt a personal responsibility for their loss. The need for oil, the prosperity of the past decade, and the burden of unmet responsibilities fostered a dissonance that would weigh heavily on Alaskans in the aftermath of the spill. The fouling of the Sound and its creatures would prove more than many could bear.

The numbers of birds lost as a result of the spill can never be known although wildlife biologists used a general rule of thumb to calculate the effects of oil on bird deaths in the Sound. The rule projected that the number of dead birds recovered would equal approximately 5 percent of the total bird mortality. By summer solstice, twenty thousand oiled birds had been carefully collected and catalogued.[1] An incinerator constructed along the old Dayville road leading out to the Alyeska terminal destroyed thousands of bird and animal carcasses in the initial days and weeks of the cleanup.

In the days after the spill, workers found 520 dead birds of fifty different species on four miles of Green Island alone. Identifying the birds among the heavily oiled grass and rocks of the beaches proved challenging, however. One worker reached down to set his camera on an oiled rock only to discover it was a cormorant when it pulled its long neck and head out from under its wing.

Workers found it difficult to differentiate between the species, as the mat of black oil masked the russet, brown tweed, white, emerald, and turquoise feathers that distinguished them. They sorted birds by those with long and graceful necks, those with short stubby beaks, and others with elongated piercing mandibles. Yet despite the best efforts of workers to collect and count carcasses, agreeing on a method for calculating the actual number of birds would ultimately prove intractable. It could be argued that every beach, bay, and island had a unique population, which could not directly lead to accurate conclusions about the total death toll in the Sound.

Dave Kennedy, a representative from the National Oceanic and Atmospheric Administration (NOAA) pointed out, "What they have done is, they have taken Green Island, which is a dot in the Sound, which has been very heavily hit, which was very biologically rich, and you can't extrapolate from that."[2] Kennedy's statement foreshadowed significant problems that would come to plague a true assessment of the spill's effects on the environment.

Scientists had very little baseline data identifying the number of most birds and mammals in the Sound prior to the spill, although they knew that approximately ten million shorebirds were due to settle along Orca Inlet and across the Copper River delta in the next few weeks. And they knew that murres would soon settle along the Barren Islands between the Kenai Peninsula and Kodiak Island to hatch their young. But for the most part, scientists had no specific documentation of the pre-spill numbers of most birds, much less their location within the Sound.

The same was true for sea otters, stellar sea lions, fur and ringed seals, river otters, mink, bear, and deer. Estimates of the population of sea otters in Prince William Sound ranged from four thousand[3] to twenty thousand[4] making it difficult to judge how otter deaths might impact the population in the longer term.

Because this catastrophe was a manmade disaster, questions of liability would color the investigations and cooperation between Exxon and its cleanup contractor, government regulators and nongovernmental organizations. Regulators had to rely on workers hired by

Exxon or their cleanup contractors to report the number of dead birds and animals. Yet this evidence could ultimately be used against Exxon in court.

One biologist working for the National Marine Fisheries Service (NMFS) said he received a memo directing him not to talk about environmental assessments with reporters or anyone outside the agency. NMFS biologist Byron Morris, who established a multi-agency cooperative effort to evaluate long-term damage from the spill, said he hadn't received any memo to that effect. However, he acknowledged that he had been directed to consult with the general counsel for NOAA before publicly releasing any information. "The information that will be generated will be used in litigation, so it is privileged," Morris said. "It can't be released to any one person, because then it would have to be released to the opposition."[5]

Scientists also differed in their opinions about what—if anything—should be done to rescue wildlife. Many expressed concern that holding birds, otters, and seals in closely confined quarters would only impose more stress on animals that might otherwise survive if left alone. Others cited concerns about bioaccumulation, in which rehabilitated and released animals that had ingested oil might be eaten by other animals, passing on and accumulating toxicity in the food chain. Finally, scientists warned that rescued animals might be susceptible to contracting any number of diseases from each other or from domestic animals. These diseases could spread back to others in the population once they were released. But for those who picked up a bird on the beach, or even watched them on the evening news as they clung to life, there was little question about what should be done.

Exxon contracted with the International Bird Rescue Center of Berkeley, California, which set up bird cleaning operations in Valdez, Seward, Homer, Kodiak and Anchorage. Workers and volunteers from Alaska and around the country used Dawn dish soap to carefully cleanse oil from the fine inner down and outer feathers. Because it took over an hour to carefully wash, rinse and dry each bird, workers were only able to treat 180 to 230 birds per day. A total of 1,589 birds were treated, although half of them died before they could be released. The effort cost Exxon $30,000 per bird.

The satisfaction of watching a rehabilitated murre, red-necked grebe, harlequin duck, or cormorant fly back out over the Sound likely did more to help people combat a sense of helplessness in the days following the spill. Fewer than a thousand birds were saved, although for those birds, the effort meant the difference between life and death. Scientists estimate that between 260,000 and 580,000 birds died in the wake of the spill.[6]

If the sheer number of birds lost wasn't enough to break a heart, the sight of an oiled otter could finish the task. In the days and weeks following the spill, 430 veterinarians and volunteers came from around the country to help rehabilitate sea otters. Because otters lack a layer of fat and rely solely on their fur to keep them warm, a coating of oil was a death sentence. And it meant that cleaning and drying them was only the first step in the rehabilitation process. Once clean, they were held in floating pens until their fur regained natural oils and insulating strength. The first rescue center was set up in Valdez at the community college, then others followed in Seward, Homer, and Kodiak.

A total of 344 otters were treated at a cost to Exxon of $80,000 per otter. About half of the rehabilitated otters were sent to zoos or aquariums and the rest were tagged and released into the Sound. Within a year, nearly all of those in captivity would be dead, along with about half of those released into the Sound. Scientists would disagree about the cause of their deaths—whether from the stress of handling, or from the toxic effects of hydrocarbons that had permeated their systems. All told, an estimated 3,500 to 5,500 sea otters died in oiled waters, along with two hundred harbor seals and twenty-two orca whales.

As Bobby stood on the deck of the *Lady Lynne* in Siwash Bay, he wondered how long it would take the Sound to restore itself, how long before it was filled again with the songs of shorebirds, until it was clean and *felt* clean. Because Unakwik was further north than Bligh Reef and the oil had spread to the south and west, he could almost fool himself into thinking the spill had never really happened.

Looking north up the bay, the bend in the land concealed the Meares Glacier that spanned the width of the bay at its end—nearly a mile across. It loomed several stories high above the water and calved off in magnificent hunks of mineral-rich turquoise ice. Like so many of the narrow fjords and inlets in Prince William Sound, the glaciers that carved and shaped it still remained, and the story of the Sound's formation could almost be inferred from their existence.

The Meares Glacier deposited a reef across Unakwik Inlet upon its retreat and Bobby had come to know the reef as a rich feeding ground for spot and stripe prawns and red crab. He wondered if places like Unakwik, which had been spared in the oil's swath, would ultimately suffer fallout from the disaster as well.

Would otters that had survived the spill find their way here to nourish themselves with untainted clams and mussels and eventually deplete the resources in the clean parts of the Sound? Or would places like Unakwik serve as a sanctuary and help to heal the rest of the Sound in time? What he couldn't know is that these questions would ultimately never be unequivocally answered in a scientific sense. There were simply too many variables, too little baseline data, and an infinite number of ways to interpret results depending on your perspective.

The sound of jumpers splashing intensified, drawing Bobby's attention back to the task at hand. They're marching, he thought, and he retreated into the foc's'le to wake the others. Before the early summer sun broke over the top of the eastern rim of Unakwik, the *Lady Lynne* sat low in the water, laden with fifty thousand pounds of humpies. They'd used the hydraulic lift to roll the seine aboard—stretched tight and full of flapping fish. As the crew worked to release the fish into the hold and restack the seine, Bobby called the skipper of the *Theresa Marie*, the tender boat waiting for him over at Esther.

"Dan, we're plug loaded here in Siwash Bay. It only took one set, and they're still marching up the bay. How fast can you get here?"

The fish wouldn't all fit in the hold so the deck was piled high with humpies and occasionally one slid overboard and splashed back into the water that was almost level with the deck now. Sitting in the wheelhouse Bobby thought this felt right. This felt like old times. He settled back in the captain's chair and sipped his coffee, watching jumpers still marching up the bay. He hoped Dan would hurry, that he would get here before the other boats got wise to where he was going.

The *Theresa Marie* could pack 150,000 pounds of salmon in refrigerated seawater. A seventy-foot Delta, Bobby had her built in 1983 and named her after his daughter. When the boat was finished in late 1983, already inflated interest rates bounced up another two percentage points and his interest payments alone came to more than $100,000 for a couple of years.

Fortunately, salmon prices had jumped along with interest rates, and although he had quite a bit of equity in the boat now, he still had payments. A big catch here at Unakwik would go a long way toward meeting all his obligations this year. If Dan hurried, he might be able to make a couple more sets before the ebb tide.

As he pulled out of Esther, Dan called back on the radio, "I'm on my way. It looks like they might close fishing here at Esther. I've heard on the radio a few boats saying they've run through oily water here by the hatchery. So, I'll probably have company when I leave."

"Okay, buddy. Pour the coals to her! " Bobby called back.

One of the crewmembers who also doubled as the cook brought a ham sandwich and a fresh cup of coffee up to the wheelhouse. A cook isn't necessarily the highest paid position on a fishing boat, but he or she can have a significant effect on the mood of the crew and captain.

Salmon season usually opened early on Monday morning and closed late on Friday night. The crew worked sometimes twenty hours a day and what they lacked in sleep to replenish their energy, they made up with meals. Breakfasts of eggs, bacon, biscuits, fruit cocktail, and coffee. Dinners of steak or grilled fresh red snapper, frozen peas and corn, mashed potatoes, and thick-sliced wheat bread. The physical work, the smell of the ocean, and competition with other boats for the highest catch made for hearty appetites and deep sleep when they got a chance.

The captains knew when salmon would return to certain areas. When the season opened in June, they knew they could find early salmon in the northeastern part of the Sound—Jack's Bay, Galena Bay, and Valdez Arm. Port Wells in the northwestern corner was next and by mid-July, you'd better be fishing at Long Bay, Unakwik, and Glacier Island. In August, fishing was best at Knight, Culross, and Montague Island. By the end of the month, chum salmon would pour into Fidalgo Bay on the Sound's eastern edge.

As Bobby sipped his coffee and devoured the ham sandwich, he thought back to the past couple of years. Fishing wasn't like it was when he started on the *Demetra M* in the early 1970s. Back then the season opened for the summer and fishermen went where the salmon ran. They depended solely on the rhythms of nature—hoping that fall rains wouldn't wash the fertilized salmon eggs from their gravel nests, that plankton would bloom just as fry emerged from the streams, and that the currents would carry the fry into a bountiful ocean and return them as mature adults to the streams from which they spawned. It took wits, fish sense, and plain hard work to scrabble out a living on the Sound's natural salmon runs.

But the volume of fish produced in the last few years by the hatcheries required more hands-on management. Each hatchery hired fishermen to catch salmon returning to their spot in the Sound and the proceeds from the sale of their catch would fund another year of operation. The fish sometimes milled around in the Sound before honing in on their specific place of origin. By the time the salmon came within the bounds where the hatchery was allowed to catch them, they could be turning dark as they approached their time to spawn. Darker fish were less firm and attractive to consumers and many of the fishermen believed that Prince William Sound salmon were becoming less marketable because of the way they were managed.

Bobby and many of the other fishermen had lobbied to simply open up the Sound and catch the fish when they were bright and firm. In exchange for the freedom to fish in any location, the fishermen could simply tax themselves to pay the hatchery expenses. But so far it hadn't happened and it seemed to some that managing the fisheries was becoming more bureaucratic and less in tune to either natural or market forces.

Even though fish biologists and regulatory agencies increasingly had a hand in managing the fisheries in the past couple of years, nothing could compare to this summer. This season was like no other. Although the fish kept pouring into the Sound, exceeding the predictions for a record run, not all areas were open to fishing. Boats would sit idle for days or weeks on end waiting for the Department of Fish and Game to ensure areas were free of oil before they opened them up for fishing.

Areas as far away as Kamishak Bay, 250 miles away in Cook Inlet, were closed when the wind and currents carried in tar balls on the tide rips. At Kodiak Island, nearly 250 miles to the southwest of Bligh

Reef, most areas were closed for fishing. In 1988—just last year, five hundred fishermen caught $94 million worth of salmon, equaling about one seventh of the state's entire catch. This year, fishermen were concerned about the potential long-term impact on the reputation of Alaskan salmon. "Our main concern is for the consumer," Kodiak fisherman Stan Duncan said. "We really would like to take a hard stand against fishing because...of the oil that we got here."[7]

In Bristol Bay, north of the Alaska Peninsula and safely out of reach of the spill's swath, sockeye salmon were returning in record numbers. The harvest had nearly doubled from the previous year's run, but the price paid to fishermen was nearly half. Fishermen wondered if the low prices were due to fear in the marketplace of contamination of all Alaskan salmon. Or were the low prices instead, as the processors claimed, due to a large carryover of frozen salmon in Japan from the previous year and a weakening of the Japanese yen?

Exxon funded a public relations effort by the state to prop up prices for salmon on the global market. But the weak prices for salmon made negotiations for fair compensation between Exxon and the fishermen difficult. Exxon wanted to compensate for lost fishing based on current year prices. Fishermen demanded last year's prices. As area after area closed to fishing, the parties finally reached an agreement about compensation for the 1989 fishing season only. Exxon would pay based on each fisherman's two-year historical catch matched against this year's lost fishing opportunity and an average price per pound to be determined at the end of the season. Fishermen would not give up their right to sue for additional damages.

Seven fishermen's associations participated in the negotiations with Exxon, including the Cordova District Fishermen United. "I think this is a really strong commitment by this company," CDFU representative Phil McCrudden said. "They're talking about real, meaningful payments. They're not forced to do this by law or anything."[8] A few dissenting voices could be heard, but the majority agreed the arrangement represented a good-faith effort by the company. Cook Inlet seiners and driftnet fishermen still sought to quantify damages and collect compensation from the 1987 *Glacier Bay* spill and one of their representatives doubted the scheme would provide fair recompense. Some thought they should just forget the entire season and let Exxon pay them all off.

In harbors from Valdez to Homer and Kodiak, attorneys walked the docks, handing out cards. They offered to help fishermen file claims with Exxon and to file suit for longer-term damages. But most fishermen wouldn't have traded a check for any amount with to the chance to go out and fish as they always had.

"We're not just producing income. We're producing food, supporting a lifestyle. And we're proud of it. A check from Exxon won't work. It would hurt our hearts," Armin Koenig said. Koenig had been instrumental in developing the salmon hatcheries in the early 1970s and the hatchery at Sawmill Bay bore his namesake. "We produce about one pound of seafood for every American. We are not interested in having Exxon just pay us off on a straight dollar-and-cent loss. We know these same oil companies have safer operations elsewhere in the world. Here in Alaska they have tried to buy us with bullshit, expensive ad campaigns. Neither the state nor the federal government had enough poop to stand up to them."[9]

As Bobby sat in Unakwik, he turned the dials on the radio. He wanted to hear what was happening at Esther, and he needed to hear familiar voices.

He was glad to be sitting there with a net full of fish, and grateful for the feeling of solidarity that fighting a common cause fostered among the fishermen. They had all, at one time or another, rejoiced in a big set, felt their heart pounding as they sought shelter in a storm behind the nearest island, or even lost loved ones. Bobby remembered the first set he ever made on his own boat, sitting there waiting for the tender just as he was now, and his own close brush with tragedy.

It was 1971 and he'd sat at the galley table of the *Donna R* while the crewmembers slept in their bunks below, his brother Pat, and Bobby's nine-year-old son, Eddie, among them. Cold coffee spilling on his hand woke him, and he realized the *Donna R*—his first seine boat—was going under and fast. He'd bolted down into the foc's'le, screaming for everyone to get out. Pat had never learned how to swim but he managed to get the crewmembers into the skiff and cut it loose.

He couldn't find Eddie in all the commotion and the water in the foc's'le nearly filled the bunkroom. Suddenly he heard the boy cry out as the water engulfed him. Scooping him up in his arms, he told him to hang onto his neck no matter what, and they made their way out of the cabin. The boat was completely submerged now. At least the water no longer came through the cabin door in a rush of white water. He struggled to hold his breath and he wondered if the boy in his arms would live to see his tenth birthday.

Bubbles floated to the surface around them and as Bobby looked up, he could see the seine billowing out in the water behind the sinking boat. How would they ever make their way through hundreds of feet of net? An odd sense of calm filled him as the water around them grew darker. He tucked the boy under his arm, and with his one free arm started swimming toward the dimming light of the water's surface. The web seemed to part around them as if by some mysterious force and Bobby worked methodically to push it aside with his free hand, all the while struggling to continue upward. He felt Eddie's body go limp.

His own lungs threatened to betray him, to convince him of the need to succumb to an almost irresistible desire to swallow the water that surrounded them. He fought back the urge. Kicking. Arm flailing. Kicking. He sensed a rim of whiteness around the edges of his vision and he almost embraced the feeling of traveling into a different realm. With a splash and a gasp, they surfaced and he discovered that the halcyon glow he'd just experienced was really light on the water's surface.

His brother was sitting in the skiff, shoulders heaving, convinced that they would never come up after being under so long. They heaved the boy up into the skiff and began to cheer as he gasped, eyes fluttering, as he coughed up water.

As he sat in the wheelhouse now, waiting for the *Theresa Marie* to come up the bay, Bobby thought about Eddie. He was a grown man now and fished his own boat—the *Bobbie Jo*. He held down the button on the microphone, trying to raise Eddie on the radio. He hoped Eddie would follow Dan in the *Theresa Marie* to Unakwik. He took a sip of coffee, wishing that together they would scoop up all these jumpers before others got there.

A southeast wind was rolling whitecaps across the Sound when an announcement came over the marine radio. It had been three weeks since the big catch in Unakwik and now Fish and Game announced an opener at Fidalgo Bay. Earlier in the summer, Fish and Game indicated no areas in the eastern Sound would be open, so this was a welcome surprise.

The mouth of Fidalgo Bay was only ten miles from Bligh Reef, but the oil had moved in the opposite direction. With the volume of chums that seemed to be pouring into Fidalgo, it wouldn't be wise to simply let them pile up on the beaches and in the streams. A big run like this could actually mean a smaller return in the next cycle if some weren't harvested.

A stiff wind that carried a hint of early fall rippled across the water. Bobby checked the barometer and decided it wasn't likely this wind would let up anytime soon. If he could buck into the wind and waves and beat everyone over to Fidalgo, he reckoned he might fill a tender with elusive chum salmon before the wind laid down and other boats showed up. He set the auto-pilot south by southeast and got ready for a long trip across the Sound.

He could see lights glowing against the gray skies to the southwest off Knight Island and he remembered fishing in a storm not unlike this one. He and the Butler brothers from Cordova were the only ones fishing off of Point Helen. Waves rolled across the decks of their boats as they tried to haul their seines aboard. He'd learned from old-timers like Don and Harold Butler and he did as they did, he fished when they did, and drank with them in the bars. Most of his closest friends were a generation older and they had taken him on as an apprentice, proud to be passing along knowledge they had learned over a lifetime of fishing.

In that storm, the stay on Don and Harold's boom broke and they nearly rolled the boat. Bobby raced to help right them—something any fisherman would do for another whose life was in danger. He missed them now in their retirement. He wondered what they thought of the mess in the Sound.

Point Helen was now overrun with cleanup equipment. Just like other places all around the Sound, the beaches crawled with workers in oil-soaked orange raingear. They sprayed hot and cold water on the rocks, washing it back down into the sea to be sucked up by skimmers that worked between the beaches and protective boom.

There were eleven thousand people spraying and scrubbing rocks that summer. They seemed to Bobby to be swarming the beaches wherever he turned. Sounds of civilization replaced the calls of shorebirds. Barges such as the *Cinmar, Sockeye,* and *Donkey II* erected booms fifty- to sixty-feet tall, spraying rocky cliffs too steep for workers to navigate. Workers with hoses and pressure washers attacked the shiny black crude left on the rocks by the high tide, as if the sheer force of water and will could make it disappear.

Tugs transported oil boom and skimmers, and seine boats and bow-pickers carried workers outfitted in Helly Hansen raingear and supplies. Ferries and military vessels housed workers, medical personnel, and cooks. Inflatable Zodiacs scurried through the waters carrying supervisors, Coast Guard observers, reporters, and representatives of VECO—the contractor Exxon hired to manage the cleanup.

To Bobby and others who lived there, the onslaught of workers and equipment felt like an invasion of privacy, and only magnified their anger over the spill. Many of the fishermen doubted that oil could ever be washed off, that the only thing to do now was let nature heal itself. They feared that the hot washes, the thousands of workers' boots, and heavy equipment would actually do more damage to the delicate ecosystems within the Sound's rocky beaches than the oil itself.

High-pressure washes seemed only to drive the oil deeper into the sediments and substrate—making it disappear from view but prolonging the impact. But they suspected making it disappear from view was Exxon's foremost priority. The fishermen's instincts were backed by recommendations of the American Petroleum Institute which recommended "natural cleansing."

But doing nothing didn't seem right either and in any event, Federal law requires that a spiller clean up the oil. At its annual shareholder meeting in May, Exxon executives showed a fifteen-minute video asserting that 75 percent of the eleven million gallons of oil had dissipated shortly after the spill, or had been cleaned up. Oil toxicity, the video claimed, was no longer a problem. It concluded with dramatic scenes of clean beaches and whales swimming through ocean waters. The video claimed that the initial grief and shock over the spill "is giving way to a feeling that Prince William Sound can be cleaned up soon, not later."[10]

But to some the video and tone of the shareholder's meeting felt more like a public relations effort than a sea change in corporate culture. "What they are doing is a cover-up, not a cleanup," said a representative from Trustees for Alaska—one of eleven environmental organizations that filed a notice of intent to sue if the Sound wasn't cleaned up. "This videotape is just one more piece of the deception."

As cleanup workers and equipment were deployed over the summer, Exxon estimated that twelve hundred miles of coastline had been oiled. Yet this figure represented distance as the crow flies. Because of the many islands and inlets throughout the Sound and southwestern Alaska, the National Oceanic and Atmospheric Administration (NOAA) estimated that 5,372 miles of coastline had actually been oiled.[11] Some called into question whether eleven million gallons of crude could have had such far-reaching effects.

An investigation on file with the Alaska Resources Library and Information Services, alleges that the true amount of oil spilled was actually closer to thirty million gallons. According to this report, the ships used to lighter oil off the *Exxon Valdez* after the spill—the *Exxon Baton Rouge, Exxon San Francisco,* and *Exxon Baytown*—were actually filled with such a high percentage of seawater that refineries refused to offload it. The report claims that instead of delivering lightered oil to refineries, 24.32 million gallons actually returned to the Alyeska terminal in Valdez as ballast water, was logged on the survey forms, and treated for release into the bay.[12]

Whatever the amount, the oil fouling the beaches in Prince William Sound called into question what Alaskans—and Americans—value. Are we willing to hand over local control of resources to regulators in Juneau and Washington, D.C.? Are we willing to stand by as corporations assess whether protecting the environment will align with their quarterly goals for profitability? Do we value rising stock prices over accountability?

As people from Los Angeles to Maine watched one of the largest environmental disasters unfold on the evening news, many sought ways to say, "these are not our values." People from Peoria, Illinois, sent towels to help wash and clean birds. Talk show hosts from Seattle to New York City called on consumers to boycott Exxon.[13] From every corner of the country, Americans seemed to reach out and wrap their collective arms around Alaskans.

By the summer's end, Exxon would announce the end of cleanup activities. Workers would retreat from the beaches in mid-September, having cleaned approximately eight percent of the oil spilled, according to estimates by the DEC. The cleanup efforts would require forty times more fuel to run boats and other equipment than the amount of oil recovered. Absorbent materials would be burned in incinerators along the old Dayville road and 31,000 tons of oily debris would be transported to a hazardous waste dump in Oregon. The cleanup cost would total over $2 billion, including $300 million in payments to fishermen for their efforts on the cleanup.

Bobby reached down and switched off the auto pilot, then grasped the wheel and wrestled it starboard twenty degrees. The swells were heavier now and it took all his strength to keep the bow of the *Lady Lynne* pointed into the waves. He thought about all that had happened this summer and knew that someday a jury would seek to put a value on the damage to the Sound. They would try to place a value on all that fishermen had lost this season and on what might be lost in the years to come.

If a representative from Exxon came to him now and asked him to put a price on what had been lost, could he do it? If he could no longer make a living fishing in this Sound, he would have lost more than just his income until he retired. But how could such a thing be fairly quantified?

A wave broke over the bow of the boat and sprayed the wheelhouse window. As he grasped the captain's wheel and felt the *Lady Lynne* settle into the next trough, he looked down at his hands. They had come to look more like bear paws after a lifetime of hard work, fingers short and thick, palms square and strong. These hands had untangled salmon from a freezing cold gill net on the Copper River flats, dug clams along Orca Inlet and Unakwik Inlet, and wrestled the captain's wheel through waves that buffeted his boat.

These hands had on them the blood of salmon, otters, seals, and deer from this Sound. They had landed with a rousing smack in bar fights in nearly every port from southeast Alaska to the Kenai Peninsula. These hands had come to the aid of fellow fishermen in need.

But they did not look old. They belonged to a robust man who was not ready to leave this Sound. He had spent a lifetime learning the most intimate features of this place. He'd learned from Don and Harold Butler that the ebb tide would sometimes carry a school of salmon back south through Knight Island passage toward the Gulf, which meant he should set his net backward. Other old-timers had taught him that when chum salmon show up at Glacier Island, they'll be in Fidalgo Bay in seven to ten days. He'd learned how to navigate through the reef and shoals inside Fairmont Island without impaling his hull on a rock.

Loved ones had died in the tsunami after the 1964 earthquake, and other close friends had drowned as their boats sank in a freak storm. He'd come within a few breaths of losing his own son when the *Donna R* sank.

Sudden fall storms that caught him with his boat hold full of herring never caused him fear—only respect and humility. He'd shared the season's returning salmon with killer whales and humpbacks and watched in awe at the rituals of shorebirds courting in the springtime.

With his boat at full throttle, he'd tried to outrun the eruption of Mount Augustine, only to be forced to turn off his engines and let the ash settle on his boat and in the waters around him in silence. He'd watched blood-red sunsets shimmer across deep green waters in the chill of late August evenings.

In this Sound, he had fished with his father and father-in-law, his brother, brother-in-law, nephews, sister, son, and daughter. Someday he hoped to fish these waters with his grandchildren. A knowledge and intimacy of this place had been handed down from generation to generation. He could almost feel the Sound's emerald currents coursing through his veins. Could he stop the beating of this heart? Being a fisherman, he knew, was so much more than what he did for a living. It defined his very existence.

14

The Fall of Strict Liability

ESTHER HATCHERY: MID-AUGUST 1989

BOBBY GUIDED THE *Lady Lynne* eastward into Fidalgo Bay. The steep mountains ringing the fjord offered a welcome break from the winds he'd fought all the way across Prince William Sound. The rocky cliffs of Fidalgo rose sharply out of the water, shaded in places by low-slung alder and salmonberry bushes. As the fjord widened at Land-locked Bay, Bobby instinctively glanced up at the northern rim, just as he did every time he came to Fidalgo. The late afternoon sun revealed the yawning, dark opening of a long-abandoned copper mine once operated by the Fidalgo Copper Company.

Bobby always marveled at the old timbers that framed the mine opening and the decaying platform that once supported tram cars that carried ore down the steep slope to the water. He'd hiked up there one day just to get a closer look at the mine entrance and remnants of the old building and platform perched on the cliff, and puzzled over how men had wrestled the equipment and building materials up a grade that was nearly too steep for him to climb.

He turned his attention back to the clear green water, his grey eyes scanning the gentle waves for a sign of chum salmon. For as long as he could remember fishermen had referred to chum salmon as "dogs." Perhaps it was because they grew large wolf-like fangs when they neared their spawning grounds. But by Bobby's reckoning, it was because they were agile, quick, and smart, which made them the most difficult of all salmon species to catch. They moved rapidly through the water in tightly packed schools, and a good fisherman knew they were "walking" when their fins flickered above the water in close proximity to each other. In this formation, they were almost impossible to catch and any fisherman worth his salt wouldn't waste fuel or effort to chase walking dogs.

As he scanned the bay, Bobby saw the unmistakable sign of dogs walking right up the middle of the bay. The late afternoon sun shone across their fins, sparkling like diamonds atop the emerald depths. Bobby settled back in the captain's chair and decided it might be a good time for an early dinner. He called down on the radio and asked the crew if they were ready to eat. This might be a long night, he told them. With a little time and patience, these dogs would pile up near the head of the bay where the *Lady Lynne* could scoop them up in her net.

Bobby guided the boat eastward toward the head of the bay as the cook readied dinner and a fresh pot of coffee. As the sun began to fade behind the southern rim of the bay, the *Lady Lynne* eased through the gentle waves in an ever lengthening shadow. He picked up the receiver to the aircraft radio, and dialed into the private channel that he and Lori used to talk with each other. Even though they weren't working together that summer, they talked several times throughout the day, keeping each other company in the otherwise lonely work that occupied their days. Because she spent most of her time flying above the Sound, working now to shuttle oil company representatives and clean-up contractors back and forth, she knew what all the other fishing boats were up to. None of the other boats had left Esther Island yet, she told him. He grinned to himself, partly out of comfort in hearing her voice, but also at the thought of having all these chums to himself.

Fidalgo was nearly as long as Valdez Bay just to the north, and the *Lady Lynne* had nearly reached the head of the bay when they stopped to eat. It turned out to be a hurried meal as the chum started to jump and flip in the water near the boat. It looked as though these dogs weren't walking any further tonight. It was time to get to work.

The crew worked under a twilight sky, the skiff anchoring the end of the seine as the *Lady Lynne* laid it out, leaving a wake behind her. Unlike pink salmon, dogs will sense the net closing in around them and simply turn around to get out of it—either that or dive down beneath it. Bobby had a seine made especially for catching chum salmon, but since none of them suspected that Fish and Game would open Fidalgo that year because it was so close to Bligh Reef, he'd left it back on the dock in Valdez. The "deep dog seine" as he called it, had extra webbing strung between the lead and cork lines so that it billowed out further and deeper and could capture dogs seeking to escape beyond the reach of his net.

No matter, Bobby thought. He'd caught dogs with his regular seine many times. It was all about the skill of the captain and his crew he thought to himself as he brought the *Lady Lynne* around and pursed up the seine. A set made on a few jumpers could yield a few dozen fish, a few hundred, or a few thousand—it was nearly impossible to tell until you closed the net up and started rolling them aboard. But as he eased back on the throttle and looked down into the water from the wheelhouse, Bobby could see only bubbles, then a thick, flapping mass of silvery bodies. He called Dan on the *Theresa Marie* to see how far away he was, and how soon he could get the tender there to pick up their catch. By the time the *Theresa Marie* neared the head of the bay, Bobby and the crew had made another set. Young men in slickers and waterproof pants worked into the darkness, stacking the corks, releasing the net, and beating the water with long-poled plungers to scare the fish into staying in the net. By the time the *Theresa Marie* came into sight, they were plug loaded with dogs in the hold and had a net full of fish alongside.

It was close to midnight when Bobby and the crew finally loaded the tender, which was now riding low in the water with 150,000 pounds of chum salmon in her hold. The lights of the *Theresa Marie* spilled out onto the water and Bobby thought he saw more dogs jumping in the glow of the deck lights.

The chums were pouring into Fidalgo Bay like Bobby had never seen before. If he could make a big hit here, it would go a long way toward ensuring he could make his boat payments and have a little left for next year. And who knew what next year would bring? But he had no way to offload them since he'd already filled his own tender. It was a problem he hadn't faced in the past few years. Before he built the *Theresa Marie*, he'd often promised round-trip tickets to Hawaii for the next tender captain to come and offload his catch. He picked up the ship-to-shore radio. It was late but he dialed Stuart Lutton in his apartment in Kodiak. As one of Ocean Beauty's top fishermen and a close friend of Stuart's, he knew the fish buyer would find him another tender no matter what it took.

Lutton answered his line, of course. Bobby figured he must get about as little sleep as the fishermen whose catch he purchased during fishing season. He told Bobby he had the *Seabrook* headed to Esther Island to haul pink salmon, but he could divert her to Fidalgo.

Stuart also said he thought the *Sunrunner* might be in the area too. Bobby thanked him and radioed down to the crew. Let's rock and roll, he told them.

They laid out the net and hauled it in, over and over as the night wore on. With each haul they brought in five or six thousand chums, which Bobby could hardly recall ever doing in his thirty years of fishing. He couldn't think of a year when the chums had ever run this heavy before, much less having an entire bay to himself without competition from other boats. He could scarcely believe his luck. As the late summer dawn brightened the southeastern sky, Bobby and the crew of the *Lady Lynne* had caught nearly 80,000 chum salmon, filling two more tenders that were now heavily laden and heading back down the bay. Only then did they sleep.

The sun was high overhead by the time Bobby settled back into the captain's chair. He stacked his fish tickets from the night before in a folder and listened on the marine radio as his fellow fishermen grumbled that most of the chums had already been caught in Fidalgo. Picking up the microphone on the aircraft radio, he pressed down the button and said, "Hey Pop Tart, you got your radio on?"

Lori called back, "Roger roger. How'd you make out in Fidalgo? Some of the other captains are saying you didn't leave any fish for them! You ought to see it over here by Esther Island. The pinks are pouring in like I've never seen. Some of the fishermen are lobbying for Fish and Game to open this area back up. There hasn't been any sign of oil since a few fishermen spotted that sheen near the fishing grounds a week or so ago."

Bobby considered this news. Esther hatchery was predicted to yield nearly one-fourth of the entire region's harvest of an estimated forty million fish.[1] It might be worth running back over there to wait it out for a day or two until Fish and Game made a decision.

"Yeah, maybe I'll head back over there," he called into the mike. "What are your plans? You want to come pick me up this evening over by Esther?"

Lori picked him up after he made his way back across the Sound to the Esther district. She taxied around and they took off to the south, heading down the western coastline of Prince William Sound.

"We had a big hit at Fidalgo," he admitted to Lori, once they were airborne. "You should have seen the dogs pounding into that bay."

Bobby wasn't the only one hitting it big that summer. Despite all the areas closed for fishing—Cook Inlet, Kodiak, and now Esther Island—the salmon catch was on track to set a record. Fishermen were pulling in nearly 40 percent more fish compared with last year, although the dollar value promised to be much lower than the $742 million fishermen received for their catch in 1988.[2]

As the plane rose above the Sound, they could see the flotillas of barges, floating housing for the cleanup workers, and Zodiacs that skittered across the Sound. Workers wearing brightly colored gear continued to spray the rocky beaches with pressure hoses, oil boom still lined the shallow waters around the islands, and helicopters buzzed like evening gnats over the water. Tendrils of oily sheen reached into nearly every bay and around every island in the western part of the Sound. What would happen to the salmon runs in two years' time, when the next generation of pink salmon returned? Or the dog runs in four years? Despite his success in Fidalgo Bay, the uncertainty left Bobby feeling vulnerable and unable to control his own fate for the first time in his life. Lori's future as a pilot seemed somehow less uncertain than his, but he ached for her nevertheless. He doubted that the herring would ever return to Prince William Sound, which might mean an end to their working relationship.

Lori pulled the plane higher and they crested the mountains rising up from King's Bay. The high country was mostly barren except for stubby tundra bushes and sedge grasses lining the lee of the mountains and along the lake. A fiery sunset cast a bronze glow over the lake, creating a brilliant contrast against a turquoise chunk of glacier that floated at the end of the lake. They landed at the end furthest away from the ice, waded ashore, and set about building a fire and pitching the tent that Lori always kept in the tail compartment of her plane. Over a dinner of canned beans and roasted hot dogs they reveled in a peace and solitude that seemed a world away from the ever-present cacophony that accompanied the cleanup efforts.

Bobby gathered a few more twigs and small sticks to feed their campfire. A sense of uncertainty hung over them like the damp cool air of the early autumn evening settling over them. They were two people exhausted from not knowing whether the fish would show up next year, what the prices would be, and what kind of market and consumer sentiment the canneries would face. Every conversation felt infused with emotion and Bobby wondered how long he could maintain this kind of intensity in his life.

Staring into the fire, Bobby remembered the hours and days he had spent with Lori in the plane, teaching her to spot fish. The time he and his crew had gone ashore in Togiak, when the temperature dipped into the twenties, the wind howled at fifty miles an hour, and blew her tent away. She was trying to make a name for herself then, and even as Bobby and the crew offered her a warm dinner and dry clothes, she had worried about her plane. In all of the years he had known her, she had always been as positive and professional as she was on that frigid spring day. No matter the task, she had been a positive force in his life and career, always willing to put in the hours and do whatever it took to be successful. They had both worked so hard in the years since then and now they were at the top of their game.

He looked at her across the fire. "It just doesn't seem fair that we have worked so hard and sacrificed so much, to have it all be taken away like this."

She nodded. "We've tried to do our best. Not just for ourselves, but you have helped so many others in the business. It has never been just about making the biggest profits for you." Maybe it was about catching the most fish, she said grinning, but not just the bottom line.

"You're a good person Lori," Bobby said. "No matter what happens, we will both be okay. Even if we never work together to catch another fish, we will both find success."

"I can't picture you doing anything else but catching fish," she said.

"Well," he said. "I can't either right now. But who knows what life will bring?"

"How are things in Seattle?" Lori asked.

He threw another small branch into the fire, considering how best to answer her. Aside from his boats and fishing gear, all his assets and most of his cash were tied up in the forty-acre ranch north of Seattle. It felt to him as if nearly all of his personal relationships had run aground on Bligh Reef along with the *Exxon Valdez*—and he wasn't alone. Tensions altered and strained relationships from Cordova to Valdez and from Seward to Seattle—now facing similar financial pressures and an uncertain future.

"I don't know," he told her. "Nearly everything I've worked for my entire life is invested in that ranch and in my fishing operation. I'm afraid I'm going to lose everything here in Alaska because of the spill, and I just don't want to lose the ranch, too."

Lori nodded. She picked up one of the twigs they had stockpiled for the fire and began peeling it. She seemed to sense what he hadn't said, that they were both changing, becoming travelers in a place that neither of them had known before. Bobby watched her hands as she turned the stick, peeling and twisting it. He had felt certain that their friendship, the memories they shared of big herring sets, of making each other laugh over the aircraft radio, and the sense of teamwork and pride they shared in each other's work would sustain them. Yet he sensed now, in the face of so much uncertainty, that she needed some sort of commitment from him. Lori was more than a pilot—Bobby had found in her a kindred spirit with an easy laugh, and toughness tempered by a welcome feminine sensitivity. Making a commitment to her seemed the obvious thing to do, but he knew he couldn't offer it. Retreating to his ranch and leaving Alaska behind seemed an appealing escape from a new post-spill reality. But Lori belonged here and would never leave Alaska. He decided to change the subject.

"This has to be especially hard on the guys from Cordova," Bobby said.

He knew from listening to the marine radio that the dollars pouring into the Sound for the cleanup were again creating tremors along the old fault lines. Those who had worked the hardest to halt construction and later to push for more safety regulations had unfortunately been proven right, although they would have been happier to be wrong. Even though no oil had reached the shores of Orca Inlet, the fishing and canning industry that sustained Cordova was in jeopardy.

They talked about their friends from Cordova, which ones had signed contracts to work on the oil spill, and those who held out in the hopes for a decent salmon season. A new rift had emerged between those who accepted money from the oil company, and those who refused out of principle.

"Eddie and I had the *Theresa Marie* contracted for a couple of weeks, but we decided to pull her off of it to go fishing. Maybe we'll live to regret that, but goddamn it, we're fishermen, not oilmen."

Bobby paused, thinking back to bittersweet memories of living and working in Cordova. "I remember those guys in Cordova who gave their heart and soul to stop the construction of the pipeline in the first place," he said. "Mostly, they were the same guys who held out for the big money during the union strike. It seemed to me back then that their philosophical beliefs overrode all rational thinking. But now I can kind of understand. My heart really breaks for everyone in Cordova."

"Right," Lori agreed. "I guess the only thing that is certain is change."

"Yeah," Bobby said. "I remember after the earthquake, we all pulled together to move the town. There was no question about who was at fault, or who should pay damages. Nobody was busy pointing fingers. We just worked together to move on. But this is so different. This spill will tear us all apart."

"But we have to think about holding Exxon accountable," Lori said. "In a disaster like this, we simply don't have a choice."

Bobby leaned back on one elbow. "I just wonder whether we will ever be able to hold Exxon accountable for the grounding of that ship, for putting a drunk captain on the bridge—and then for the shoddy response and cleanup.

Lori considered this. "Holding them accountable is not just for our benefit. If this doesn't hurt them financially, Exxon and others will just continue to roll the dice and take their chances." "I know," Bobby said. "They have lawyers and lobbyists. What match are a bunch of independent-minded fishermen for the richest corporation in the world? You can bet they've been working on covering their ass for this spill since before the sun came up that Good Friday morning."

All that remained of the fire was a few slow-burning embers. The bronze sunset and glowing remnants of the glacier that had greeted Bobby and Lori as they landed were now shrouded in darkness. They'd sat in a comfortable silence now for a few minutes, weary of their talk of the spill and of the future. There seemed nothing left to do but crawl into their sleeping bags and welcome the stillness of the alpine night.

Exxon and the American Petroleum Institute began working to limit liability from oil spills before the first barrel of oil scuttled down the pipeline from Prudhoe Bay to Valdez in 1977. Exxon representative Don Cornett stood that same year in the Cordova High School gymnasium—just as he had faced mostly the same crowd in the days following the spill. Before tankers began plying the waters of Prince William Sound, the Cordova Fisheries Institute had convened this meeting of oil industry representatives, fisheries biologists, and state regulators to discuss the safety of oil transportation and potential liability for spills. As he stood before the crowd gathered in 1977, Cornett expressed the oil industry's frustration with a "patchwork" of state laws that created differing limits of financial liability for spills. The solution, he told the crowd, was a bill coming before Congress that would preempt all state laws and mandatory compensation funds, by creating a single federal standard.

To this the crowd gathered in the Cordova High School Gymnasium in 1977, Don Cornett explained House Resolution 3711 would create a $200 million fund to be established by a one-time, three-cent-per-barrel tax on all oil delivered to U.S. refineries. If an oil company declines to accept liability for spilled oil, citizens can turn to the fund for compensation. Liability for a single spill would be capped at $30 million.

Not everyone in the audience was convinced that Exxon's solution was best for the state of Alaska, its environment, or its citizens. Although Cornett pointed out that the oil spill fund would make money readily available to fishermen, should they ever need to file a claim, most in the crowd weren't persuaded about the benefits, including Ernst Mueller of Alaska's Department of Environmental Conservation.

As Cornett turned and took his seat, Mueller stepped to the podium to speak to his fellow Alaskans. Mueller began, "One of the promises that was made by Congress in the Trans-Alaska Pipeline Authorization Act was that the oil companies would be strictly liable without regard to fault, within certain defenses, for the damages to everybody."[3]

Mueller continued, "The point is that when the Trans-Alaska Pipeline Authorization Act was passed, the oil industry at that point was willing to make a lot of sacrifices to move the oil. People in the United States were willing to make some sacrifices because there was an energy crisis. And so we were made some promises, and one of those promises was that the Congress was not going to preempt state legislation, and strict liability from spills of oil into the environment was to be imposed, at least around Alaska. Now we see in H.R. 3711 a slow erosion of that promise, and a definite preemption of state authority.

"I think we as Alaskans have to stand up and say, 'Hey, this is what was said when you guys wanted to build this damned pipeline, and now that it's almost over and you're running oil through it, you're starting to back down.' I think that what happened here is that the oil industry went back to Congress and is pressuring them to renege on those promises. That is exactly what the gentleman from Exxon stated; the industry is now strongly supporting preemption of state authorities."[4]

Mueller paused to survey the crowd. He went on to argue, "I think that those of us who work with Alaska courts, particularly now with some of the recent insurance cases, know that our courts are going to be a hell of a lot more sympathetic on balance to the interests of the fishermen than they are to the interests of an oil company. By contrast, a federal judge may not be so sympathetic. While surely there are administrative processes that could expedite settlements, when it comes down to the nitty gritty, the oil industry lawyers are on retainers, and they're all willing to spend the extra time to drag the issue out in courts. Once it gets into the courts, I think you can see very easily that it could go on for years, until such a point at which the court costs involved may exceed any potential claims. So, what we're concerned about here is that the state retain jurisdiction over this matter, especially in the matter in which you are most closely involved, and that is to be able to go to your judge and your lawyer down here in the nearest State Superior Court and attack the polluter.

"The other issue I think that involves us is that the renewable resources impacted by oil development here in Alaska, are uniquely state resources, they belong to us, they're fishermen's fish and the people of Alaska's fish. They do not necessarily represent the proprietary interests of the remainder of the United States. So we feel that we are uniquely qualified to protect those resources. Sure, we need some general backup, help, and assistance from the federal government, particularly from administrative agencies like the Coast Guard; but we feel that since we are the ones who suffer the loss, we're the ones who should make the fundamental strong decisions on environmental protection systems."[5]

The concerns Mueller raised, particularly about state's rights, would ultimately doom House Bill 3711 and plague further attempts by Congress to preempt state regulatory authority to hold oil companies liable for spills. In fact, the issue remained yet unresolved the day the *Exxon Valdez* ran aground on Bligh Reef—nineteen years after it had first been introduced before Congress.

However, in the wake of the spill, the U.S. Senate passed a bill to strengthen federal oil spill liability and compensation laws and toughen requirements on tanker operators, with provisions specific to Prince William Sound. The bill would preserve the rights of Alaska, Washington State, and sixteen other states to maintain unlimited liability for spills in their waters. However, Alaska Senator Ted Stevens feared it would be "tough sailing" in the House, which preferred to preempt state's rights on the issue of liability.[6] Although the Senate bill passed in early August by a 99-0 vote, it would be another year before the issue could be agreed upon and resolved as part of the Oil Pollution Act of 1990.

As concern over the *Exxon Valdez* oil spill echoed in the chambers of Congress in the summer of 1989, the Anchorage District Court was inundated with lawsuits. On August 15, 1989, following five months of investigation, the state of Alaska filed a forty-two-page suit, charging that Exxon and Alyeska Pipeline Service had grossly misled the public about their ability to safely move oil. From the beginning of the pipeline planning in the early 1970s, the suit said, the public had relied on oil industry assurances that concern for the environment would be of paramount importance to their operations.

As the trustee for all Alaskans, the state's suit sought damages for environmental, economic, and social damages resulting from the worst tanker accident in U.S. history. Announcing the suit, the state oil spill coordinator, Robert LeResche, predicted a final judgment in the "multi-billions" of dollars.[7]

The suit sought compensation for emotional distress of its citizens "from having witnessed the destruction of the environment in which they live and work and having their livelihoods threatened and their personal and family lives disrupted." It also sought further monetary damages for the "intentional and negligent" actions leading up to and following the spill.

Finally, the suit alleged that the "defendants' inability to respond to the oil spill was due in large part to defendants' conscious, deliberate, negligent and reckless decisions to save money by reducing manpower, training, equipment and maintenance of equipment below those levels which defendants knew, or should have known, were necessary to respond to a major oil spill."[8]

As the state filed their suit, Exxon attorneys responded to over 140 lawsuits filed with the Anchorage District Court and state and federal courthouses throughout south-central Alaska. Exxon attorneys essentially argued that the plaintiffs deserved no compensation. The *Anchorage Daily News* described the following six themes consistent in Exxon's responses:

- Claims for lost earnings, such as by fishermen or cannery workers, should be offset by money that workers earned by participating in the spill cleanup.
- Other parties share in the blame for what happened, and they should also be held liable.
- Tort reform measures passed by the state legislature should limit Exxon's payments.
- A punitive damage award in one case should bar similar awards in others.
- Exxon conducted the cleanup under direction of government officials and shouldn't be held responsible for their decisions and priorities.
- Maritime law strictly limits payment of damages to those who can prove direct physical injury to property.[9]

Exxon attorneys said they hoped claims could be settled promptly to avoid costly and protracted litigation. However, Exxon attorney Dick Clinton promised, "If people want to litigate, we'll have to litigate and use all the vehicles we have."[10] As the chill of early fall began to settle over Alaska, the legal battles were just beginning to heat up.

15

Deception

CAPITOL HILL: NOVEMBER 4, 1991

I N ROOM 2226 OF THE RAYBURN HOUSE Office Building, Congressman
George Miller rapped his gavel to convene a hearing before
the Committee on Interior and Insular Affairs. The hearing began
promptly as scheduled at 9:45 a.m.. The purpose of the hearing, Chairman Miller informed the committee and members of the audience,
would be to learn more about a covert operation authorized by Alyeska Pipeline Company. Testimony would be heard regarding allegations that the Wackenhut Company, one of the nation's largest private
security firms, conducted undercover surveillance of former independent oil broker and environmental activist, Charles Hamel, and others
on behalf of Alyeska and its owner companies.

"Charles Hamel," Miller explained, "has been a source of information for Congress, State, and Federal regulatory agencies, and
the media, concerning environmental, health, and safety violations
by Alyeska and its oil company owners. Mr. Hamel has served as a
conduit for whistleblowers, including Alyeska employees, to make
public information on oil industry practices. At the same time, Mr.
Hamel has at least two significant business disputes with Alyeska and
Exxon."[1]

That Alyeska and its owner companies had attempted to discredit,
humiliate, harass, or fire whistleblowers surely came as no surprise
to many Alaskans. Since the *Exxon Valdez* oil spill over two years earlier, headlines about the oil industry, regulatory activities, and political posturing regularly commanded above-the-fold headlines. Just
months after the spill, on August 3, 1989, the front page of the *Anchorage Daily News* announced that Dan Lawn, the state's chief environmental watchdog, had been transferred to the Anchorage DEC office.
Lawn believed he had been demoted for blowing the whistle on Alyeska, particularly during the cleanup operations, and he suspected

that his presence in the Valdez office made access by reporters and politicians a little too convenient for Alyeska and Exxon's taste. In his new capacity reviewing oil spill contingency plans, Lawn would no longer oversee Alyeska operations or the cleanup efforts.

Larry Dietrick, Lawn's supervisor at DEC, assured Lawn and the press that it was not a demotion, but rather the agency's effort to fill a much-needed position with someone who possessed his experience and expertise. But when the *Anchorage Daily News* filed a public records request to obtain a copy of a memo from Larry Dietrick regarding Lawn's transfer, they found Lawn described as "unobjective" and "difficult to work with." These terms, Lawn said, were often applied to whistleblowers. Critics of the move by DEC suggested the agency was simply caving in to pressure from Alyeska and Exxon.

Despite the ongoing media attention on whistleblowers, few Alaskans could have imagined the chain of events that ultimately required Alyeska, its owner companies, and the Wackenhut Company to testify before a Congressional Committee for allegedly carrying out an illegal spying operation. In addition to Chuck Hamel, objects of the illegal covert activity allegedly included Dan Lawn, Riki Ott, Alyeska employees, the owner of a Valdez-based tour boat company, a Valdez bartender, and even a member of Congress.

Working through a phony environmental organization known as Ecolit (a combination of the words ecology and litigation), Wackenhut operatives sought to find the source of information leaks inside Alyeska. Over the past decade, leaked evidence confirming environmental wrongdoings, such as deficiencies in the ballast water treatment plant and illegal pollution of the Valdez airshed, had incurred significant costs for Alyeska and its owner companies—both in terms of dollars and public trust. But when a confidential internal memo regarding the *Exxon Valdez* cleanup appeared in the media, it prompted Alyeska to spend an alleged $1,000,000 to stop the flow of information from whistleblowers within the company to the media, regulators, and members of Congress.

It apparently began with an attractive woman flirting with Chuck Hamel and Rick Steiner in the Fletcher Bar of the Captain Cook Hotel in Anchorage in March of 1990—nearly a year after the oil spill. She struck up a conversation with the two men, well-known critics of the oil industry, as they were discussing the *Exxon Valdez* oil spill and the current state of Prince William Sound.

The woman introduced herself as a journalist from Ecolit, an environmental organization in Florida, suggesting she was in town to attend the "Frontier Thinking" conference on business and the environment. She wanted to learn more about the environmental impacts of the spill, she said, but her approach seemed to suggest to them another kind of interest. It wasn't long before the two men left to continue their conversation elsewhere.

Hamel noticed the same woman sitting in the seat just behind him on the plane to the east coast the following day. Her name was Ricki Jacobson, though she used an alias. She and Hamel began talking, and she told him that she was a single mother, looking to start a new career though she had not fared well at the conference. She told Hamel that she hadn't had much luck getting to know others at the conference because nobody had heard of the environmental firm "Ecolit." Perhaps Hamel would agree to share some of his documents related to operations at the Alyeska terminal and during the *Exxon Valdez* cleanup, Jacobson suggested. He promised at least to grant her an interview when he returned home to Virginia, but he never received a call from her.

The following month, Hamel received a letter from Wayne Jenkins, PhD, (who was actually Wayne Black). Jenkins described himself as Ecolit's research director and he sent along a brochure about the firm. Jenkins said the firm was interested in exposing wrongdoings by Alyeska. They would be willing to fund some of Hamel's efforts in exchange for his documentation. Hamel called his friend Rick Steiner, enthused about the opportunity and convinced that the firm seemed legitimate.

What happened next was later revealed by investigators employed by Wackenhut who came to believe the actions they were directed to take in the investigation were at best ethically questionable, and at worst illegal. Wackenhut investigators said they recorded Hamel's conversations "in his home and at the office of the Ecolit Group, a phony environmental organization set up for the sting. They wooed him with cash for his expenses, stole his garbage, took documents from his house and tricked him out of others. They listened in on his telephone conversations, they said, and surreptitiously got records of his long-distance calls."[2]

The details of this deception might never have been revealed were it not for Ann Contraras, Sherrie Rich, Gus Castillo, and others within Wackenhut who blew the whistle on its investigative practices. Their story spilled into public view on the front page of the *Anchorage Daily News* on September 1, 1991. The article, along with hundreds of other news sources, memoranda, phone records, and tape recordings, was introduced into evidence for the Congressional committee now gathered on Capitol Hill.

After opening the floor to statements by his colleagues on the Committee on Interior and Insular Affairs, Congressman Miller called the first witness, Mr. Wayne Black, Vice President, Investigations, The Wackenhut Company, Coral Gables, Florida.

Black was sworn in and advised of his rights before the committee, and asked if he wished to be represented by counsel.

Black replied that he wished to be represented by Jon Sale. Sale went to work immediately, requesting that all cameras and recording devices be turned off immediately. Congressman Miller agreed that was the right of the witness, and requested that all cameras and recording devices be turned off. Sale then requested the committee go into executive session and that Black's testimony be excluded from the public record.

Based on the roll call vote, questioning of Mr. Black would proceed in executive session, without members of the audience present, or a public record. The open hearing reconvened the following morning at 9:45 a.m. sharp.

The CEO and founder of the Wackenhut Corporation was called as the first witness on the morning of November 5. A former member of the FBI, George Wackenhut had started the company in 1954. Mr. Wackenhut assured the members of the committee that at no time had his company investigated Congressman Miller or other members of Congress. Alyeska was a regular client of the Wackenhut Corporation, which provided security services for the terminal and pipeline. He told the members of the committee that out of Wackenhut's annual revenues of $560 million, the Alyeska account brought in between $15 and $16 million. Mr. Wackenhut had no information about how much the covert investigation had cost Alyeska, no knowledge of the contract, and was uncertain as to whether his company had separate contracts with any of Alyeska's owner companies.

During the question-and-answer period, Congressman Harry Johnston, Democrat from Florida asked, "You were given a charge by Alyeska to find the leaks. Did you find any?"

Mr. Wackenhut responded, "Yes sir."

When asked the source of those leaks, Wackenhut responded that his company had identified several employees who had been supplying Chuck Hamel with information. Other members of the Committee inquired about the nature of the documents that were provided to Hamel or others outside Alyeska.

When asked, Wackenhut described the documents as "stolen" and potentially valuable to competitors. Wackenhut assured the members of the Committee, "It was just a total leak. A flood of information coming out of the bowels of the company and they wanted it stopped, naturally."

Later in the day, the committee heard from James Hermiller, president of Alyeska Pipeline Service Company. In his remarks to the committee, Hermiller explained, "I became president of Alyeska shortly after the *Exxon Valdez* spill. Public confidence in the large oil companies and in Alyeska was low. I considered it a top priority to do everything in my power to restore that public confidence.

"I took aggressive steps to deal with the aftermath of the Valdez spill, including the development of a spill prevention-response plan in Prince William Sound which I consider to be the finest such plans in the world. I believe I have been open and attentive to the concerns of all Alaskans, and that I have been successful in demonstrating to them that Alyeska shares their determination to protect and preserve our environment."

The Valdez spill gave rise to an extraordinary amount of litigation. Alyeska and the other oil companies found themselves defending literally dozens of lawsuits. In the course of deciding how to deal with these lawsuits, Alyeska—like any other defendant in litigation—consulted with legal counsel. Among those counsel were lawyers from the Los Angeles law firm Gibson, Dunn & Crutcher. Those consultations with counsel were, of course, highly privileged and confidential.

"To my great distress, and to the distress of the owners of Alyeska, we learned at the beginning of 1990 that certain legal documents containing our confidential communications with our counsel in the Valdez litigation had been stolen or leaked. One such document was actually shown on a British television program called the *Scottish Eye*. The owners of Alyeska and I viewed the unauthorized dissemination of these highly confidential documents as intolerable. The theft or leaking of these documents...led me to conclude these steps should be taken to determine who was stealing or leaking the documents from Alyeska."[3]

Mr. Hermiller explained the details of securing the services of the Wackenhut Corporation for the investigation which began in March of 1990. "At all times," Hermiller assured the committee, "it was my intention that the investigation proceed in strict compliance with the law."[4]

Throughout the course of the hearing, it became clear that the investigation extended far beyond Alyeska employees or Chuck Hamel. In a February 23, 1990, memo to Wayne Black, Alyeska's Manager of Corporate Security, Pat Wellington included a copy of an article about Riki Ott. Wellington wrote, "This girl had been a real pain in the ___. She is very active in all Alyeska issues... I think she is also receiving inside information."[5]

Other evidence submitted for the record included a May 1990 memo from Wayne Black to Pat Wellington, diagramming a web of interactions between Chuck Hamel, Alyeska employees including Bob Scott, Riki Ott, Dan Lawn and other DEC employees and Congressman George Miller.[6] Yet representatives from Wackenhut and Alyeska adamantly denied that the investigation had extended to Congressman Miller. As James Hermiller, president of Alyeska, drew his remarks to a close, he explained the abrupt end of the covert operation. "On September 25, 1990," he said, "I met with representatives of several Alyeska Owner Companies in Denver to discuss these options (which legal counsel had presented, including a possible civil lawsuit against Hamel). After discussion, the owners directed that the investigation be halted...I complied at once with the owners' instructions... In retrospect, while the Wackenhut investigation was legal, its implementation may not have been wise. It is not enough for Alyeska to operate within the law. The company must also operate within the limits of a public consensus about the conduct of large corporations. It is now clear that the damages to Alyeska's reputation in Alaska and in Congress outweighs the benefits that have resulted from the investigation."[7]

The following day, William Rusnack of ARCO confirmed the directive to end the investigation. Furthermore, he said, the owners requested a review of the investigation by a special independent counsel to determine "whether the results of the investigation required notification to any public official or other person, or the taking of some further action."[8] However, Mr. Rusnack reminded the committee that "the investigation disclosed that one person had in his possession over 20 privileged documents that had been prepared by Alyeska's lawyers in connection with the defense of Alyeska in over 100 lawsuits stemming from the *Exxon Valdez* oil spill. No organization, in my view, can operate without procedures to ensure that its privileged and proprietary information will remain privileged and proprietary."[9]

"Before closing," the ARCO representative continued, "I would like to emphasize that Alyeska's management encourages employees to freely express concerns they may have about workplace safety and environmental compliance. If an employee believes Alyeska is doing something wrong, something in violation of the law, we want to know about it."[10]

In his testimony, Darrel Warner, representing Exxon, added that the owners directed Alyeska not to use the evidence gathered in the course of the investigation to take action against its employees, or for any other purpose. Warner insisted he had no knowledge of the investigation until the September 25, 1990, owner's meeting, although questioning of Warner later suggested that the investigation had been authorized by Exxon's legal counsel.[11] Fred Garibaldi, representing BP America, concurred with the others, reminding members of Congress that it was proper and necessary for Alyeska to take action to stop the improper dissemination of information. "However," Garibaldi concluded, "I did not agree with the methods employed. Based upon my 30-plus years of experience with Standard Oil and now BP, this is not the way we do business."[12] On the last afternoon of the three-day hearing, committee members heard from Chuck Hamel. He began by telling members of Congress about his background, which included serving as executive assistant to Senator Mike Gravel. "Among my duties as his assistant," Hamel said, "I worked relentlessly to convince Alaska residents, commercial fishermen, Natives and the public that the oil industry would be good for Alaska."[13] He then explained the course of events that brought him before the committee. He began with a business-deal-gone-bad between himself, as an independent oil broker, and Exxon.

Hamel began by staying that his investigation of Alyeska began in 1985. He was concerned that the oil contained high water levels, and apparently suffered financial losses as a result. "By this time, I had also come to the conclusion that the oil industry was turning Alaska into an environmental disaster. Employees I talked to in Valdez, friends I knew in the industry, people I had worked with for years, were all discussing the dismal performance of Alyeska in regards to their commitment to environmental and worker safety.

"I realized that I was not the only victim of dishonesty of the oil industry in Alaska. We were all victims, and no one was doing anything about it."

Hamel said he feared that Alaskans were waiting in silence for an environmental disaster, and he decided to speak out. "The more I learned, Hamel said, "the angrier I got about what was going on. Alyeska was polluting the water by introducing toxic sludge, including cancer-causing benzene, into the pristine waters of Port Valdez and Prince William Sound.

"Alyeska was poisoning the Valdez fjord's air by venting extremely hazardous hydrocarbon vapors directly into the atmosphere. There was no regulatory oversight, and thus no regulatory violations. It was [as] if the environmental regulations of the United States did not even apply north of the Canadian Border—no regulators, no oversight, no enforcement, nothing..."[14]

Hamel described some of the evidence he had gathered against Alyeska, and who had helped him. "Bob Scott was one of the first of many employees that provided me information about violations of environmental regulations by Alyeska. As I learned of these abuses, I in turn provided the information to the appropriate Government agencies responsible for investigating these matters, including EPA, the

General Accounting Office, and the Alaska Department of Environmental Conservation, the Attorney General of the United States, and the Director of the GAO.

"In the beginning, it was very difficult to get any Government action on the employees' allegations. I then turned the information over to the press, and sometimes to Members of Congress.

"There was a profound skepticism everywhere that the oil industry would knowingly pollute the environment and harm their own employees in Alaska.

"The Alyeska public relations campaign was working. Few newspapers would print the facts. Few regulators would even listen. Alyeska tried hard to discredit me by attacking my motives, my sources of information, my credibility, and attempted to portray me as a vengeful, if not slightly insane, opponent of the oil industry.

"But their 'kill the messenger' approach backfired. It seemed that the harder Alyeska tried to discredit me publicly, the more their employees came to me with information privately. In fact, frequently the public denial of facts, known to be true to Alyeska employees, led those employees to my doorstep.

Rather than just addressing the allegations and resolving them, Hamel said, Alyeska had resisted compliance through litigation. "Alyeska had to be dragged, kicking and screaming, through each corrective action. However, it was apparent to the fishing community leaders like Riki Ott and Rick Steiner of Cordova, my loyal supporters throughout the years, that a major disaster was eminent."

Then the *Exxon Valdez* oil spill happened, he said, and everything changed. "The allegations I had been pointing out to the EPA for years to no avail were suddenly 'high priority,' and even the public began to doubt the public relations departments of the oil industry.

"The day after the spill, leaders of the fishing community and the fish processors telephoned for my help. I immediately flew to Valdez to do what I could.

"In addition to helping the fishermen, I assisted this committee and its majority and minority staff and counsel with housing and support services during their outside investigation, and also provided a network of information to members of the media who were attempting to provide accurate coverage."

Hamel then went on to explain to the committee how he had become involved with the firm Ecolit, which was specifically set up to deceive him. He'd been relieved to find what appeared to be a well-funded and well-intentioned group of attorneys who could protect whistleblowers and conduct investigations. Hamel admitted to the committee, "I thought it was too good to be true."[15]

He continued, outlining the tactics of the secret investigation and its consequences.

"Bob Scott was fired.

"He lost his home.

"And he lost his retirement."

Others lost their jobs too, he said.

"Today, I am simply saddened and disgusted but, in a strange way, grateful and relieved that this entire incident has come to light because it demonstrates better than I could ever do that Alyeska and its owners cannot be trusted.

"The last ten years of my life have been spent trying to warn the public that Alyeska and Exxon cannot be trusted with our natural resources." Hamel told the committee that the Alyeska and other members of the consortium appeared to operate based on a belief that profitability depends on cutting corners on environmental protection. "I refuse to believe that fallacy..." Hamel said. "I refuse to believe that the only way to advocate for a clean environment and regulatory compliance is to take a vow of poverty and join a not-for-profit environmental organization."

In closing, Hamel acknowledged the honesty and courage of the Wackenhut investigators who, he said, "came forward and told the truth... The Nation and Alaska are better because of the integrity of these people."

"Each of these employees, Hamel said, "like the many Alyeska employees who took similar risks to bring forward the truth about Exxon and Alyeska's activities, have more integrity than the oil industry could ever buy, and more courage than Alyeska could ever defeat. Thank you for giving me the opportunity to testify."[16]

16

The Voice of the Sound
PORT ETCHES: NOVEMBER 1991

THE SONAR PINGED IN THE OTHERWISE DARK and silent wheelhouse of the *Theresa Marie*. Bobby glanced up at Walt and Gloria, and his brother Pat, their faces cast in the soft bluish glow of the sonar's screen. "Looks like there's nobody home," he told his family. "This is really unreal. The fish used to ball up here and there would be nothing but solid herring for five miles."

The waters were deep here just south of Bligh Reef. In the darkness brightened only by a crescent moon, they could just make out the gently rounded coastline of Knowles Head, dwarfed against the dramatic rise of the Chugach Range behind it. It was late October and the Chugachs glowed under the season's first dusting of snow. More than two years had passed since a row of tankers anchored here, awaiting the reopening of Port Valdez to marine traffic after the grounding of the *Exxon Valdez*.

"Maybe they're further south, down by Red Head," Walter suggested.

"Could be," Bobby said, turning the captain's wheel. "Let's go see." The seventy-foot Delta cut easily through the gentle waves. The night was crisp and still, the Sound calm.

As the Cat diesel engine propelled them southward, none of them wanted to say what seemed obvious. That perhaps the herring were gone and that things had changed as a result of the oil spill. Because there were both local stocks of herring that never leave the Sound, and herring that live most of their life in the Pacific and return only to spawn, perhaps some had survived.

But the oil that covered the surface of the Sound two years earlier had darkened the waters as though it was nighttime, prompting the schools of herring to come to the surface—and to their death. The herring had returned from the Pacific just as oil coated the kelp and shoals where they traditionally spawn. Because they return to spawn at three to four years of age, it was too soon to tell yet whether the spring roe herring fishery would be affected. But it would soon be crystal clear that the fall bait herring fishery would close, perhaps forever.

Bobby kept a close eye on the sonar screen, but his instincts told him that the Sound had not healed from the enormous spill even though the waters now appeared mostly clear and clean. Earlier that summer, DEC had declared an end to the cleanup. The state's on-scene coordinator Ernie Piper announced, "It's over, although I've been wary of saying we or anybody else can declare victory over the oil spill."[1] At the same time, DEC also acknowledged that the coming years "may result in oil resurfacing at places such as Herring Bay, northern Latouche Island, Knight Island, and Green Island."[2]

Only days ago, the *Anchorage Daily News* announced that the state of Alaska had settled its lawsuit against Exxon. Governor Walter Hickel celebrated the billion dollar settlement, which would fund restoration projects in the Sound. Having served as Alaska's second governor before resigning to serve as Richard Nixon's Secretary of the Interior, Hickel was now back in office as the state's eighth governor. "We are whole again," Hickel declared. "For the last two and a half years we have been divided."[3]

The settlement agreement was approved in Federal District Court on October 8, 1991. As he faced reporters, lawyers, environmentalists, and Exxon CEO Lawrence Rawl in his courtroom, Judge Russel Holland suggested that Exxon should be given credit for the $2.5 billion it had spent to clean up the spill. "What is now very clear to me is that Exxon has been a good corporate citizen," Holland said. "It is sensitive to its environmental obligations."[4] According to the agreement, Exxon and its shipping subsidiary would pay $125 million in fines and plead guilty to four misdemeanors. The company would pay $900 million over a ten-year period for the preservation and restoration of Prince William Sound. If environmental damage proved worse than predicted, the state could re-open the agreement and claim up to an additional $100 million before 2006.

Environmentalists criticized the outcome, arguing that the billion-dollar settlement would neither serve as a deterrent for future spills, nor restore what had been lost in the Sound. Congressman

George Miller said, "This is a continuation of checkbook justice." As chair of the House Interior Committee, and later allegedly a target in the Wackenhut investigation, he'd become quite familiar with the causes and consequences of the spill. Miller declared, "Exxon has bought its way out of one of the worst environmental insults in this country's history."[5]

But Alaska's Attorney General Charlie Cole reminded critics that Exxon had filed a countersuit. Exxon's suit claimed that the state of Alaska should pay for damage resulting from the oil spill because DEC would not agree to the use of dispersants in the hours and days following the spill.[6] Cole said, "It is not inconceivable the state could face a judgment requiring it to pay certainly in the tens, if not the hundreds, of millions from the state treasury. That is a risk that responsible public officers, the governor and the attorney general, must consider."[7] The agreement foreclosed the state's liability by settling Exxon's countersuit.

Sitting before Holland, Lawrence Rawl assured the judge that the oil business was far too competitive to pass on the criminal fines to its customers. The leader of one of the world's largest corporations, Rawl leaned forward on his elbows as Judge Holland acknowledged the economic harm inflicted on Exxon by the spill. "There is no question," Rawl responded quietly, "I am sure we've regretted this spill very much."

As the *Theresa Marie* cut through the waters of the Sound, the sonar screen remained devoid of the yellow and red formations that should have hinted at the presence of fish. To an untrained eye, it could be difficult to distinguish the shapes and shades of underwater formations from a thick school of fish. But Bobby had spent hours memorizing how the bottom of the Sound looked on the sonar, where the reefs and mud-banks were that could fool a fisherman into setting his net on a phantom school. As they made their way toward Red Head, there was simply no sign of life.

"You know," Bobby said, "It is really eerie that the herring are simply gone. But it is more than just the herring. I can't put my finger on it, but the Sound is just not right."

"I agree," Walter admitted. "When your mom and I make our halibut trips, I've noticed it seems quieter now, like there aren't as many birds. You hardly ever see ducks or cormorants diving for fish anymore. And you hardly ever see an otter."

"You're right," Bobby said. "The year I had the *Theresa Marie* built, we caught thousands of pounds of king crab in the Sound. I've hauled around a crab pot all the years I've been fishing just to catch some for dinner. We've always been able to get a few at Snug Harbor, or Bay of Isles, or Montague Straits. But we haven't caught a one since the spill."

"What about prawns?" Gloria asked.

"There are still a few spot prawns left," Bobby said. "I can still find them up behind the reef in Unakwik Inlet and a few other places that were protected from the oil."

"Actually, everything just feels different," Bobby said. "There are lots of big, fast boats in the fishing fleet now. Guys from Cordova and Cook Inlet got big money for working on the spill and they turned around and bought boats that they could never have afforded otherwise. Now the fleet is totally over-capitalized and we don't even know if there will be fish to sustain it."

"You know," Walter said, "instead of paying people to contract their boats, Exxon could have paid off the debt for the salmon hatcheries. Since we don't yet know what the effect will be on the natural runs, they could have at least made sure the hatcheries were sustainable in the future."

"I'll tell you, I think a lot of things are different in town,," Gloria said. "Who knows whether the Sound will fully recover, or how long it might take. But I can tell you I worry that people in town may never be the same."

"How so?" Bobby asked.

Walt and Gloria traded glances. Pat's gaze remained fixed on the rounded rise of Red Head as it grew nearer out the port side window. It was hard to describe to someone who no longer lived in town. How could they explain the social impacts of the oil spill, the allegations of environmental wrong-doing by Alyeska, and espionage on private citizens, oil terminal workers, government officials, and even a member of Congress? How could they describe the fissures of silence that developed between friends and neighbors, and even among families? Nearly every person in town had a close friend or family member who worked for Alyeska. And virtually everyone in Valdez benefited at least indirectly from the economy it generated in town. Criticizing the oil industry or Alyeska simply made others uncomfortable.

The wheelhouse grew quiet but for the steady thump-thump of the Cat engine. A rogue gust of wind blew down from the Chugachs and rattled the wheelhouse windows. To their left, the coastline gave way in a sharp turn to the east as it opened up into Port Gravina. Gravina had been protected from the oil spill by the counter-clockwise currents, as had Orca Bay just to the east. Directly ahead lay Hinchinbrook Island and Port Etches, a protected cove on the western side of the island. At a cruising speed of about ten knots, they'd be anchored in Port Etches within the hour.

It wasn't unusual in the late fall for stillness to suddenly give rise to gusts, then to high sustained winds. With the passage of the equinox, the calm of a crisp evening could become a wintry gale within the blink of an eye. Just as the *Theresa Marie* left the relative protection of the coastline to cross more open waters of the Sound on the way to Hinchinbrook, whitecaps began to splash against her hull and the anemometer reported winds of sixty miles per hour.

"At least we can call the response vessel stationed at Port Etches if we get in trouble," Bobby joked.

"Right," Pat teased back. "I doubt they'd pull anchor for a rogue vessel like this."

The tug escorts and response vessels now stationed around the Sound represented a new effort by Alyeska to help tankers safely traverse the seventy miles from Port Valdez to the Gulf of Alaska. The Ship Escort Response Vessel System (SERVS) was established on July 10, 1989, four months after the *Exxon Valdez* oil spill. SERVS maintained equipment and response vessels at hatcheries and other sensitive areas such as Lake Bay, Cannery Creek, Solomon Gulch, Main Bay, Sawmill Bay, Valdez Duck Flats, Naked Island, Port Etches, Chenega Bay, and the Native village of Tatitlek. In addition to escort tugs, response vessels and skimmers, SERVS contracted with hundreds of fishing vessels, training and equipping their captains to respond to a potential spill.

"C'mon," Bobby said. "Doesn't having a nephew on the crew of a response vessel buy a guy anything?"

Pat's son, Mike, started working for SERVS in the winter of 1990. Before that, he'd fished salmon and herring with Bobby and his dad. Mike was stationed now at Port Etches on the response vessel *Constitution* and they had planned to pick him up on the *Theresa Marie* and take him deer hunting on Hinchinbrook Island tomorrow during his off hours.

The wind howled against the wheelhouse windows and the boat rose and fell on swells that were increasing in height and intensity. Pat made his way down to the galley and came back with four mugs of coffee, steaming in the enclosed wheelhouse that had become noticeably chilled. Pat glanced down at the radar screen which indicated that the *Theresa Marie* was closing in on Hinchinbrook Island.

"With wind like this," Pat said, "we'll be lucky if we don't drag our anchor tonight."

"I think you're right," Bobby agreed. "Port Etches will give us a little protection, but not enough. There's a buoy that tugs and barges use to anchor up in bad weather. We'll tie off on that."

The following morning dawned gray with low clouds brought in by the previous night's wind. A light drizzle dampened the deck of the boat and the marine air felt thick. Bobby and Pat lowered the skiff into the water and set off across the bay to where the *Constitution* was anchored. Once they had Mike aboard, Pat guided the skiff toward a gravelly beach—one of the few points of access in Port Etches, which was otherwise surrounded by sheer rocky cliffs.

By nightfall the smell of fresh deer liver and onions simmering on the gas stove filled the galley. The warm and hearty aroma was especially enticing after a chilly day in the woods. Walt, Gloria, Pat, and Mike gathered around the table in the galley, warming their hands on mugs of coffee while Bobby sliced potatoes for frying, and fresh tomatoes for an appetizer. He listened absently as they chatted, thinking back to a time when he'd caught boatloads of salmon in the protected waters of Port Etches.

It was 1971, the same year the *Donna R* sunk. He had leased a small wooden boat from a fisherman in Cordova as a replacement. *The Vi* leaked from the roof of the cabin and water slowly seeped through the floorboards, requiring the crew to take regular watches to keep the water pumped out. The summer of 1971 had delivered wind and rain that lasted for weeks, but he'd found refuge—and a great deal of salmon—here at Port Etches.

Now twenty years later, he found himself thinking of leaving the Sound, never to return. The rock cliffs of the islands in the western Sound were still stained dark with streaks of crude oil where the surf had carried it in the violent windstorm that followed the spill. If the light was just right, you could still see an occasional sheen of crude oil in bays along the western side of Prince William Sound. Bobby picked up a wooden spoon and stirred the liver and onions, then threw the potatoes into a cast iron skillet now bubbling with butter and olive oil. As he shook pepper and garlic salt over the potatoes, he wondered how many more times he would make a meal on the *Theresa Marie*. He'd built her specifically for the bait herring fishery that he suspected would soon cease to exist. The boat was worth a million dollars the day they put her in the Duwamish River at Delta Marine in south Seattle. That was only six years before the oil spill. Now he'd be lucky if he could sell her for half that amount. The bottom had fallen out of the market for seine boats, tenders, and Prince William Sound fishing permits after the spill and they remained low. Fishermen joked now that a highliner was no longer the guy who caught the most fish—it was the guy whose wife had the best job at the Alyeska terminal.

His thoughts turned to his nephew Mike, one of the smartest people he'd ever known, steady and calm with a strong work ethic and a dry sense of humor. One of the best hands ever on a seine boat, Mike would now be the first in three generations of Days to leave the fishing industry. Bobby had probably worked with a hundred crewmembers throughout his career, but there were a few that would always have a place in his heart. Mike Day would be one of them, nephew or not. Others he'd worked with over the years, including Pat and Eddie, now had their own boats and he felt proud that he'd had some influence on their ability to work, to fish, and to succeed in a tough business. Like Dale Dawson, most of them were family in spirit if not blood. If he lost Day Fisheries Incorporated and all of its assets, it would be more than the loss of a career or business. It would feel like losing his family and his sense of place in this world.

The galley windows had steamed over with the warmth of cooking, conversation, and damp canvas overcoats drying on the wall pegs. Outside the clouds grew darker as nighttime set in. Bobby dished up the plates he had warming in the oven. Liver, onions, and potatoes steamed as he set them on the galley table. Then he slid into the booth-style bench next to his mom.

"Hey Mike," he said, "were you with me on the *Theresa Marie* the time we were heading out to go bait seining, and Stan Stephens stopped and gave us all his leftover groceries?"

Mike nodded. "Yup," he said, grinning. "I remember Stan bringing all the tourists on the *Glacier Spirit* over to watch us make a set. You put on a real show for them."

"How is Stan's business doing?" Bobby asked. "The fishermen and processors will get compensated for whatever we lose. But what about the tourists? Are they still coming to Valdez?"

"I think his business is picking up," Pat said. "The first year was pretty tough. After the spill, he ferried Exxon people back and forth between Valdez and Bligh Reef on the *Glacier Spirit*. But that was mostly over within a few weeks. Then he had a contract to watch the *Exxon Valdez* when it was anchored up in Outside Bay for repairs before they towed it south."

"Right," Gloria added. "He went to California and bought the *Nautilis* that year, then leased it to DEC for a while. You know, he really took the spill pretty hard. I think he feels like a lot of us, that the regulators and politicians weren't listening to the citizens who were concerned about a spill."

In fact, the city of Valdez had been precluded from initiating greater control over the terminal and tanker operations. The city had assessed an extra property tax of three mills on the Alyeska terminal (equivalent to 0.3 percent of the terminal's assessed value) to fund the purchase of city-owned oil spill containment equipment.

By 1989, the town of Valdez had $26 million set aside to purchase equipment. But the state of Alaska challenged the tax in court and ultimately determined that the city couldn't tax the terminal at a rate higher than other tax-payers. The litigation was pending in the courts in 1989 when the *Exxon Valdez* ran aground on Bligh Reef.

"You know, Stan was the one chairing the meeting that night in the city council chambers," Gloria reminded them. "Since then, he has spent a lot of time trying to put together the new citizen's council."

Walter added, "I think a lot of us feel like we should have paid more attention to the oil companies and the government before the spill happened. Some of us worried about a spill happening, and whether it could be cleaned up, but we never sat down and studied the documents." The new council would make reviewing the specifics of spill prevention and contingency plans its primary goal.

The Regional Citizens Advisory Council (RCAC) began to take shape in the days and weeks following the spill. Stan Stephens, Riki Ott, Mayor John Devens and others who had been outspoken about the possibility of a spill recognized that citizens with the most to lose had no formal voice in determining cleanup priorities or techniques. They had no formal seat at the table to express local priorities or concerns about the use of dispersants, the importance of the hatcheries, or other sensitive areas. Instead, Alyeska, Exxon, the Coast Guard and DEC made decisions largely uninformed by Native and fishermen's knowledge of the Sound's tides, wind patterns, wildlife, and fish.

Even as they worked to ensure their voices were at least present in the town hall meeting held at the Civic Center in the weeks following the spill, they met with Senator Frank Murkowski, and along with several Cordova fishermen, testified before Congress. Stephens, Ott, Dan Lawn, and Devens again approached Alyeska about participating on a citizens' council. This time, just two months after the spill, Alyeska agreed.

Although encouraged by Alyeska's change of heart, the four also wanted to ensure that a citizens' advisory council would be formally codified in new legislation to establish limits of liability and a compensation fund as a result of the *Exxon Valdez* spill. In 1989 Dan Lawn and Stan Stephens traveled to northern Europe to observe terminal operations and tanker safety in Norway and the Shetland Islands. As a result, the council was modeled after a similar partnership at the Sullom Voe terminal in the Shetland Islands, considered to have the safest operations in Europe. Thanks in large part to the efforts of Stephens, Lawn, Ott and Devens, the RCAC was formally chartered in the Oil Pollution Act of 1990.

The findings within the legislation asserted that "only when local citizens are involved in the process will the trust develop that is necessary to change the present system from confrontation to consensus."[8] The findings also acknowledged that many citizens believed that complacency on the part of industry and government officials contributed to the spill. Congress concluded that "one way to combat this complacency is to involve local citizens in the process of preparing, adopting, and revising oil spill contingency plans. A mechanism should be established which fosters the long-term partnership of industry, government, and local communities in overseeing compliance with environmental concerns in the operation of crude oil terminals."[9]

With the exception of challenges in court, citizens had little opportunity to affect the implementation of policies and agreements to protect the Sound prior to the spill. During the years before the pipeline was constructed, environmentalists and the CDFU were actively involved in litigation to halt construction of the pipeline. Although Congress had ultimately preempted further judicial review of the permits needed to construct the pipeline, the Supreme Court ultimately weighed in on a narrow aspect of the dispute.

In a separate suit, the CDFU and environmental groups sought reimbursement of the legal fees they had incurred. In 1974, the Washington, D.C., Court of Appeals upheld a lower court's granting of fees to these groups, noting that the appeal served to "vindicate important statutory rights of all citizens whose interests might have been affected by construction of the pipeline." [10]

Had this been the final ruling, it would have helped defray the costs of those citizens who had organized to ensure the protection of the resource they shared in common. Perhaps reimbursement of their legal fees would also have provided an incentive to continue their oversight of the pipeline and tanker safety through the courts.

However, the Supreme Court reversed the appellate court decision, stating that only Congress and not the courts could authorize such reimbursement under the "American rule."[11] Although the court's majority opinion ruled against the fishermen, Justice Thurgood Marshall dissented in a minority opinion. He noted the importance of the fishermen's claims under the National Environmental Policy Act (NEPA). Their suit, he argued, played an important role in ensuring that the Department of Interior complied with the law's requirements for impact assessment and due process. Marshall wrote, "Although the NEPA issues were not actually decided, the lawsuit served as a catalyst to ensure a thorough analysis of the pipeline's environmental impact." The fishermen's suit, Marshall asserted, delayed the construction of the pipeline until appropriate safeguards for the environment were codified as conditions in the right-of-way permit.

Justice Marshall opined that these "beneficial results" might not have occurred in the absence of the fishermen's suit because the record showed that "Alyeska was unwilling to observe and the Government unwilling to enforce congressional land-use policy." Although the fishermen would benefit from the additional safeguards they sought in their lawsuit, Marshall suggested that their efforts were largely altruistic. Perhaps most importantly, Marshall acknowledged that the extensive factual discovery, expert scientific analysis, and legal research required to undertake legal action to ensure compliance required significant resources. Implicit in Justice Marshall's opinion was the suggestion that the majority opinion denying reimbursement of costs to the fishermen could discourage other public interest groups from holding government accountable in the future.[12]

Clearly, the CDFU and environmental groups had played a pivotal role in developing policies intended to protect the Sound. During the period from the first major oil strike in 1968 through enactment of the Trans-Alaska Pipeline Authorization Act in 1973 and resolution of the Supreme Court case in 1975, citizens and organized interest groups claimed rights for the environment in court and mobilized in part through the pipeline hearings. But such an organized effort to ensure the implementation of those policies was noticeably absent in the years that followed.

Perhaps the Supreme Court decision denying reimbursement of fees to litigants served as a critical juncture in the protection of Prince William Sound. Had the rest of the court agreed with Justice Marshall, perhaps citizens would have organized to ensure that policies in place to protect Prince William Sound were implemented as intended by Congress during the 1980s when it was most needed. The Supreme Court's 1974 *Alyeska* decision may have dissuaded public interest groups in other areas of the country from taking action to ensure compliance with environmental regulations in the courts.

The provisions for a citizens' advisory council in the Oil Pollution Act of 1990 sought to overcome the structural disadvantage that citizens and public interest groups face in participating in the regulatory process. While it would not directly override the *Alyeska* decision by reimbursing legal fees in successful court challenges, it did provide funding for citizen oversight and participation in the regulatory process. The RCAC established a formal mechanism for overseeing the activities of both the oil companies and regulatory agencies.

According to the provisions outlined in the Oil Pollution Act, members of the council would be Alaska residents appointed by the Governor to serve a three-year term. The council's membership represents a balance of local interests including local commercial fishing industry organizations, aquaculture associations, Alaska Native Corporations, environmental organizations, recreational organizations, and the Alaska State Chamber of Commerce, representing the locally-based tourist industry. Other voting members include representatives from Cordova, Whittier, Seward, Valdez, Kodiak, the Kodiak Island Borough, and the Kenai Peninsula Borough. Members of the council are not paid for their work, but are compensated for travel and expenses.

In addition to voting members, the council included non-voting, ex-officio members from the Environmental Protection Agency, Coast Guard, National Oceanic and Atmospheric Administration, United States Forest Service, Bureau of Land Management, Alaska Department of Environmental Conservation, Alaska Department of Fish and Game, Alaska Department of Natural Resources, Division of Emergency Services, Alaska Department of Military and Veterans Affairs.[13] By including representatives from state agencies, the council ensured that citizens' voices and priorities were heard and considered by regulators, providing a counterbalance to the influence and priorities of industry. The Act also established an identical RCAC to oversee terminal operations and tanker safety in Cook Inlet.

The legislation mandated that Alyeska fund the Prince William Sound RCAC with up to $2 million annually, although the council would operate as an independent, self-governing nonprofit organization. The council's formal mandate is to undertake independent scientific research or review research conducted by government agencies or others. The council also monitors environmental impacts of the terminal and tanker operations, reviews oil spill prevention and response plans, and provides a forum that gives voice to the people and communities around the Sound. The funds provided by Alyeska are used to hire professional staff and researchers to carry out the council's mandate.

Alyeska is not bound to accept or adopt recommendations made by the council. However, if it does not accept recommendations, or significantly alters them, it must provide notice and a rationale in writing within five days. As John Devens and the other founders acknowledge, the concerns and priorities of citizens inherently differ from those of the oil companies. Yet they all recognized the possibilities for finding common ground.

Pat pushed his empty plate toward the center of the galley table, and told his family he had been attending the start-up meetings for RCAC. Like others, he had a hard time imagining that the council could to be dedicated to citizen interests while being funded by Alyeska.

Mike nodded, carefully considering how to best describe some of the challenges the two entities faced in working together. "Although the hope was to work together to improve operations," he said, "there is a lot of tension now between RCAC and Alyeska. The council has worked with whistleblowers from the terminal to gain access to information to set priorities for monitoring and additional research."

Bobby reached to fill empty mugs. He said, "Well, there were a lot of people from Cordova who argued that fishermen and others who make a living from the Sound should have a voice in how it is regulated. At least this is a start."

"That's right," Walter said. "We can get a lot done if we all participate and talk about problems and potential solutions. Alaska benefits from the oil industry, but we all have a responsibility as citizens to make sure our environment is protected."

Mike glanced down at his watch. "It's about that time," he said. "I better get back aboard the *Constitution*."

He said goodbye and he and Pat lowered the skiff into the waters of Port Etches. The *Constitution* was tied to the SERVS buoy only a few hundred yards away. The lights of the response vessel laid down a path across the water in the darkening evening. The dishes were clean and put away by the time Pat returned and pulled the skiff into place on deck. They decided to pull anchor and head back to Valdez.

As the light at Busby Island came into view on the starboard side of the boat, the Day family gathered in the wheelhouse of the *Theresa Marie* must have shared the same thought—that of a missed turn by the *Exxon Valdez*. The simple maritime canon "red, right, returning" had failed to prevent the ship's professional operators from the historic grounding of a supertanker. In retrospect, many citizens, regulators, and politicians blamed themselves for the grounding of the *Exxon Valdez* on Bligh Reef. Updated legislation, a mechanism for citizen oversight, and newfound political will would help to prevent another *Exxon Valdez*. Yet nothing could be done to recover the damage to the lives and livelihoods of more than 32,000 fishermen, Alaska Natives, seafood processors and cannery workers. Nothing could undo the actions of one captain—and one company—that resulted in one of the largest oil spills in U.S. history. It would now be up to the judicial system to hold these actions to account.

17

Disappearing Act

PRINCE WILLIAM SOUND: JULY 1992

T
HE HULL OF THE *Lady Lynne* emerged from the water, cradled in the straps of the hydraulic boat lift. Bobby and Lori stood watching on the dock in St. Paul's harbor on Kodiak Island, as the lift plucked her gently from the water. The hull of the boat shone a brilliant white in the mid-summer sun, water cascading down off her sides. But her beauty belied the glitch in one of her engines, the repairs she needed that her owner could not afford, and her paltry catch of sockeye salmon for the season. The seine boat would rest in dry dock for the remainder of the summer.

Rather than going to Togiak Bay on the edge of the Bering Sea to fish spring roe herring, Bobby had instead leased a salmon seine permit in Kodiak for the spring salmon season. Fish and Game rules prevented a captain from fishing the same boat on two separate permits, so Bobby planned to work with Ed in Prince William Sound later in the season, just as Ed had worked for him to fish the Kodiak permit. The fishing in Prince William Sound would prove to be equally dismal, with their catch for the entire season equaling what they would normally catch in a single set. The 1992 pink salmon season proved to be a bust—for Bobby and for most other fishermen. They were all doing everything they could to stretch dollars and conserve fuel, but the fish simply weren't there.

Before he left Seattle to head north earlier this spring, Bobby got a phone call from his banker in Ballard. "Bank of America is buying Seafirst," the voice on the line said. "They're calling in notes on fishing vessels."

"You're kidding," Bobby said. "Last fall you said it was no problem. I could just make interest payments for a few years until we see how things shake out after the oil spill."

"Sorry, Bobby, Bank of America has decided it doesn't want to be in the fishing business."

"Well," Bobby said. "I didn't have any money last fall at the end of fishing season, so how do you expect me to pay off my note in the spring?"

The pressure to catch fish weighed heavily on his mind. Although he hoped it would never come to this, Bobby decided to take Stuart Lutton up on his offer to help. For twenty years he'd caught fish for Ocean Beauty and he wanted to think of Stuart's offer of financial assistance as a business partnership rather than a bailout. When he had stood in the Ballard sunshine with Stuart and his family only weeks after the oil spill, Bobby had little idea that the fall herring fishery would soon close, that spring herring would return to Prince William Sound in ever decreasing numbers, or that the salmon runs would all but collapse in three short years.

It was hard to believe how things had changed so quickly. In early 1989, Day Fisheries had assets totaling several million dollars, a healthy cash flow, and a sound amount of equity. Now just three years later, Bobby didn't know how much longer he could hold off the bank from foreclosing on both of his boats. Today, he resolved, he would try to find Stuart before he and Lori left for Valdez.

The boat lift slid horizontally, carrying the *Lady Lynne* over land, ready for dry-docking. As the boat lowered and came to rest squarely on the blocks beneath her, Bobby wondered whether he would ever be back for her. Whether he wanted to come back, or if he could afford to keep fishing even if he wanted to. His eyes met Lori's as the boat lift retreated. "Let's go get some lunch," he said.

As they walked up the harbor boardwalk toward town, a few puffy clouds raced across the sky, sending shadows scuttling across the water and deep green forests of the surrounding islands.

"I wonder if Stuart is in town," Lori said. "Maybe he'd like to go to lunch with us." Her suggestion caused Bobby to wonder if she could read the thoughts racing through his mind.

"Let's just you and I go to lunch," he suggested. "Then we'll see if we can find him." As they settled into a booth at the Kodiak Inn coffee shop, they both knew the task of finding Stuart might not be easy. Stuart hadn't been answering the phone at the Kodiak apartment he usually kept in summertime. They had an uneasy sense that Stuart simply hadn't been the same in the past year or so. One incident in particular had left lingering tensions between them.

As they sipped coffee and set the menus aside, Bobby couldn't put that incident out of his mind. He said, "I wish I could understand why Stuart sent the tender right past us at Port Heiden last year, when we had 250 tons of herring in our net."

Bobby and Lori had both worked hard for that set. For weeks, Lori had circled the plane in the turbulent spring air, looking for the unmistakable dark shadows of herring arriving to spawn along the shoreline. With Bobby or one of the crewmembers riding along, Lori logged hundreds of hours without any sign of a sizable school of fish. When she finally noticed something that looked promising, Bobby was in the co-pilot's seat. They landed the float plane and jigged a few of the herring with a pole Lori kept in the plane. They sliced a few small, silvery fish open as samples, and found that the roe were in prime shape for harvesting.

Not wanting to attract other boars by calling Stuart on the marine radio, they flew to Port Molar to call on a land-line. Stuart seemed pleased with the news and said he would dispatch a tender, that it would arrive the following day. As if to signal their luck was about to change, the next morning dawned clear and still, a day perfect for fishing herring. Bobby and his crew set the net in slack water, knowing a big catch would be easier to hold if the tide wasn't running.

They estimated the set was at least 250 tons. As they strapped the nets to the seine boat and skiff, securing the catch to offload, they noticed the tender was moving silently past them in the distance. In disbelief, they tried in vain to call the tender's captain on the marine radio, but it stayed its course.

As the stern of the tender disappeared from view, so did their hopes for a catch that could have put Day Fisheries, its crewmembers, and spotter pilot back on solid financial footing. Bobby would never forget the sound of the straps breaking against the force of the tide as it began to run, spilling fish back into the sea.

Lori nodded at the memory, knowing that losing those herring had not only hurt Bobby financially, but had left his ego badly bruised. The trip from Valdez to Togiak was longer than the trip from Seattle to

Valdez, and she didn't blame him for opting out this year when working capital was short. Although Stuart later said it had all been a miscommunication, Bobby had never been able to reconcile in his mind what had transpired to cause him to lose the catch.

"It really doesn't make any sense," she said. "Since Ocean Beauty gave you an advance that year, you'd think they would have wanted you to succeed. Seems they would want you to earn enough revenue to cover your advance."

"Right. It would have been in their interest in several ways," Bobby agreed. "We both took big risks to set that net," Lori said. They both knew that crossing the Bering Sea in a seine boat was risky. "The most ironic thing," Bobby said, "was that the tender went to one of the other boats that only had a few tons in its net. Ocean Beauty lost out on our 250 tons because we couldn't hold it any longer. It just didn't make sense for Ocean Beauty's tender to pass us by."

"Maybe it had nothing to do with you," Lori said. "I've heard some of the other fishermen talking over the marine radio. Stuart just isn't himself. Some of the guys think that he might be really sick or something. Or maybe Ocean Beauty is having its own financial troubles as a result of the *Exxon Valdez*. There were lots of salmon last year, but the prices were low."

What neither Lori or Bobby knew was that Ocean Beauty Seafoods had negotiated a secret agreement with Exxon in the past year. Along with several other fish processors who would ultimately come to be known as the "Seattle Seven," the processors had accepted a $70 million dollar payment from Exxon. In return for this prompt settlement, the processors agreed not to pursue any punitive damages that might ultimately be awarded in the ongoing litigation against Exxon. As a top executive with Ocean Beauty, Stuart Lutton likely knew about the settlement, or perhaps even participated in its negotiation. But this secret settlement would remain undisclosed for many years to come. Bobby and Lori paid for lunch and set about finding Stuart Lutton, but their efforts proved fruitless.

The float plane sped easily through the gentle waves of Chiniak Bay before lifting off the water and heading north toward Prince William Sound. Bobby and Lori scanned the water, looking for any sign of pink salmon. Last year, the pink salmon were smaller than usual, but there had been so many of them, fishermen glutted the market and the processors declined to take any more fish. To keep the pinks from rotting on the beaches in front of the hatcheries, fishermen caught them and dumped them into deeper waters. The glut was in some ways a relief, as those salmon appeared to have successfully returned through Prince William Sound in the summer of 1989. However, the generation before them, which emerged in the spring of 1989 only days after the spill, would have returned in 1990, providing the brood stock for this year's run. For that reason, scientists and fishermen believed that the 1992 pink salmon run would reveal whether there had been genetic damage to a generation of salmon as a result of exposure to crude oil.

As this year's run shaped up to be the smallest in decades, many fishermen feared it was a foreboding sign of long-term damage. Though the fish were large and of good quality, only twelve million pink salmon would ultimately be caught in south central Alaska this season, much lower than the thirty million predicted by the Department of Fish and Game. As the plane gained altitude, Lori asked Bobby what he thought accounted for the small runs.

"I think everything about the ecology of the Sound has changed," he said. "The whole thing seems sterile. The herring and crab have all but disappeared. There is probably very little plankton for the fry to feed on even now, and that was surely the case when the fish returning this year emerged as fry from the streams and hatchery holding pens."

In fact, a scientist studying pink salmon partly confirmed this suspicion. Ted Cooney of the University of Alaska announced that tests showed very little plankton available in the Sound when the fry emerged in 1991. However, Cooney also noted that the water temperature at the time was colder than normal, which could also have accounted for lower plankton levels. While crude oil from the *Exxon Valdez* may have affected wild salmon in some streams and rivers directly in the wake of the spill, Cooney doubted that the oil spill could be entirely blamed for the dismal returns in 1992.

The Gulf of Alaska currents run in cycles, Cooney explained, chilling Prince William Sound to below-average temperatures every twenty years or so. The currents could have lowered the water temperatures, resulting in slower growth of salmon fry in their initial stage of life, making them more vulnerable to predators or disease. His theory seemed to be supported in part by the low returns of hatchery fish too. Compared to their average return of five percent, the Prince William Sound Aquaculture Corporation hatchery runs were a mere one and a half percent this year.[1]

The plane eased northward above the Gulf of Alaska, flying easily atop gentle zephyrs in the late afternoon sun. Lori pointed out her window toward Mount Augustine, which from their vantage point appeared to rise directly out of Kamishak Bay. A wisp of steam rose above the majestic peak, and Bobby thought back to the day many years ago when it erupted, turning the skies dark with ash, forcing him and the crew to hunker down in the cabin, engines silent and windows drawn tightly shut.

"The thing that is most troubling," Lori said, "is that we'll probably never know what caused the salmon to nearly disappear."

"Right," Bobby said. "It is just like that mountain. It is part of the Sound's ecosystem. If the ash falls on the water, we'll never know what kind of chain reaction an eruption creates, or what effect it has on the birds and fish."

Lori nodded, taking in the scenery below. They flew on, in silent acknowledgement of the complexities of the Sound. It had the power to make humans feel small and powerless in its seemingly endless expanse of water, islands and jagged horizons. Yet with the small act of a missed turn by a supertanker, humans had altered the complex biological relationships within it. By itself, the Sound was constantly changing. Glaciers scouring out rocks and fjords, earthquakes heaving rocky coastlines and the seabed into new shapes, ash scattering across the waves and filtering through glacial streams, generations of salmon returning based on nature's selection of the healthiest and most robust fish, seabirds plucked from their rafts by raptors, and otters and seals devoured by killer whales.

But these changes, while occasionally sudden, take place at nature's pace. Now humans had disrupted the natural progression and selection of life within the Sound. Altering relationships between the land and waters, between the fish and wildlife, between man and the Sound, and perhaps just as importantly, between people. This place, which once nurtured relationships, trust, and common memories, felt as though it had lost its ability to nurture, to provide and make whole the people and wildlife most dependent upon it. And it was this sense of loss that Bobby felt most acutely.

Just like the ecosystem, the fishing community still struggled to adjust. A culture that had formed over several generations had been punctuated by a single tragic event. While financial pressures, low salmon returns, and fluctuating prices were common challenges for fishermen, these concerns generally evened out over the years, slowly seeking and finding a new equilibrium. But the oil spill had created a sudden shock and equilibrium proved elusive, despite the passage of three years' time.

In the weeks remaining before the close of summer salmon season, Bobby and Lori would often find themselves flying above the Sound, just as they were today, looking in vain for the schools of salmon that would normally be flooding into the Sound. This summer he'd caught fewer fish than he had at any other time since he'd helped build the hatcheries in the early 1970s. The more they looked, and the more the nets came up empty that summer, the more Bobby became convinced that things would never be the same for him.

The place that had once supported his livelihood, fed his soul, and nurtured relationships with his family, business partners, fellow fishermen, and with Lori, no longer seemed to be the place he once knew. Tensions remained between fishermen who took money to work on the spill, those who bought new boats with oil money but now couldn't afford them, and those whose boats had foreclosure signs on them. Bobby felt as though Stuart, a trusted friend and business partner, had abandoned him, a highliner who had provided Ocean Beauty with thousands of tons of fish in the past two decades. He had less work for Lori to do as a pilot, forcing them both to make decisions about what their relationship looked like in the future in the absence of professional ties. And in these tough times, what had once been friendly competition with other fishermen, turned to accusations of illegal fishing. Perhaps the place and its people would someday again reach equilibrium. But how long would it be?

When Lori flew him to Anchorage at the end of the salmon season, he hugged her goodbye with a sense of finality. She moved back, holding him at arm's length.

"You'll be back," she said, tugging playfully on the bill of his baseball cap.

18

Blockade

A LINE OF FISHING BOATS STRETCHED hull to hull across the Valdez Narrows. With their sterns toward Valdez Bay and the Alyeska terminal, their bows facing out into Prince William Sound, the captains of sixty-five fishing boats refused to move. Though dwarfed by the *Atigun Pass*, a British Petroleum owned supertanker bearing down on them, the captains held steady in their act of defiance.

For three days now—since August 23—fishermen had effectively blocked the narrow entrance, denying two Exxon tankers, two ARCO tankers, and three BP tankers passage to the terminal to fill their holds with North Slope crude. Oil continued to pour into the Alyeska storage tanks at a rate of 1.6 million barrels per day, but their capacity was only 8.7 million barrels. Unless the fishermen relented, Alyeska officials would be forced to slow down or even halt the flow down the eight-hundred-mile pipeline.

But the fishermen refused to back down. The 1993 fishing season in Prince William Sound marked the third year of sharply declining catches. Only six million pink salmon were harvested, the worst run in over two decades, and only a fraction of the 25 million predicted by the Alaska Department of Fish and Game. The fishermen received fifteen cents a pound for pinks—less than half the price they had received five years ago. In 1988, the catch had been worth $46 million. This year, it was worth just $5 million. The herring run was so weak that the spring roe season was cancelled. Of the herring that did return to Prince William Sound, many were diseased or deformed with heads unusually large compared to their bodies.

The fishing fleet was slowly dying along with the Sound, and many fishermen were now facing bankruptcy. In 1988 a salmon seine permit had been worth $300,000, but today would only sell for about $85,000. Cordova had been the eighth largest seaport in U.S. in 1988, but had fallen to twenty-eighth. By the end of the season, Prince William Sound Aquaculture Corporation would be $4 million short of the operating capital it would need to produce next year's fish because of the poor runs.

The fishermen demanded that Exxon negotiate in good faith to compensate them for their losses, as Don Cornett and Frank Iarossi had promised to do in the days following the *Exxon Valdez* spill. Alaska Governor Wally Hickel said of the fishermen's blockade, "They feel it's sort of the end of the road. I don't think they want to be confrontational, but they want Exxon to do something."[1] But Exxon denied that poor returns of salmon and herring were caused by the spill. Furthermore, Exxon spokesman Les Rogers explained, because the fishermen had initiated litigation against them, Exxon was unwilling to negotiate. In a statement released from Houston, Texas, Rogers said, "Our position would be, because the fisherman-plaintiffs initiated the lawsuits, it's something that's going to have to be left to the courts."[2]

ARCO and BP, Exxon's majority partners in the Alyeska consortium, agreed to meet with fishermen, hoping that their efforts would bring Exxon to the table. The two oil companies negotiated a $12 million loan package for fishermen, though they were careful not to pin blame for the poor runs on the *Exxon Valdez* spill. Representing Exxon's position, Rogers pointed to the record salmon runs in 1990, one year after the spill, as proof that the oil spill had no relationship to the declining salmon runs. Exxon held firm in its refusal to meet with fishermen.

At the request of the fishermen, Governor Hickel called on Interior Secretary Bruce Babbitt to intervene and mediate a discussion. At a meeting with a few of the protesting fishermen on the third day of the blockade, Hickel promised lower-interest state loans and increased spending on restoration projects. Later that day, Secretary Babbitt also met with fishermen, but was unsuccessful in prompting Exxon into the discussion. Babbitt said, "I think it's outrageous that an American company with the size and sophistication of the Exxon company doesn't have the will to sit down and talk with a bunch of fishermen on this sound."[3]

Although neither Governor Hickel nor Secretary Babbit was ultimately able to bring Exxon to the table, Babbitt pledged to continue working with the fishermen to negotiate a deal. "The message I've been peddling all over Alaska this week is that we need to talk more, that all groups need to increase communication," Babbitt said. "I think that applies to Exxon, too." In his meeting with the fishermen, Babbitt also pledged to encourage holistic studies of the Sound's ecosystem, including salmon and herring runs.

This promise met another of the fishermen's demands. After the state and federal governments and Native Corporations settled with Exxon, scientific studies had been scaled back. In 1992 the Oil Spill Trustee Council, which administered the $900 million settlement from Exxon, focused instead on repaying state and local government entities for their litigation expenses. Some scientists expressed concern that litigation had driven the science.

Ted Cooney, a University of Alaska researcher, had presented a proposal for analyzing the natural cycles in the Sound as a means for separating out the effects of the oil spill and natural phenomenon. But his study was denied funding. "There's a very good chance we'll come away from this without knowing very much at all about how oil affected the natural environment," Cooney said. "It's a legacy of the kind of studies that have been approved since the spill."[4] Riki Ott concurred. "We had the perfect lab, with oiled bays and intertidal spawners, and we blew it," Ott said. "I think the litigation really messed up the science that got initiated."[5]

That the true effects of the oil spill may never be fully understood or quantified only served to heighten a sense of uncertainty and distrust among the fishermen. But Babbitt's pledge to continue negotiations and encourage additional studies served to de-escalate the conflict. A spokesperson for the fishermen expressed optimism that Babbit, Hickel, and Exxon's two partners in the Alyeska consortium would convince Exxon to negotiate. The fishermen agreed to stand down.

"Exxon isn't that dumb," a spokesperson for the fishermen said. "I don't think they have too many options. We stepped down in good faith. We can always head right back out there. Right now we're willing to let Exxon step back and listen to those who are talking to them, but we're going to have to see some action within a few weeks. Within about sixty days here, some people are going to be losing their boats."

The fishermen also faced consequences for the blockade. The Coast Guard Commander said that they had recorded the names and numbers of the fishing vessels that blocked the Valdez Narrows, and planned to issue civil fines with maximum penalties of $25,000. If the fishermen moved to block the Narrows again, however, the Coast Guard said they could face criminal penalties up to six years in prison and $250,000 in fines.

By sundown the following day, supertankers were again tied at their berths at the Alyeska Marine Terminal. But Exxon never agreed to come to the table to negotiate with the fishermen, despite ongoing efforts by Governor Hickel and Secretary Babbitt. Perhaps Exxon believed that 10,000 fishermen with a strong sense of independence and self-reliance would never agree amongst themselves on a settlement amount. If they didn't agree with each other, how could Exxon ever settle their claims?

Or perhaps Exxon believed that rebuffing the financial and environmental concerns of the fishermen would cost the multinational corporation little in terms of their public image. Finally, their analysis of the costs and benefits of continued litigation may have suggested that even a protracted legal battle would cost less than a settlement.

Whatever their thinking, Exxon attorneys continued to prepare for a high-stakes court trial scheduled for April of 1994. Instead of settlement talks, fishermen continued to be deluged with a sea of paperwork. With more than seven hundred attorneys working on the case, Exxon kept the fishermen's legal team busy. The plaintiffs now numbered thirty-four thousand, including cannery workers, deck hands, and others whose livelihoods had been affected by the spill. In preparation for the upcoming trial, the fishermen's attorneys responded to 275 discovery disputes, retained five hundred experts, recorded two thousand depositions, and reviewed ten million documents.[6]

For many fishermen, preparing for the trial nearly became a part-time job. Since the spill, hardly a week had gone by that the fishermen weren't asked to submit fish tickets, processor statements, records of equipment and permit purchases, and income tax returns. They sat for depositions and prepared statements. Even if they wanted to put the *Exxon Valdez* spill behind them and go on with their lives, the ongoing litigation refused to let them.

19

Reckless Decision

ANCHORAGE, ALASKA: MAY 9, 1994

T HE NORTHERN SUN WAS ALREADY UP at six in the morning as fishermen, journalists, and other interested onlookers lined up in front of the Federal Building on Fourth Avenue in Anchorage. They stood waiting, only a little impatiently in the knowledge that Judge H. Russel Holland would not allow standing spectators in his one-hundred-seat courtroom. The outcome of this trial could prove to be one of the most important pieces of environmental litigation of the century.

For the fishermen who had flown in from Cordova, Cook Inlet, Tatitlek, Kodiak, and Valdez, their hunger for accountability had only grown more ravenous in the five years since the oil spill. The jury had been selected and seated last week, and in two short hours, the doors to Courtroom Number Two would be flung open to the fishermen and to the possibility that they would be made whole, at least financially. Perhaps more importantly, this trial offered a chance at redemption for a corporate philosophy that gave rise to the largest oil spill in U.S. history, and for a political and regulatory system that had otherwise failed one of the last unspoiled places on earth.

The legal team for the fishermen and other plaintiffs was led by Brian O'Neill, an attorney from Minneapolis, Minnesota. His firm, Faegre and Benson, traditionally represented corporate interests from its offices located in Minneapolis, Denver, Des Moines, Washington, London, and Frankfurt.

Most commonly, the firm defended its clients against plaintiff lawsuits such as the one filed against the Exxon Corporation. Having spent most of their time on the corporate side, the firm's experience and expertise uniquely prepared them to litigate this case. And their client base and practice provided the financial backing for the Exxon litigation. Before they even arrived at Courtroom Two on that day, O'Neill estimated that the plaintiffs had spent $125 million preparing to go to trial. The Exxon defendants, he estimated, had spent several times that amount.

The lead attorney for Exxon, Patrick Lynch, hailed from the Los Angeles firm O'Melveny and Myers. Lynch had defended clients ranging from the National Football League to Gallo and IBM, and the firm's client list included Wells Fargo Bank, Manufacturers Hanover Trust Company, Paramount Pictures, Columbia Pictures, and Federal Express. Lynch was accompanied by other Exxon trial lawyers including James Neal of Nashville, Tennessee. Neal's record included successful defense of Louisiana Governor Edwards against notorious corruption charges, and the Ford Motor Company when they made a calculated decision to produce Pinto cars despite a heightened risk of explosion upon a rear-end impact.[1]

The scene in Courtroom Two on that day left no doubt that the country's top lawyers would be at work here for the next two to four months. The show of technology was state-of-the-art and unprecedented at the time. As spectators crushed through the door and raced for seats in the gallery, they were greeted by a six-foot-by-six-foot television screen that would display recorded depositions and other visual evidence. The huge screen was accompanied by two thirty-seven-inch Mitsubishi televisions positioned at each end of the jury box, along with screens at the judge's bench and witness lectern. The courtroom was wired for sound and visual effects, and alive with the electricity of anticipation.

Judge Holland entered the courtroom and approached the bench. At six foot three, this thin, long-limbed figure of a man with a white beard exuded both an air of confidence and respect for the proceedings about to take place. Legal counsel for both sides had done their homework on Judge Holland and discovered that he had been the law partner of Ted Stevens prior to his election to the U.S. Senate. After Senator Stevens left for Washington, D.C., Holland had taken over the practice and client list heavily populated with oil companies, including Mobil.[2]

Although these prior affiliations likely prompted some nervousness on the part of the plaintiffs, Judge Holland was also known to be fair-minded and hard-working. Having overseen the settlement between Exxon and the State of Alaska, Holland was no stranger to the circumstances surrounding this case. Both plaintiffs and defendants could only hope that his integrity and attentiveness to the facts presented during this trial would prevail over former affiliations or prior involvement in the matter of the *Exxon Valdez*.

Judge Holland faced the packed courtroom. He introduced himself and announced the case number for the record. He then turned to the jury box and proceeded to explain to jurors their responsibility to evaluate the facts of the case.

The trial would take place in three phases, Judge Holland explained. "In phase one," he said, "plaintiffs will seek to prove, one, that the Exxon defendants' conduct leading up to the grounding of the *Exxon Valdez* on March 24, 1989, was reckless; and two, that the reckless conduct was a legal cause of the grounding of the *Exxon Valdez*."

The second phase would task the jury with determining the dollar value of compensatory damages that should be paid to fishermen and others for direct economic harm the spill had caused. If the jury found that Exxon had acted recklessly in phase one, the third phase would determine whether punitive damages should be levied, and if so, how much. If the jury did not find recklessness in the first phase, there would be no phase three.

Judge Holland also cautioned the jury, saying, "Punitive damages are not favored in the law, and are never awarded as a right, no matter how egregious the defendant's conduct but may be imposed for that conduct which manifests reckless or callous disregard for the rights of others. Punitive damages serve the purpose of punishing a defendant, of teaching a defendant not to do it again, and of deterring others from following the defendant's example."

In closing Judge Holland instructed the jury. "The burden is on the plaintiff in a civil action such as this to prove every essential element of his claim by a preponderance of the evidence. If the proof should fail to establish any essential element of plaintiffs' claim by a preponderance of the evidence in the case, the jury should find for the defendant as to that claim."[3]

Judge Holland turned the proceedings over to Brian O'Neill. The Minnesota attorney was a likeable person, with fair hair, a clearly audible voice, and an easy smile. As the lead for the plaintiffs, he would solely carry the burden of oral presentation and arguments. Unlike the legal team representing the defendants, which would take turns on the courtroom floor, O'Neill's strategy as the sole litigator would both benefit and cost him. The jury would come to know him well over the next few months, but the effort would tax his mental and physical endurance.

O'Neill began by introducing some of the members of his legal team, many of whom had followed him to Alaska from Minnesota and devoted the last five years of their professional and personal lives to this cause. He then turned the focus of his attention to the jurors' fellow Alaskans. "My clients include ten thousand fishermen and four thousand Natives, the municipalities in the spill area, Native Corporations in the spill area, and Natives who live in remote villages whose subsistence lifestyle was impacted by the wreck of the *Exxon Valdez*," O'Neill said. "Now, I can't introduce you to all fourteen or fifteen thousand of these folks, but I am going to introduce you to a few."

O'Neill introduced Prince William Sound herring fishermen Snooks Moore, Kory Blake, Jamie Henderson, and Tom Cochran; Upper Cook Inlet fishers Jere Eidem, Bobby Correia, and Liz Schmidt; and Richard McGahan and his son Richard Jr., Dave Horn, Timmy Keener, and Dean Osmar, a fisherman and 1984 Iditarod champion, among others.

He said, "The plaintiffs in this case represent the full fabric, the full tapestry of life in and around Prince William Sound and indeed Alaska life. Now, how did we all get here? How did you get here, how did we get here, and how did the Exxon defendants get here? How did we get to the point to where twelve citizens will be judging the actions of one of the biggest corporations in the world? A disaster happened, and why did the disaster happen? The disaster happened because of the recklessness of Exxon Corporation."

O'Neill began to lay out the case, going back to the hours before the *Exxon Valdez* pulled away from her berth on the night of March 23, 1989. He retraced Captain Joseph Hazelwood's steps, beginning at the office of the shipping agent in Valdez. Along with two of his crewmembers, Hazelwood completed some paperwork, made a few phone calls, and then called Ed Murphy, the harbor pilot who had brought them into port the night before. They'd agreed to meet for lunch.

The four men headed Mike's Pizza Palace for lunch, which advertised the "best pizza in Alaska." Overlooking the small boat harbor, the Pizza Palace was dimly lit, its wood walls offering a warm and cavernous escape from the damp snowflakes that had begun to fall outside. Hazelwood's two shipmates ordered beer with their lunches, and Murphy and Hazelwood stuck with iced tea.

Although they had originally been scheduled to leave at nine that evening, they learned that their departure would be pushed back another hour. It was still early—only 2:00 p.m.—and the crew decided to spend a few more hours in town. Murphy dropped the three off at the Hobby Hut, a florist and knickknack shop. They agreed to reconvene at the Pipeline Club later that afternoon. Hazelwood stayed longer than his crewmembers, placing an order for flowers to be delivered to his wife and daughter for Easter.

O'Neill's gaze on the jury was intent now. The facts as he had just described them were undisputed, he claimed. "From two to four thirty," O'Neill explained, "the evidence is going to be scrambled about what happens."

By some accounts, Hazelwood had gone to the Pipeline Club early. When he arrived, Hazelwood discovered that one of his crewmembers had already found a table, and was sipping a gin and tonic. Hazelwood allegedly set his attaché case down next to a chair and approached the bar to order himself a drink. He'd like a Stolichnaya on the rocks, he told Lisa Harrison, the bartender. She replied that the Pipeline Club didn't carry that brand, and offered Smirnoff, their house brand, instead.

Exxon's rulebook forbade alcohol consumption more than four hours before departure. Since their departure had been pushed back an hour, they could enjoy a drink or two until five o'clock and still comply with the rules. They were soon joined by the third crewmember and they ordered two more rounds.

The dim lighting, the rounds of darts thrown by other patrons, and the sound of the jukebox obscured the passage of time. It had grown late, and the three decided to go back to Mike's to order pizzas to go. They placed their order and found that the lobby of Mike's had grown crowded with families awaiting a table. They decided to wait for their order in the Harbor Bar next door. They didn't want to just take up a table without spending money on something, so they each ordered a drink.

O'Neill railed about the "boozy afternoon" Hazelwood spent in Valdez. He told the jury, "From 4:30 to 6:30, he admits to being in the Pipeline Club and having three Vodkas, possibly doubles. He admits that. He'll testify to that. And about 7:00 they go to pick up a pizza next door to another joint called the Harbor Club, and he admits to having a vodka at the Harbor Club. So he admits to anywhere between four and seven or eight shots. If you put together the testimony of the bartenders, who saw him at various times, it's as many as sixteen shots."

A tanker captain who made a judgment error—had a few too many drinks, too late in the day—could have seemed like a tragic human error leading to an historic accident. But it was more complicated than that.

Widely regarded among other captains and crewmembers for his nautical abilities, it was no secret that Joseph Hazelwood was becoming increasingly dissatisfied with Exxon's cost-cutting corporate culture. With each tanker now operating as its own "cost center," paperwork and other administrative responsibilities competed for his time at the ship's helm. Crews were expected to work seven days a week, twelve hours a day, for a total of eighty-four hours per week. When the *Exxon Valdez* was launched in 1986, it was manned by thirty-four crewmembers. By 1989, the crew had been cut back to twenty, with plans to further cut back to only fifteen. When Hazelwood and two of his mates were in Valdez drinking on that afternoon, the rest had stayed behind to load the ship. O'Neill told the jury, "So they load the vessel all afternoon, and the evidence will be that towards the end of that day, they're exhausted."

But O'Neill had yet to hone in on what might prove to be the most damning of all evidence: that Exxon had acted "recklessly" in its operation of the *Exxon Valdez*. In July 1984, Hazelwood had a hit-and-run accident and was arrested in the driveway to his own house. He refused to take a breathalyzer test and was later convicted of drunk driving. His driver's license was later revoked in 1985. Hazelwood agreed to a twenty-eight-day inpatient stay at South Oaks Hospital Alcoholism Clinic in Long Island. One of the doctors at South Oaks found him to be "depressed and demoralized" and prescribed aftercare and participation in Alcoholics Anonymous upon his release.

And it was on this very prescription, and on the time from 1985 forward, that O'Neill would focus. When Hazelwood returned from disability leave, O'Neill told the jury, he met not with the company medical doctor, but with a representative of Exxon Shipping Company who simply told him not to violate any company policies. "And the first meeting he has with the representative of Exxon Shipping Company is where?" O'Neill asked the jury. "It's in a bar. The first meeting he has on return from his disability leave is in a bar."

O'Neill grew serious, placing the weight of company's burden about what to do with a tanker captain who is known to be an alcoholic, and in fact, doesn't even have a license to operate a vehicle. Outlining what was at stake in the company's decision making for the jury, O'Neill said, "The captain's in charge of the crew, the cargo, the vessel, and the safety of those around that vessel. It's a lot of responsibility and he is the sole one in charge.... Ship captains can't be monitored because they're out at sea, and the crew of a ship isn't going to tattle on the captain, so... here you have Captain Hazelwood ninety days after treatment and there's no treatment on that ship for ninety-nine days..."

O'Neill then began to make the case that Exxon's policies led to the grounding of the tanker, and to the economic losses of the fishermen. He estimated that the actual economic damages to the fishermen totaled about $1.5 billion, and he let the jury know he would be asking for $15 billion in additional punitive damages. O'Neill concluded by outlining for the jury the arguments Exxon would make against his clients' case. First, he said, Exxon would argue that Hazelwood leaving the bridge had nothing to do with the accident. "But," he said, "the proof will be the bridge manual required him to be there, the pilotage rules required him to be there."

Exxon would also argue that drinking had nothing to do with the accident. "Everybody in the company knew he was drinking," O'Neill said. "His superiors knew he was drinking, he didn't know he was being monitored, and there will not be one piece of paper that Exxon Corporation can provide for you that says, 'I talked with Joe and we went over these problems.' Not one." O'Neill then explained to the jury that when the Coast Guard finally tested Hazelwood's blood alcohol level—nine hours after the grounding—it measured .06. "But," O'Neill emphasized, "this is nine hours after the accident. Coast Guard requirement is .04. If you're above .04, that's a violation of the law."

There would be the blame-it-on-the-third-mate-strategy, O'Neill explained. Then, he said, "They'll say 'we relied on the Coast Guard, so it's the Coast Guard's fault.' The evidence on this will be the Coast Guard and its manual. In its manual says, don't rely on us."

"And then the last one," he said, "will be the wreck had nothing to do with Exxon shore-side management. Sort of a—it was all the vessel's fault—and the guys on the shore had no responsibility, but the evidence will be that shore-side management hired him, assigned him back on the vessel, created the conditions for relapse, failed to support him after his treatment, failed to monitor him, ignored evidence of the relapse, and evidence of the relapse goes in the high ranks of the company, that they regularly used overworked and fatigued mates on their vessels, that they failed to intervene in the disaster waiting to happen, that shore-side management was recklessly indifferent to how they treated this man. They were recklessly indifferent to how they treated the public, that they were recklessly indifferent to a tragedy in the making.

"And as to these people and these people," O'Neill said, wildly sweeping his arm across the gallery, pointing to the fishermen, Natives, and representatives of the municipalities he represented, "they didn't want Exxon—they didn't hire Hazelwood, they didn't supervise him, they didn't monitor him, they didn't make tens of billions of dollars off of the public's oil. They didn't spill the oil and they've had their livelihoods destroyed and their way of life altered, and Exxon will say they're sorry, but the evidence will be that they're only sorry enough to get by this trial and to get by this proceeding… And Exxon will say that 'we were negligent, but it was only negligence that caused the harm.' But I submit to you if we prove what I've said we're going to prove, it wasn't just negligence, it was recklessness, it was recklessness to the captain, it was recklessness to them," O'Neill said, pointing again, "…it was recklessness to the people of Alaska, the biggest mess by the people that had the wealth and power and size to do better."[4]

After a short recess, it was Exxon's turn to deliver opening statements. Patrick Lynch stepped forward to address the jury. He told them that he was in the unique position of representing a client that had accepted responsibility for the accident, and had agreed that the plaintiffs are entitled to compensation.

"But it…is a step from that, as His Honor instructed you this morning, from responsibility to pay[ing] actual damages, which Exxon has admitted that it has, to the obligation to pay large sums of money," said Lynch. "You'll remember that Mr. O'Neill was talking about billions of dollars, over and above any loss that these fishermen suffered and over and above any loss that these Natives suffered by way of punitive damages."

Lynch admitted that Exxon could have done better. But were the actions of Exxon employees reckless, or were they simply doing the best job they could, given the challenges they faced? "I think you will see," Lynch said, "that these are people who had no motive to be reckless and who had every motive, and who did, in fact, try every day they got up to do a good job. They made some mistakes, they may have been guilty of simple negligence, but they were not guilty of recklessness."

Lynch retraced the voyage of the *Exxon Valdez* that night, showing the jury a chart of Valdez Arm, Potato Point, the Narrows, the light at Busby Island where third mate Gregory Cousins was to commence the turn back into the shipping lanes. With pictures of the bridge and chart room up on the large screen televisions, Lynch pointed to the captain's quarters, where Hazelwood was working to complete some paperwork. "It takes eleven seconds, let's round it fifteen seconds," Lynch said, "to get from the captain's quarters to the bridge."

At this point, Lynch took a break from recounting the events of that fateful night, to emphasize Exxon's position. He said, "We agree that Captain Hazelwood should have followed our bridge manual and should have stayed where he was, but the question here is reckless. Was Captain Hazelwood acting like a man racing a train through an intersection? Was he aiming a ship at Bligh Reef and going below to sleep or something? Or is this both Captain Hazelwood and Mr. Cousins trying carefully to assess the situation and concluding that this was not a dangerous situation, or more than they could handle?"

Lynch explained to the jury, that the tragedy of the case was "that there were so many chances for this accident not to happen, and it took all of those chances to go wrong for this accident to occur. I suggest to you…that if you look at what happened here, you try to put behind you this label of alcoholism or drunk that the plaintiffs try to package this case with, you see that this is a very tragic accident. But it really involved the kind of simple mistakes that you see in car accidents every day. It involves one person making a mistake and another person making a mistake and all those come together, unfortunately, for this accident to happen."

Lynch said he wanted to wrap up, but before doing so, he wanted to again address the issue of alcohol. As O'Neill had suggested in his opening comments, Exxon would argue that drinking had nothing to do with the accident, that the tanker captain was not impaired as he took the helm from harbor pilot Ed Murphy outside the Narrows that night.

Despite his arguments that drinking had not played a role in the grounding, Lynch defended the company policies that left Captain Hazelwood at the helm of the newest supertanker in Exxon's fleet. Certainly, the company would not choose to risk the $130 million investment in the *Exxon Valdez*, he reasoned. In fact, the company had consulted experts in the field who had advised the company on dealing with the problem drinking on board the ships, or returning to the ship in a drunken state. Alcoholism was a problem that had plagued shipping companies for over a hundred years, he said.

And it was the call of the president of Exxon Shipping, Frank Iarossi, to make, Lynch explained. And Frank Iarossi had made the right call, he said. It was a call influenced not only by expert advice, Lynch explained, but also by legal obligations. "In 1978," Lynch told the jury, "the attorney general of the United States ruled that a person who has been treated for alcohol problems is a handicapped person and is entitled to the benefit of laws protecting the handicapped from discrimination."

Furthermore, Hazelwood was protected by confidentiality laws, and Frank Iarossi had asked his managers to monitor his job performance. This request was carried out with a great deal of discretion, Lynch said, which would explain where there was little or no paper record of company monitoring activities.

Frank Iarossi had placed Hazelwood on the Valdez-Long Beach run, where he would be in town more often, and agents could monitor his drinking in a private and confidential manner. "There are jurors in this country who think about awarding punitive damages against companies like Exxon," Lynch told the jury, "for treating their employees unfairly for violating the employee's rights, and I guess all of us have seen when you travel around there are ramps and various other things that recognize the rights of the handicapped to participate in society fully."

Lynch was holding firm to the notion that Exxon had little choice but to leave Hazelwood at the helm and do what it could to watch and evaluate his performance from the shore. And so, this was an accident, a tragic culmination of events that resulted from Exxon employees doing the best they could to deal with a difficult situation. It was Frank Iarossi balancing a need to comply with laws and follow the advice of experts, Joseph Hazelwood to safely navigate a ship despite increasing pressure to cut costs from corporate headquarters and struggle with his own personal addictions, Gregory Cousins to commence the turn entrusted to him, Robert Kagan to execute the turn, and Maureen Jones to warn of an impending catastrophe.

Lynch said in closing, "This was an accident that didn't have to happen, and wouldn't have happened except for a chain of mistakes from Exxon people, Mr. Cousins, Captain Hazelwood, others, and from other people...the Coast Guard and others, it's a tragedy. The plaintiffs, Natives and the fishermen are entitled to full compensation for their loss. This is not a case in which punishment is warranted."[5]

As the days lengthened, separated only by a few twilit nighttime hours, the trial wore on. It was mid-June, after four weeks of testimony and four days of jury deliberations. Judge Russel Holland read the verdict of phase one of the trial. The jury had found Exxon and Joseph Hazelwood's actions to be reckless, opening the door to punitive damages. Courtroom Number Two erupted in cheers from the gallery—from the fishermen, Natives, and other Alaskans who had waited five years to hold this company to account.

But the plaintiffs' jubilation was all but quashed nearly eight weeks later with the closure of phase two, which revealed a somewhat less pleasing verdict. The compensatory damages of $287 million represented less than a third of what the plaintiffs had asked for. The jury agreed that depressed salmon prices in 1989 could be attributed to the spill, but didn't agree that depressed prices for salmon and herring could be blamed on the spill in the following years. There were simply too many possible intervening variables.

"After five years of this, I can see all of this is going to amount to nothing," the president of Cordova District Fishermen United told an *Anchorage Daily News* reporter. "When you boil the numbers down, it looks like we are going to get hardly anything out of this."[6] But Exxon representatives were pleased with the verdict, and Patrick Lynch said the company would argue for zero punitive damages. "We believe that Exxon's response to the spill was really a unique show of corporate responsibility from Day One," Lynch said. "It made an unlimited commitment to clean up."[7]

The trial had begun in the waxing days of summer, and now in the waning days, it would conclude. After four months of testimony, evidence, and even a helicopter tour of Prince William Sound for the jury, the attorneys would summarize their cases at the end of phase three, and leave the fate of their clients in the hands of the jury.

On August 29, 1994, James Neal presented the closing arguments for the defendants. Neal said, "Members of the jury, the Court will instruct you, as I've said several times, that punitive damages are not favored in the law. I submit to you a reason punitive damages are not favored in the law." The gravest risk of assigning punitive damages, he argued would be punishing innocent employees and shareholders.[8]

Brian O'Neill would offer the last word. The jury's verdict in this phase of the trial, he explained, would not just be about the plaintiffs in this case, but rather a statement of what our society values most, and what behaviors we as Americans seek to reward or punish. "Your verdict," O'Neill said solemnly, "is going to be a validation of society's values, and that includes values on people, the environment, honesty...."

O'Neill emphasized to the jury that theirs was an awesome task, not just to award those who had been harmed by the spill, but to deter the members of the board of directors of corporations across America from acting recklessly. "And in point of fact," O'Neill said, "these people in these board of directors' rooms are going to look to what you do, and the day after you do it, it will be discussed in every major board of director's meeting in the country that exists. And your fellow citizens are going to look to what you do, and it is a very, very important task."[9]

Epilogue

A FTER A THREE-MONTH TRIAL IN THE SUMMER of 1994, the Anchorage jury awarded the largest punitive damages to date. At the time, the jury award of $287 million in compensatory damages, and $5 billion in punitive damages equaled approximately one year's profit for Exxon. With the announcement of the jury verdict, Exxon's stock price dropped $3 a share, equating to a $3.5 billion dollar loss in market value. Following the verdict, U.S. District Judge H. Russel Holland received a thirty-five-pound stack of appeals and counter-motions. This stack hinted at the complex entanglement of legal wrangling, conflicting rulings from district and appeals courts, and secret pretrial agreements that would soon emerge.

Three years before the jury verdict, the fish processing companies known as the "Seattle Seven" settled with Exxon for $70 million. In 1996, these companies filed in U.S. District Court to participate in receiving a share of the $5 billion punitive damages. The Seattle Seven had not participated in the punitive damages portion of the 1994 trial, but now decided to stake a claim to them. However, the processors would return nearly all of the award back to Exxon per their confidential 1991 agreement. When the secret agreement came before Judge Holland, he declared the processors' request to be "pernicious and flagrant violations of public policy" and "an astonishing ruse."[1] Holland admonished Exxon, which he said had "acted as Jekyll and Hyde, behaving laudably in public and deplorably in private."[2]

In his ruling, Judge Holland declared that the processors had no right to retroactively lay claim to the punitive damage award. He said, "Exxon intended to share in the very punitive damages award which the jury deemed necessary to fulfill society's goal of punishment and deterrence." If he gave his legal blessing to the clandestine deal, Holland said he would have allowed Exxon to take back $745 million in damages. In exchange, the processors would keep $12.4 million as a "performance bonus."[3] The deal would have effectively allowed Exxon to reduce their punitive damage liability by 15 percent.

In his decision, Holland stated, "The jury determined that $5 billion, and not a penny less, was the amount reasonably necessary to punish and deter Exxon." Further, Holland declared, "Public policy will not allow Exxon to use a secret deal to undercut the jury system, the court's numerous orders upholding the punitive verdict, and society's goal in punishing Exxon's recklessness."[4]

In November 2001, the Ninth Circuit court ruled the $5 billion in punitive damages awarded to the fishermen excessive and reduced the damages by half. On June 25, 2008, the Supreme Court further reduced the punitive damages award to $507 million, all but dismissing the original $5 billion awarded by the Anchorage jury in 1994. Because an appeals court reversed Judge Holland's earlier decision regarding the Seattle Seven, the processors would return $107 million of the $507 million punitive damages award to Exxon. The Supreme Court decision yielded an average of $15,000 per claimant in the fishermen's lawsuit.

The Supreme Court did not address the matter of interest on the punitive damages award, which had been set in an earlier court ruling at 5.9 percent. Interest on the $507 million award would effectively double the dollar amount paid to fishermen. In early fall 2008, Exxon appealed to a lower court to overturn the earlier order to pay interest on the punitive damage award. Further, Exxon requested that the $70 million in bank fees to ensure payment of the original jury award be deducted from the fishermen's award.

After nearly twenty years of litigation, the case *Baker v. Exxon* earned the distinction of longest running non-criminal court case in U.S. history. Of the thirty-four thousand plaintiffs, six thousand fishermen have died, many have declared bankruptcy, and most still have debts hanging over their heads as they struggle to make a living fishing in still-recovering waters.

The implications of the Supreme Court ruling extend beyond the fishermen's case. In their decision, the Supreme Court justices ruled that in maritime cases such as the *Exxon Valdez*, the appropriate ratio of compensatory to punitive damages is one-to-one. As primary author for the court's majority opinion, Justice David Souter opined that punitive damage awards in the United States are too unpredictable. As a general rule, Souter argued, punitive damages should be pegged at approximately three times compensatory damages. This opinion not only denies justice to the fishermen, its precedence may thwart future efforts to hold corporations legally and financially accountable for reckless risk-taking.

One lesson we might learn from the *Exxon Valdez* spill is that assigning blame, putting a dollar value on a pristine environment, and cleaning up an environmental disaster are all fruitless endeavors. The failure to prevent such a disaster calls attention to the deeper-rooted problems of short-sighted goals for corporate profits, accountability to shareholders over local communities, and the inability of politicians and regulators to resist succumbing to pressure from special interests.

Yet out of the *Exxon Valdez* disaster, hope for solutions to these dilemmas within our democracy arose like a phoenix from the oiled beaches of the Sound. The Regional Citizen's Advisory Council (RCAC) has succeeded in bringing balance to the interaction between industry and regulators, which often becomes too cozy. "A lot of times regulators see citizens as amateurs and that is certainly not true in this case," said John Devens, former mayor of Valdez, who served for many years as the organization's executive director. Although the working relationship between RCAC and Alyeska hasn't always been smooth, the group has been successful in helping to ensure cleaner air and water in Port Valdez, and the purchase of escort tugs. Most importantly, the RCAC gives voice to those whose lives and livelihoods most depend on local resources.

Reflecting on the early years of RCAC's operations, board member Stan Stephens attributed some of the success to the willingness of Bob Malone, then Alyeska's CEO, to work with members of the community. In particular, he noted that Malone, formerly of BP, helped to improve the culture within Alyeska. Stephens said the answer is to train a workforce that is more concerned about environmental problems, and a work culture that encourages them to bring concerns to the attention of the CEOs.[5]

Alyeska may have been prompted to change its culture, in part, by the money it paid to settle claims related to its failure to clean up the oil spill as outlined in the contingency plan. In November 1992, Alyeska settled lawsuits with the State of Alaska for $30 million and the federal government for $1.6 million. In 1993, Alyeska agreed to pay $98 million to settle legal claims raised by fishermen, business owners, Native corporations, and others affected by the spill.

Alyeska may also have been prompted to change as a result of the draft report issued by the House Committee on Interior and Insular Affairs. The July 1992 report signed by Congressman George Miller blasted Alyeska and its involvement in the covert Wackenhut investigation. In the summary of findings, the Committee stated, "It appears from the record that while Alyeska's covert activities may have been designed in part to identify and plug leaks within Alyeska, that was not the only goal."

The report determined that the focus of Alyeska's covert activities extended to those outside the organization as well. The primary focus, the Committee concluded, centered on Chuck Hamel, the "most vocal and effective critic and conduit of information from Alyeska's employees to state and federal officials about serious allegations of environmental wrongdoing." The report found that other individuals and organizations known to be critics of Alyeska were also targeted, including a public interest law firm Trustees for Alaska, DEC official, Dan Lawn, and marine toxicologist and board member of the Cordova Fishermen District United, Dr. Riki Ott.

During the course of the investigation, Alyeska had insisted that documents and other evidence provided to the Committee by a company insider were trade secrets that had been wrongfully divulged. To this argument, the Committee responded by finding that "to the extent documents and information provided to government officials concerned matters of public health, safety and the environment, they were not 'trade secrets' and 'corporate assets.' Since Congress has passed laws encouraging the disclosure of such information to government officials, the Committee has also concluded that neither Hamel nor any government official to whom he may have provided the information or documents were in possession of 'stolen' property."

The Committee offered little support for Alyeska's arguments, instead expressing their belief that Alyeska had violated the law prohibiting obstruction of a Congressional investigation. In the report's summary, the Committee concluded: 1) Alyeska's goal was not only to find the internal source of information, but also to interfere with the Committee's investigation, 2) Alyeska sought to gather information that could be used to discredit its critics (including Congressman Miller), thereby blunting the effect of disclosures, and 3) Alyeska and Wackenhut interfered with the Committee's investigations by altering or destroying evidence of covert operations.

The Committee closed by stating, "Although it appears that Alyeska left most of the day-to-day undercover work to Wackenhut, the Committee believes that Alyeska must nonetheless bear great responsibility for the conduct of the operation. The Wackenhut agents regularly reported their activities to Alyeska, which must have known of and approved the investigative techniques employed." Whether or not Alyeska had specific knowledge of Wackenhut's activities, the Committee believed that Alyeska bore the responsibility for setting the "tone and goals of the undercover operations."

The report was approved on a voice vote, but many Republicans on the committee disagreed with the findings in a 186-page minority report. Alaska Representative Don Young, the Committee's minority leader said, "This is a legislative body, not a judicial one."[6] In their minority report, Republicans suggested that the Committee lacked evidence to support its findings that the investigation sought to interfere with the ongoing investigations of the *Exxon Valdez* oil spill or the Trans-Alaska Pipeline System.

The findings of the congressional committee prompted Hamel and others who had been implicated in the covert operation to file civil suits against Alyeska. During the court proceedings before U.S. District Judge Stanley Sporkin, Alyeska requested that Hamel be required to reveal his informants within the company. Judge Sporkin denied the request.[7] Chuck Hamel ultimately settled his claims for an undisclosed sum of money, as did Stan Stephens, Dan Lawn, and Riki Ott. After they received their settlement, Stephens, Lawn and Ott used their funds to start the Alaska Forum for Environmental Responsibility, an organization "dedicated to holding industry and government accountable to the laws designed to safeguard the environment, provide a safe and retaliation-free workplace, and achieve a sustainable economy in Alaska."

In 1992 Dan Lawn's union filed a grievance for removing him from his position as head of the Valdez office. An arbitrator found in Dan's favor, directing DEC to restore him to his old position, awarding damages and attorney fees. Yet DEC declined to offer him his old position, and in 1996, the Alaska State Supreme Court upheld the arbitrator's decision directing that he be reinstated in his previous position. Lawn is now retired, but continues to advocate for safe environmental and workplace practices at the Alyeska terminal.

Stan Stephens passed away in 2013. The company he owned and operated still bears his name—Stan Stephens Glacier and Wildlife Cruises—and provides visitors with spectacular views of the Sound's wildlife, glaciers, and islands. Stephens served in many different capacities on the board of the Regional Citizens Advisory Council. After twenty-two years of service, Stephens retired from the board in 2012.

Riki Ott lives in Cordova and continues to bring political and media attention to the long-term health and environmental impacts of the oil industry in Alaska and the Gulf of Mexico. She is the author of two books about the *Exxon Valdez* oil spill.

On June 25, 1992, Rafael "Gus" Castillo, a former Wackenhut employee fired for speaking out about the Hamel investigation, was one of three whistleblowers to receive the Moral Courage award from the Cavallo Foundation in Washington. Along with the award, Castillo also received a $10,000 check from the foundation.[8]

Wisconsin-based attorney Billie Pirner Garde represented Chuck Hamel and others implicated in the Wackenhut spying operation. A former whistleblower herself, Garde represents employees in the oil and nuclear industries across the country, seeking protection for them as well as changes in corporate cultures that give rise to retaliation of workers who raise health, safety, and environmental concerns. Garde later worked for Alyeska as a consultant and many attribute the changes in Alyeska's organizational culture to her efforts. Judge Stanley Sporkin, who once admonished Alyeska for its actions in the Wackenhut investigation and approved settlement of the civil case, later took a position as the employee ombudsman for BP.

Lori Egge founded Sky Trekking Alaska in 1992. Along with two other pilots, she offers tours of Alaska by air. She also guides inland bird hunts in Alaska, Idaho, Georgia, and Hawaii through the Orvis-endorsed organization Wingshooting the Wild. Along with other well-known bush pilots, Lori was featured in an *Alaska* magazine article. Tom Parker was killed in 1991 in a mid-air collision over Landlocked Bay while spotting fish for a herring opener.

Two of Bobby Day's former crew-members and close friends have passed away. Dale Dawson died suddenly of a heart attack on a sunny summer day in 2004 while operating a piece of logging equipment at his home in Northport, Washington. Mike Phillips died in a tragic accident on Robe Lake, near Valdez, Alaska. Stuart Lutton, an executive with Ocean Beauty Seafoods, died of an unknown cause in 1993.

For his role in the *Exxon Valdez* oil spill, Joseph Hazelwood was convicted of a misdemeanor for negligent discharge of oil. He was fined $50,000 and sentenced to one thousand hours of community service. On Friday, November 27, 1998, the *Wall Street Journal* announced that Exxon and Mobil were engaged in merger talks. If joined, the merger of the country's first and second largest oil companies would reunite two entities of the Standard Oil Trust—the former oil monopoly broken up into thirty-four companies in 1911. Together, the two companies would form the world's largest oil company.

On March 25, 1999, attorneys general from thirty-seven states sent a letter to Lee Raymond, Exxon's Chairman and CEO. It had been exactly ten years since the spill, and they echoed the courts' concerns that a delay in paying the fishermen the $5.3 billion granted to them by an Anchorage jury was profiting Exxon. "As our states' chief legal officers," the attorneys general wrote, "we call upon the Exxon Corporation to acknowledge its corporate responsibility to the people, businesses, and communities affected by the spill by paying the federal jury verdict awarded five years ago." Several elected officials, including Senator Slade Gorton of Washington, suggested that Exxon should pay up before merging with Mobil.

We now know that these concerns and admonitions fell on deaf ears at Exxon headquarters, the Justice Department, and Congress. In February 2008, ExxonMobil posted the highest quarterly profits on record for a U.S. company. Total earnings of $45.2 billion for 2008 set a record for the highest earnings of any U.S. or global corporation.

In 2012, ExxonMobil posted earnings of $44.9 billion, falling just $300 million short of the world-record it set in 2008.

On the beaches of some islands in the Sound, oil can still be found by digging down just a few inches. A federal study released in 2007 estimates that eighty-five tons of oil remains in the Sound, declining at the rate of about four percent per year. As of 2006, the Oil Spill Trustee Council designated cormorants, harbor seals, harlequin ducks, killer whales, marbled murrelets, pacific herring, pigeon guillemots, and sea otters as species "not recovering" from the oil spill. Common murres, pink and sockeye salmon, and mussels are designated as "recovering," and only bald eagles are considered fully recovered. The effects on many other species are unknown, due to a lack of baseline data prior to the spill.

In the years since the oil spill, fishermen have faced stiff competition from farm-raised salmon imported from Norway, Chile, and Canada. However, as consumers have begun to understand the human health and environmental impacts of farm-raised salmon, prices and demand for wild Alaska salmon have increased. The 2008 salmon season was in many ways a success and a turning point for fishermen in Prince William Sound. Hatchery-raised salmon returned in large numbers, and at thirty-five cents a pound for pinks, prices paid to fishermen were some of the highest since 1988.

Since then, the salmon industry in Alaska has experienced a welcome rebound. In 2013, the state-wide salmon catch reached a record high of 260 million fish, and in Prince William Sound alone, eighty-seven million pink salmon were netted. Big catches often result in lower prices, but fishermen expect a price of about forty-five cents per pound in 2013. After nearly twenty-five years, these yields and prices have finally surpassed pre-spill profits for salmon fishermen in Prince William Sound.

The bait herring season has never reopened in Prince William Sound. The spring roe herring fishery has been closed for nineteen of the twenty-four years since the spill. After the spill, the spring roe fishery peaked in 1992 with returning adults that spawned prior to the spill in 1988. The total catch in 1992 was thirty-three million pounds followed by a collapse of herring stocks in 1993. Spring roe fisheries in 1997 and 1998 (the first commercial seasons since 1992) yielded nine and six million pounds respectively, but the seasons have since remained closed. A pot shrimp fishery opened in 2010 for the first time since the spill but yielded far lower returns than expected.

It is difficult to know whether the Sound, its fisheries, and wild-life will ever fully recover. While we can't predict the future, we can learn a great deal by reflecting on the factors that gave rise to the spill and applying those lessons to prevent future environmental disasters. We need companies and government agencies that make decisions based on more transparent information, are more responsive to concerns raised internally, and an active citizenry sharing oversight and accountability. There is much to be learned from the model that the RCAC has developed for collaborative efforts that bring together corporations, regulators, and citizens—an equally balanced triangle—to find real solutions. This forum encourages problem solving in a truly democratic way that creates mutual understanding about common needs and interests, and contributes to the development of solutions rather than conflict.

Corporations can learn valuable lessons from the reformation in corporate culture within Alyeska in the years following the spill. Companies who encourage employees to raise concerns about environmental and worker safety and include them in the development of solutions are better stewards of the communities in which they operate. With a focus on environmental and social outcomes as well as financial outcomes, this "triple bottom line" approach can encourage trust, increased market share, and financial rewards for responsible corporations.

While we can't undo the environmental damage, heartache, and financial distress caused by an oil spill of epic proportions, the biggest tragedy would be to let the lessons of the *Exxon Valdez* be forgotten. Shortly after the *Exxon Valdez* oil spill in 1989, Senator Jay Kerttula of Palmer said, "Soon the tears will dry up and people will not pay as much attention as they should."[9] Corporations, elected officials, regulators, and citizens all share responsibility for paying attention to our limited natural resources and for working together to help prevent future environmental disasters.

We will never know what the Sound, its fisheries, wildlife, and people who make a living from it would be like today if not for the oil spill. When Bobby Day left Prince William Sound for the last time in 1992, he left behind a thirty-year fishing career and the only way of life he had ever known. Day Fisheries was forced to sell its vessels at a fraction of their former value and the remaining assets were liquidated under bankruptcy proceedings. At the conclusion of these proceedings, all creditors of Day Fisheries were paid, with interest, and most of Bobby's personal debts were paid by the sale of the ranch. However, he was ultimately unable to keep most of the personal assets he had worked to earn throughout his career. At the age of 50, he started a new life and now owns a successful feed and farm supply business in Snohomish, Washington.

Bobby's brother and son, Pat and Eddie, still fish in Prince William Sound. Ed fishes for salmon, halibut, and black cod. In 2012, Ed and a partner founded HD Marine in Valdez. The state-of-the-art shop offers repair and maintenance services for seine and gill net boats, tenders, barges, tugs, and other oil-industry support vessels. In addition to fishing for salmon, Pat works as a longshoreman. Both Pat and Ed have contracts on their fishing vessels to serve in local oil-spill response drills and are on call in the event that another major spill occurs. Pat's two sons, Mike and Tony, work for the Ship Escort Response Vessel System (SERVS) in Valdez.

Bobby's daughter Theresa works with Ed at HD Marine, managing the daily accounting and business affairs for the partnership. Bobby's two grandsons, Chase Randall and Donovan Day, and granddaughter, Kinleigh Day, live in Valdez, and he makes regular trips home to see them. Bobby's father Walter passed away in 2001. People from Valdez and across the state of Alaska filled the Civic Center to honor his life and public service to the people of the community. Bobby's mother Gloria lives in Valdez and serves on the board of the senior center.

On spring days, Bobby often finds himself standing along the west wall of Fishermen's Terminal in the Seattle neighborhood of Ballard. There he watches as crew-members load nets and supplies for the trip north—a trip he made himself so many times. The smell of the water and the pull of magnetic north prove almost as irresistible as a salmon's instinct to return to its natal waters to spawn. Yet that instinct is muted by the knowledge that Prince William Sound is no longer the same place that served as the backdrop for his childhood and sustained his livelihood.

The waters of Prince William Sound now appear pristine on the surface and some of their bounty has returned. The Sound once connected Bobby to his memories, relationships, community, and career. When the waters of the Sound were ravaged in the spring of 1989, it felt to him as through all of those connections were broken beyond repair. In that sense, his loss was far greater than could ever be counted by lost fishing seasons, markets, or retirement savings.

Bobby returns to this place he loves nearly every year, and often pulls a silver salmon on a line from the Sound's emerald waters. He embraces the love and warmth of his family. But the visits also rekindle his sense of loss, and wistfulness often overcomes him as he walks the floating docks of Valdez harbor. Leaving this place allowed him to dream again and to focus on the future rather than reflecting on what he had lost in the past. He is content to let the Prince William Sound he used to know live on in memory.

Notes

1. Red, Right, Returning

1. "Community Involvement Versus Big Oil: A Case Study of the Policy Process," presented at the 32nd Annual Michigan Conference of Political Scientists, October 26, 2000.

2. The following account of the voyage and grounding of the *Exxon Valdez* has been compiled from a number of sources including the accident investigation report conducted by the National Transportation Safety Board, a Report to the President prepared by the National Response Team, a chronology outlined in Appendix N of *Spill: the Wreck of the Exxon Valdez* prepared by the Alaska Oil Spill Commission, an *Anchorage Daily News* article "Countdown to Disaster: Events Before the Grounding," March 14, 1989, the book, *In the Wake of the Exxon Valdez*, and the documentary *Dead Ahead*.

3. "We're Going to Be Here for a While"

1. The content of this chapter is summarized from publicly available sources including the accident investigation report prepared by the National Transportation Safety Board, the Report to the President prepared by the National Response Team, the report *The Exxon Valdez Oil Spill: Final Report, State of Alaska Response* prepared by the Alaska Department of Environmental Conservation, a chronology of events outlined in Appendix N of the report *Spill: the Wreck of the Exxon Valdez*, prepared by the Alaska Oil Spill Commission, and the book, *In the Wake of the Exxon Valdez*, and accounts provided in the *Anchorage Daily News*.

2. The events and dialogue between the Coast Guard Vessel Traffic Control and on board the *Exxon Valdez* are summarized from the accident investigation report prepared by the National Transportation Safety Board, and a recording of the communication released to the public and media and recounted in *The Anchorage Daily News*, "Hazelwood Risked Sinking Ship: Tapes Reveal Captain Tried to Free Valdez," April 25, 1989.

3. This account of the response by the Coast Guard, Alyeska, and the Alaska Department of Environmental Conservation is summarized from a number of sources including *The Exxon Valdez Oil Spill: Final Report, State of Alaska Response* prepared by the Alaska Department of Environmental Conservation, a Report to the President prepared by the National Response Team, a chronology outlined in Appendix N of the report *Spill: the Wreck of the Exxon Valdez*, the book, *In the Wake of the Exxon Valdez*, and a personal interview with Dan Lawn.

4. *In the Wake of the Exxon Valdez*, 22.
5. Ibid., 23.
6. Ibid., 24.
7. Ibid., 25.
8. Ibid., 28.
9. Ibid., 28.
10. Ibid., 29.

4. According to Plan

1. This and other town hall meetings held at the Civic Center were recorded and made available to this author by the Valdez public radio station KCHU. The quotes and account of the meeting to follow have been transcribed and summarized from the recording dated March 24, 1989.
2. The following content regarding authority and responsibility for cleanup under the contingency plan is summarized and quoted from the report *The Exxon Valdez Oil Spill: Final Report, State of Alaska Response*, prepared by the Alaska Department of Environmental Conservation, a Report to the President prepared by the National Response Team, and the book *In the Wake of the Exxon Valdez*.
3. *In the Wake of the Exxon Valdez*, 33.
4. Ibid., 35.
5. Ibid., 34.
6. Ibid.
7. One barrel = 42 gallons.
8. This account of testing cleanup techniques is summarized from the report *The Exxon Valdez Oil Spill: Final Report, State of Alaska Response,* prepared by the Alaska Department of Environmental Conservation; the book *In the Wake of the Exxon Valdez*; and articles in the *Anchorage Daily News*.
9. *In the Wake of the Exxon Valdez*, 52.
10. KCHU recording, March 26, 1989.
11. Ibid.
12. Ibid.
13. *In the Wake of the Exxon Valdez*, 54.

5. Irreconcilable Views

1. *The Copper Spike*, 25.
2. "The Early Years of Alaska's Oil and Gas," 2.
3. *The Copper Spike*, 25.
4. "The Early Years of Alaska's Oil and Gas," 2.
5. *The Copper Spike*, 27.
6. Ibid., 34.

7. Ibid., 54.

8. Ibid.

7. Siege at Sawmill Bay

1. "Rescuers, Clean Up Crews Tackle Vast Size of Spill," *Anchorage Daily News*, March 31, 1989.

2. KCHU Master Cassette 32, April 1, 1989.

3. Ibid.

4. "Fishermen Keep Oil Out of Hatchery, Cordova Group, State Officers Shield One Small Corner of Sound; Slick Threatens Sea Lions," *Anchorage Daily News*, March 30, 1989.

5. KCHU Master Cassette 32, April 1, 1989.

6. "Cowper: Either Cleanup Plans Improve or the Pipeline Closes," *Anchorage Daily News*, April 2, 1989.

7. Ibid.

8. KCHU Master Cassette 32, April 1, 1989.

9. Ibid.

10. Ibid.

11. "Fishermen Keep Oil Out of Hatchery, Cordova Group, State Officers Shield One Small Corner of Sound; Slick Threatens Sea Lions," *Anchorage Daily News*, March 30, 1989.

12. "Cowper: Either Cleanup Plans Improve or the Pipeline Closes," *Anchorage Daily News*, April 2, 1989.

13. "The Thunder Mug" CDFU Newsletter, May 4, 1971.

14. Ibid.

15. *Extreme Conditions*, 83.

16. "The Thunder Mug" CDFU Newsletter, May 4, 1971.

17. Walter Day's notes from the Pipeline Hearings, February 1971.

18. "The Thunder Mug" CDFU Newsletter, May 4, 1971.

19. Ibid.

20. *The Trans-Alaska Pipeline Controversy*, 223.

21. *Extreme Conditions*, 82.

22. See *Wilderness Society v. Hickel*, 325 F. Supp. 422 (D.D.C. 1970) and *Wilderness Society v. Morton*, 479 F.2d 842 (D.C. Cir. 1973).

23. *Extreme Conditions*, 83.

24. Ibid.

25. "Trans-Alaska Pipeline Act" P.L. 93-153 Title II, Section 203(a).

26. *Extreme Conditions*, 83.

27. Personal interview, Summer 2007.

28. Proceedings of the Third Alaska Aquaculture Conference.

29. "Salmon Fish Traps in Alaska," 2.

30. Ibid., 14.

31. Proceedings of the Third Alaska Aquaculture Conference.

8. "You Have My Word on That"

1. "Valdez Folks Feel Cheated," *Anchorage Daily News*, March 30, 1989.

2. Statements by Don Cornett and members of the audience at the town hall meeting in Cordova were transcribed from a recording of the meeting posted on YouTube, titled "Exxon Lies," http://www.youtube.com/watch?v=LhC-DLleXLpo, accessed May 8, 2007.

3. "Two Fishermen File First Lawsuit Over Spill; More Suits Likely," *Anchorage Daily News*, March 30, 1989.

4. Ibid.

9. "Hang On, We're Going Around a Curve"

1. "Spill Muddies Big Oil's Reputation Clout With Legislature," *Anchorage Daily News,* April 4, 1989.

2. Ibid.

3. KCHU Master Cassette 32, April 1, 1989.

4. "Spill Muddies Big Oil's Reputation Clout With Legislature," *Anchorage Daily News*, April 4, 1989.

5. "Oil Shippers Want Looser Valdez Rules," *Anchorage Daily News*, April 1, 1989.

6. Ibid.

7. *Extreme Conditions*, 25.

8. *Crude Dreams*, 79.

9. *Extreme Conditions,* 37.

10. Ibid., 63.

11. Ibid., 69.

12. Ibid.

13. Ibid.

14. *The Trans Alaska Pipeline Controversy*, 163.

15. *Extreme Conditions*, 52.

16. Ibid., 57.

17. Ibid., 58.

18. Ibid.

19. Ibid., 70.

20. Quotes from the meeting of oil representatives were first cited in *Crude Dreams*, 296.

10. Fortune Seekers

1. *Extreme Conditions*, 76.
2. Ibid., 78.
3. Ibid.
4. Ibid.
5. Ibid.
6. Ibid., 79.
7. Ibid.
8. http://www.cf.adfg.state.ak.us/geninfo/finfish/herring/herrhome.php accessed November 14, 2013.

11. "We Can Have Our Cake and Eat It Too"

1. The account and quotes by Dan Lawn described in this chapter are based on an extensive personal interview unless otherwise cited. Lawn subsequently reviewed an initial draft of the book manuscript.
2. Dan Lawn July 13, 1982 memo to supervisor.
3. "Blueprint for Disaster: Despite Years of Warnings From Its Field Staffers About Alyeska's Poor Oil Spill Preparedness, the DEC Did Next to Nothing, Department Leaders Put No Real Heat on Alyeska," *Anchorage Daily News*, October 22, 1989.
4. *In the Wake of the Exxon Valdez*, xii, *Anchorage Daily News,* "Alaska Ear," March 12, 1989.
5. Hearing in respect to Environmental Impact of Proposed Trans-Alaska Pipeline System, Anchorage, Alaska, Transcript 2:507, Feb 24, 1971.
6. Ibid.
7. Joint Hearing of the Senate Commerce Committee and the House State Affairs Committee on Proposed Alaskan Legislation Concerning Pipeline Regulation, Right-of-Way and State Ownership, March 7, 1972, 18.
8. Testimony regarding Senate Bills 294, 313, and 315, Juneau, Alaska 1972, 3.
9. *Alyeska Reports*, 2:3, 16 July 1976.
10. "Oil and Aquatic Ecosystems, Tanker Safety and Oil Pollution Liability: Proceedings of the Cordova Fisheries Institute" April 1-3, 1977 Transcript, 211.
11. "Broken Promises: Alyeska Record Shows How Big Oil Neglected Alaskan Environment—Pipeline Firm Cut Corners And Scrapped Safeguards, Raising Risk of Disaster—Allegation of Fabricated Data," *Wall Street Journal,* July 6, 1989, 1.
12. *Alaska North Slope Oil Profits and Proposed Environmental Measures.*
13. *In the Wake of the Exxon Valdez*, 83.
14. "Broken Promises," *Wall Street Journal,* July 6, 1989, 1.
15. Ibid., 42-43.
16. Ibid.

17. Ibid., 1.
18. Ibid.
19. Ibid.
20. "Comments on the Draft of the Alyeska NPDES Permit and Fact Sheet and Technical Evaluation," Riki Ott, November 11, 1987.
21. "Broken Promises," *Wall Street Journal*, July 6, 1989, 1.
22. Ibid.
23. "Oil Industry Profitability: 1969 through 1987," Prepared for the Department of Revenue, State of Alaska March 15, 1989.
24. *In the Wake of the Exxon Valdez*, 73.
25. Dan Lawn letter to Bill Lamoreaox, DEC Regional Supervisor, December 19, 1984.
26. Letter from Congressman George Miller to Judges Russel Holland and Stanley Sporkin, April 8, 1991.
27. House Committee on Interior and Insular Affairs, *Investigation of the Exxon Valdez Oil Spill, Prince William Sound, Alaska Part I*. May 5, 7, 8, 1989, 834.
28. "In Ten Years, You'll See Nothing. That's what Exxon CEO Lawrence Rawl says will be left of the Valdez oil spill. 'A super job' of cleaning up, he hopes, will overcome Congress's new coolness to Arctic exploration." *Fortune*, May 8, 1989.
29. "Congressmen Bear Down on Alyeska's Role in Spill," *Anchorage Daily News*, May 8, 1989, A1.
30. "Countdown to Disaster: The Events After the Grounding," *Anchorage Daily News*, May 14, 1989.

12. Relying on Assurances

1. Letter from Congressman George Miller to Judges Russel Holland and Stanley Sporkin, April 8, 1991.
2. Ibid.
3. Ibid.
4. Ibid.

13. The Heart of the Sound

1. "A Fear of Spill Lawsuits Scientists, Officials Careful With Words," *Anchorage Daily News*, June 2, 1989.
2. "State Biologists Say Death Toll Extensive," *Anchorage Daily News,* April 2, 1989.
3. Ibid.
4. *Darkened Waters*, 24.
5. "A Fear of Spill Lawsuits Scientists, Officials Careful With Words" *Anchorage Daily News*, June 2, 1989.
6. GAO Report "Natural Resources Damage Assessment," 1991, 2.

7. "Oil Puts Prime Salmon Grounds Off Limits," *Anchorage Daily News*, June 14, 1989.

8. "Exxon, Fishermen Strike Deal: Company Agrees to Pay if Spill Prevents Fishing," *Anchorage Daily News*, June 24, 1989.

9. *In the Wake of the Exxon Valdez,* 103.

10. "Critics Slam Exxon at Meeting," *Anchorage Daily News*, May 19, 1989.

11. J. Michel and M. O. Hayes, "Geomorphological Controls on the Persistence of Shoreline Contamination from the Exxon Valdez Oil Spill" (prepared for the Hazardous Materials Response Branch of NOAA, Feb. 1991), 33. Table reproduced in the Federal On-Scene Coordinator's Report, 4.

12. "Size of Exxon spill remains disputed," *Anchorage Daily News*, June 5, 2010.

13. "Alaskans Not Alone in Anger Over Spill: Spill is a Live Issue Outside," *Anchorage Daily News*, April 26, 1989.

14. The Fall of Strict Liability

1. "Officials Close Salmon Fishery," *Anchorage Daily News*, July 30, 1989.

2. "Despite Spill, Fishermen Pull in Plenty of Salmon," *Anchorage Daily News*, August 30, 1989.

3. Proceedings of the Cordova Fisheries Institute: Oil and Aquatic Ecosystems, Tanker Safety and Oil Pollution Liability, April 1-3, 1977, 211.

4. Ibid., 210-211.

5. Ibid., 212.

6. "Senate OKS Oil Liability Bill: Measure Would Stiffen Rules," *Anchorage Daily News,* August 5, 1989.

7. "State Sues Exxon," *Anchorage Daily News,* August 16, 1989.

8. Ibid.

9. "Exxon Responds to 140 Lawsuits," *Anchorage Daily News*, August 16, 1989.

10. Ibid.

15. Deception

1. Oversight Hearings Before the Committee on Interior and Insular Affairs, Serial No. 102-13, 1.

2. Richard Mauer, "The details of deception, dirty tricks, used against Alyeska critic Hamel leave him bruised," *Anchorage Daily News*, September 1, 1991.

3. Oversight Hearings Before the Committee on Interior and Insular Affairs, Serial No. 102-13, 105-106.

4. Ibid., 106.

5. Ibid., 186.

6. Ibid., 445.

7. Ibid., 107.

8. Ibid., 207.

9. Ibid.

10. Ibid., 207-208.

11. Ibid., 235-236.

12. Ibid., 216.

13. Ibid., 259.

14. Ibid., 260.

15. Ibid., 262.

16. Ibid., 264-265.

16. The Voice of the Sound

1. "Oil Cleanup Concludes: DEC Calls In Most Crews From Spill-Soiled Beaches," *Anchorage Daily News,* July 14, 1991.

2. Ibid.

3. "Judge OK's Oil Spill Settlement: Exxon's 2nd Try Satisfies Court But Not Critics," *Anchorage Daily News,* October 9, 1991.

4. Ibid.

5. Ibid.

6. "Exxon Lawsuit Blames State for Delay in Oil Spill Response," *Anchorage Daily News,* October 24, 1989.

7. "Judge OK's Oil Spill Settlement," *Anchorage Daily News,* October 9, 1991.

8. Oil Pollution Act of 1990, Section 5002 (H).

9. Ibid. (C, D).

10. *Wilderness Society v. Morton* 495 F.2d 1026; (D.C. Cir 1974).

11. *Alyeska Pipeline Service Co. v. Wilderness Society,* 421 U.S. 240 (1975).

12. Ibid.

13. Oil Pollution Act of 1990, Section 5002 (d).

17. Disappearing Act

1. "Pink Harvest a Bust Again: Seiners, Processors, Strapped by Weak Run of Good Salmon," *Anchorage Daily News,* August 29, 1992.

18. Blockade

1. "Fishing Boats Block Tankers From Terminal: Three Ships Halted," *Anchorage Daily News,* August 22, 1993.

2. Ibid.

3. "Alaska Fishermen Blockade Tankers," *New York Times,* August 23, 1993.

4. "Measuring Up the Sound: Biologists Cannot Explain Collapse of Pink Runs, Fishermen Blame Spill," *Anchorage Daily News,* September 5, 1993.

5. Ibid.

6. *Fighting for Public Justice,* 270.

19. Reckless Decision

1. *Cleaning Up*, 119.
2. Ibid., 92.
3. Quotes by Judge H. Russel Holland are from a transcript of proceedings in re Case No. A89-0095 CIV (HRH) in the United States District Court for the State of Alaska, Preliminary Instructions and Opening Statements, May 9, 1994, 7-10.
4. Quotes by Brian O'Neill and a summary of his opening arguments are from a transcript of proceedings in re Case No. A89-0095 CIV (HRH) in the United States District Court for the State of Alaska, Preliminary Instructions and Opening Statements, May 9, 1994, 20-55.
5. Quotes by Patrick Lynch and a summary of his opening arguments are from a transcript of proceedings in re Case No. A89-0095 CIV (HRH) in the United States District Court for the State of Alaska, Preliminary Instructions and Opening Statements, May 9, 1994, 57-93.
6. "Damage: 287 Million, Fishermen Unhappy, Exxon Says It's Pleased," *Anchorage Daily News*, August 12, 1994.
7. Ibid.
8. Quotes by James Neal and a summary of his closing arguments are from a transcript of proceedings in re Case No. A89-0095 CIV (HRH) in the United States District Court for the State of Alaska, Closing Arguments, August 29, 1994, 7591.
9. Quotes by Brian O'Neill and a summary of his closing arguments are from a transcript of proceedings in re Case No. A89-0095 CIV (HRH) in the United States District Court for the State of Alaska, Closing Arguments, August 29, 1994, 7643-7644.

Epilogue

1. "Judge Blasts Seven Fish Processors and Exxon Secret Deal to Give Back Some Damages in Spill Suit," *Seattle Post-Intelligencer*, June 14, 1996.
2. "Exxon's Secret Valdez Deals Anger Judge," *Wall Street Journal,* June 13, 1996.
3. "Judge Blasts Seven Fish Processors and Exxon Secret Deal to Give Back Some Damages in Spill Suit," *Seattle Post-Intelligencer*, June 14, 1996.
4. "Exxon is Accused of 'Astonishing Ruse' in Oil-Spill Trial," *New York Times*, June 14, 1996.
5. Personal interview, 2007.
6. "Committee Report on Alyeska Draws Fire from Republicans," States News Service, July 29, 1992.
7. "Judge Denies Alyeska's Requests to Uncover Hamel's Sources," *Anchorage Daily News*, October 9, 1993.
8. "Ex-Security Worker Cited for Courage," *Miami Herald*, June 23, 1992.
9. "Spill Muddies Big Oil's Reputation Clout With Legislature," *Anchorage Daily News,* April 4, 1989.

Bibliography

Alaska Department of Environmental Conservation. 1993. *The Exxon Valdez Oil Spill: Final Report, State of Alaska Response*. Anchorage, AK: Prepared by Ernest Piper.

Alaska Department of Fish and Game, Division of Commercial Fisheries. 2005. *Commercial Fisheries of Alaska*. Juneau, AK: Prepared by Doug Woodby, Dave Carlile, Shareef Saddeek, Fritz Funk, John Clark, Lee Hulbert. Special Publication No. 05-09.

Alaska Oil Spill Commission. February 1990. *Spill: The Wreck of the Exxon Valdez, Appendix N, T/V Exxon Valdez Oil Spill Chronology*. Anchorage, AK: Alaska Resources Library & Information Services.

Alaska Sea Grant Program. April 27-28, 1982. *Proceedings of the Third Alaska Aquaculture Conference*. Cordova, AK: http://nsgl.gso.uri.edu/aku/akuw82001.pdf, accessed November 14, 2013.

Armstrong, Robert H. 1995. *Guide to the Birds of Alaska*. Anchorage, AK: Alaska Northwest Books.

Alyeska Pipeline Service Company. January 1987. *Oil Spill Contingency Plan, Prince William Sound*.

Coates, Peter. 1993. *The Trans-Alaska Pipeline Controversy: Technology, Conservation, and the Frontier*. Fairbanks, AK: University of Alaska Press.

Colt, Steve. January 11, 1999. *Salmon Fish Traps in Alaska: Economic History*. http://www.iser.uaa.alaska.edu/people/colt/personal/FISHTRAP.PDF, Accessed September 29, 2013.

Congressman George Miller, Vice Chairman, House Committee on Interior and Insular Affairs. April 8, 1991. *To Honorable H. Russel Holland and Honorable Stanley Sporkin, Re review of pending cases.....* Washington D.C.: http://www.alaskaforum.org/rowhist/Congress/103Congress.pdf, Accessed September 29, 2013.

Davidson, Art. 1990. *In the Wake of the Exxon Valdez: The Devastating Impact of the Alaska Oil Spill*. San Francisco, CA: Sierra Club Books.

Deakin, Edward. March 15, 1989. *Oil Industry Profitability: 1969 through 1987*. Institute of Petroleum Accounting, University of North Texas. Prepared for the Department of Revenue, State of Alaska.

Fineberg, Richard. 1994. *Alaska North Slope Oil Profits and Proposed Environmental Mitigation Measures*. A paper prepared for presentation at the 15th Annual North American Conference of the International Association for Energy Economics, Westin Hotel, Seattle, Washington, Oct. 11-13, 1993 [revised 8/1 8/93], with a February 1994 update to certain data.

Government Accountability Office. 1991. *Natural Resources Damage Assessment: Information on Study of Seabirds Killed by Exxon Valdez Oil Spill.* Washington D.C.: GAO/RCED-92-22.

"Hearing in respect to Environmental Impact of Proposed Trans-Alaska Pipeline System, Anchorage, Alaska." 1971.

House. Committee on Interior and Insular Affairs. House; Subcommittee on Water, Power, and Offshore Energy Resources, Committee on Interior and Insular Affairs, Serial No. 101-5. 1989. *Investigation of the Exxon Valdez Oil Spill, Prince William Sound, Alaska Part I.* May 5, 7, 8, 1989.

House. Committee on Interior and Insular Affairs, Serial No. 102-13. 1991. *Alyeska Pipeline Service Company Covert Operation.* November 4-6, 1991.

Janson, Lone. 1975. *The Copper Spike.* Anchorage, AK: Alaska Northwest Publishing Company.

LaChance, Karen. 1995. *Valdez: A Brief Oral History.* Fairbanks, AK: University of Alaska Press.

Lasley, John. 2005. The Early Years of Alaska's Oil and Gas. *Oil & Gas Investor* (October): 8-15.

Lawn, Dan. December 19, 1984. *Letter to Bill Lamoreaox, DEC Regional Supervisor.* http://www.alaskaforum.org/rowhist/Djl/103DJL.pdf, Accessed September 29, 2013.

Lawn, Dan. July 13, 1982. *Memo to Steve Zrake, DEC Anchorage Office.* http://www.alaskaforum.org/rowhist/Djl/101DJL.pdf, Accessed September 29, 2013.

Lebedoff, David. 1997. *Cleaning Up: The Story Behind the Biggest Legal Bonanza of Our Time.* New York, NY: The Free Press.

Lord, Nancy. 1992. *Darkened Waters: A Review of the History, Science and Technology Associated with the Exxon Valdez Oil Spill and Cleanup.* Homer, AK: Homer Society of Natural History/ Pratt Museum.

National Response Team. May 1989. *The Exxon Valdez Oil Spill: A Report to the President.* Samuel K. Skinner, Secretary, Department of Transportation and William K. Reilly, Administrator, Environmental Protection Agency.

National Transportation Safety Board. 1990. *Marine Accident Report: Grounding of the U.S. Tankship Exxon Valdez: on Bligh Reef, Prince William Sound, near Valdez, Alaska, March 24, 1989.* Washington D.C.: NTSB/MAR-90/04.

"Oil and Aquatic Ecosystems, Tanker Safety and Oil Pollution Liability: Proceedings of the Alaska Fisheries Institute." In. April 1-3, 1977. Cordova, AK: Alaska Sea Grant Program, University of Alaska.

Ott, Dr. Fredericka, Member of the Board, CDFU. 1988. *Cordova District Fishermen United's Concerns with Alyeska.* http://www.alaskaforum.org/rowhist/Ott/103Ott.pdf, Accessed September 29, 2013.

"Prevention, Response, and Oversight Five Years After the Exxon Valdez Oil Spill: Proceedings of an International Conference." In. March 23-25, 1994. Anchorage, AK: Alaska Sea Grant College Program, University of Alaska.

Public Law 92-203. 1971. *"Alaska Native Claims Settlement Act".*

Public Law 93-153. 1973. *"Trans-Alaska Pipeline Authorization Act"*.

Public Law 101-380. 1990. *"Oil Pollution Act of 1990"*.

Public Meetings. 1989. Valdez and Cordova, Alaska: Recordings by Valdez Public Radio Station KCHU.

Roderick, Jack. 1997. *Crude Dreams: A Personal History of Oil & Politics in Alaska.* Fairbanks, AK: Epicenter Press.

Smith, Wesley J. 2001. *Fighting for Public Justice: Cases and Trial Lawyers That Made a Difference.* Washington D.C.: The TLPJ Foundation.

Strohmeyer, John. 1997. *Extreme Conditions: Big Oil and the Transformation of Alaska.* Anchorage, AK: Cascade Press.

Townsend Environmental. March 1994. *The Promises Issue: Commitments and Representations by Alyeska and its Owner Companies Regarding the Trans-Alaska Pipeline System.* Otis, OR: http://www.alaskaforum.org/rowhist/ Rt/101RT.pdf, accessed November 14, 2013.

Townsend Environmental. January 1995. *The Promises Issue Part II: : Commitments and Representations by Alyeska and its Owner Companies Regarding the Trans-Alaska Pipeline System.* Otis, OR: http://www.alaskaforum.org/ rowhist/Rt/102RT.pdf, accessed November 14, 2013.

United States Coast Guard. September 1993. *Federal On Scene Coordinator's Report: T/V Exxon Valdez Oil Spill Volume I.* Washington D.C.: Department of Transportation, Report DOT-SRP-94-01.

United States Department of the Interior, Minerals Management Service, Environmental Studies Section. 2001. *Exxon Valdez Oil Spill, Cleanup, and Litigation: A Collection of Social-Impacts Information and Analysis.* Prepared by Impact Assessment Inc.

Index